THE HI... AME...N C...R 1865

EXECUTIVE EDITOR - JULIAN BROWN
SENIOR EDITOR - TREVOR DAVIES
CREATIVE DIRECTOR - KEITH MARTIN
EXECUTIVE ART EDITOR - GEOFF FENNELL
PICTURE RESEARCH - ELLEN ROOT
PRODUCTION CONTROLLER - LOUISE HALL

ARTWORKS DESIGNED BY KEVIN JONES ASSOCIATES

FIRST PUBLISHED IN GREAT BRITAIN IN 2000 BY HAMLYN A
DIVISION OF OCTOPUS PUBLISHING GROUP LIMITED
2–4 HERON QUAYS, LONDON E14 4JP

COPYRIGHT © OCTOPUS PUBLISHING GROUP LIMITED 2000, 2002

DISTRIBUTED IN THE UNITED STATES AND CANADA BY
STERLING PUBLISHING CO., INC.
387 PARK AVENUE SOUTH, NEW YORK. NY 10016-8810

ISBN 0 600 60778 X

A CIP CATALOGUE RECORD FOR THIS BOOK IS AVAILABLE FROM
THE BRITISH LIBRARY

PRINTED AND BOUND IN CHINA

10 9 8 7 6 5 4 3 2 1

hamlyn

THE HISTORY OF THE

AMERICAN CIVIL WAR

1861-1865

PHILIP KATCHER

CONTENTS

STALEMATE IN THE EAST, MOVEMENT IN THE WEST 122

DEATH OF THE CONFEDERACY 158

INTRODUCTION

The American Civil War captures today's imagination because of the sheer scope of the event, how it changed the path of a nation, and the leaders it produced. Its stories have led to the creation of some of the greatest films of all time, such as *Birth of a Nation* and *Gone With The Wind*, while serious histories fill entire libraries. Well over 20,000 individuals in the US, UK, France, and even in the Ukraine don copies of Civil War uniforms to put on mock Civil War battles and encampments. Relics of the war cost large sums and have ended up in major collections all over the world.

INTRODUCTION

In all millions of Americans put on uniforms for one side or the other and fought against each other for four long years. The involvement of the country was almost total. In all some 75 to 85 per cent of all southerner males, around 900,000 men, served in the Confederate armed forces, while half of all northerner males, for a total of 2,898,304 men, also served. Moreover, one in three Confederates died in the war, creating a generation that was missing many of its best men. Had such a proportion of American soldiers died in World War Two, the country would have suffered as many as six million casualties. The Federals, being better supplied with medicines, still had casualties of one in six.

In the process, they brought warfare out of the Napoleonic ages into the modern era. Telegraphs and other signalling methods used by professional signal corps and telegraph operators on both sides kept even small units in obscure parts of the field in constant touch with War Departments in capital cities. Railroads transferred large bodies of troops, complete with their equipment, from theatre to theatre in a matter of days almost regardless of geography rather than the months marching men would have taken. Warriors on both sides struck at civilians. From the north soldiers torched southern stores, homes, and farms in places as far apart as Virginia and Georgia to destroy southern morale as well as the ability to continue armies in the field. At the same time, southern naval cruisers struck at the northern civilian merchant marine, driving the US flag largely from the seas. Anesthetics made operations to save lives easier and quicker, while railroads brought wounded men to rear echelon hospitals sooner than ever before. Mines planted in earth and sea made warfare a less personal event. Airborn balloonists telegraphed news of enemy positions which in years before would have been hidden. Repeating weapons, including various versions of what would become machine guns, with increasing ranges made the battle field a deadlier place then ever and changed tactics from the assault in line of battle to a matter of digging in whenever possible.

The people whose lives were changed dramatically were giants in their own times. Some, such as Abraham Lincoln, US Grant, and Stonewall Jackson, rose to prominence from unpromising

beginnings. Others, such as famed US Supreme Court chief justice Oliver Wendall Holmes and author Ambrose Bierce, began their careers during this war and what they saw permanently affected them. Indeed, years later Holmes, said that during the war, 'Our hearts were touched with fire.'

Moreover, the war changed America itself dramatically. A version of universal service in the form of a draft or conscription, became mandatory for both sides, changing what had always been an all-volunteer fighting force into a national one. Human bondage would be forever banned, although reminders of it in terms of racism still exist in the country and are still being dealt with. Income taxes and legal currency changed a society used to local bank notes and a minimum of taxes to a modern financial one. Large manufacturing and banking concerns became standard, especially in the north, where before the country was mostly agricultural and industry was little more than cottage industry. The very concept of the country being a collection of towns, counties, and states hanging together as it seemed expedient, changed to being 'one nation.'

Indeed, the very status of women changed from a being whose life was limited to kitchen, nursery, and church, to a valued member of the community. Women, following the example of Forence Nightingale in the Crimea, entered hospitals to do what before had been largely man's work. Socially acceptable women began working in places as varied as arsenals where they assembled ammunition to offices where they served as clerks. Those who remained at home were in many cases left to be the chief of the home, deciding what and when to plant, hiring and supervising contractors for needed repairs, and taking charge of domestic financial matters. Many wartime marriages afterwards fell apart, and women were no longer afraid to face single life as a divorced woman as whole social norms changed. In many ways, finally, the war has not ended. William Faulkner, whose grandfather commanded a Mississippi infantry regiment, once said for every southern boy it was always just before July 3, 1863, in those moments just before Pickett's men began their long march across the Emmitsburg Pike and into history.

	Infantry units
	Infantry units (former positions)
	Cavalry units
	Infantry attacking
	Army headquaters
	Sea going Warship
	River gunboat
	Forts
	Field fortifications
	Intended line of advance
	Actual line of advance
	Church
	Site of battle or skirmish
	Town
	Major town/city
	State border
	Railway line
	Bridge

THE WAR BEGINS

6 NOV	**1860** Abraham Lincoln elected President
20 DEC	South Carolina votes to leave the Union
26 DEC	Federal garrison occupies Ft Sumter, in Charleston Harbor
9 JAN	**1861** Mississippi secedes
10 JAN	Florida secedes
19 JAN	Georgia secedes
25 JAN	Louisiana secedes
1 FEB	Texas secedes
9 FEB	The newly formed Confederate States of America adopts a provisional Constitution
18 FEB	Jefferson Davis is inaugurated President of the Confederate States
4 MAR	Lincoln is inaugurated
12 APR	Confederate troops fire on Ft Sumter – The garrison surrenders a day later
17 APR	Virginia secedes
6 MAY	Arkansas secedes
20 MAY	North Carolina secedes
3 JUNE	Battle of Philippi – The fight in western Virginia begins a series of Confederate losses in that part of the state
8 JUNE	Tennessee is admitted to the Confederacy
10 JUNE	Battle of Big Bethel – Confederates score their first victory in eastern Virginia
11 JULY	Battle of Rich Mountain, western Virginia
21 JULY	First Battle of Bull Run – The first large Northern Army is turned back before Richmond, Virginia, in a rout
10 AUG	Battle of Wilson's Creek, Missouri – The Federal commander is killed, but saves the state for the Union
21 OCT	Battle of Ball's Bluff, Virginia – Yet another Federal defeat, with the Union commander killed
6 FEB	**1862** Capture of Ft Henry, Tennessee – Naval forces alone take a major fortification in the western theatre
8 FEB	Capture of Roanoke Island, North Carolina – Union forces grab a foothold on the North Carolina coast to use to stage raids and refuel blockading ships
7&8 MAR	Battle of Pea Ridge, Arkansas – Another Federal victory in the west
9 MAR	Battle of the U.S.S. *Monitor* and CSS *Virginia* – The world's first battle of ironclad ships
6&7 APRIL	Battle of Shiloh – Confederate troops fail to destroy Grant's army
8 MAY	Battle of McDowell, Virginia – Stonewall Jackson's men are in the Shenandoah Valley
23 MAY	Battle of Front Royal, Virginia
25 MAY	Battle of Winchester, Virginia

The practice of slavery came to the New World shortly after the arrival of the first Europeans. It persisted through the formation of the republic, the United States of America. Yet it often threatened to tear the nation apart as the South embraced the practice and the North rejected it. As North and South were politically fairly equal, a compromise had been possible until 1860 when an anti-slavery Northern President, Abraham Lincoln, was elected and the South's political power eclipsed. Shortly afterwards South Carolina voted to leave the Union and was quickly followed by other slave states. Lincoln resolved to fight to maintain the Union and, when the newly formed Confederate States of America fired on a United States fort, called for thousands of volunteers to put down the rebellion. While Southern troops won the first big battles, Union forces began to nibble away at the edges of the vast South.

AMERICA IN 1860

The founders of the nation that would become the United States of America brought the seeds of its own destruction with them. Largely British, landing on a huge continent ranging from a subtropical area where life moved slowly to a rock-bound woodland where bitter winters meant short growing seasons, they brought slavery to their new world. Slavery soon died in the North, where it did not work for a society based on small farms and shops. But it did well in the South, where large plantations became the focus of development.

At first this was unproblematic as the two areas were virtually equal in terms of numbers, land and economic value. Indeed, in the nation's first census in 1790, two of the five largest states in terms of population were Southern (Virginia and North Carolina), while three were Northern (Pennsylvania, Massachusetts and New York). But by 1860 this balance of power had changed radically. In that year's census, Virginia alone remained as one of the largest states, only it was now number five. The first four most populous states were New York and Pennsylvania, followed by states that had not existed in 1790, Ohio and Illinois.

The South was not only losing the population war, it was also losing its political equality with the rest of the country. Where Virginia produced most of the country's first presidents, now presidents were being elected from the North and West. And they were being elected without Southern votes being required.

The two areas were vastly different. Widespread schooling in the North produced a literate population, while the lack of education in the South hindered its growth. In 1860, there were 372 daily newspapers in the United States; yet only 65 were in the Southern states that would eventually make up the Confederacy. Southerners were quicker to take offence, and would settle matters with firearms. In 1860, of two relatively equal states, North Carolina (with a population of 631,100) and New Jersey (with a population of 646,699), North Carolina reported the deaths of 14 males and two females from gunshot wound in the year ending 1 June. New Jersey had only four males and one female dead from gunshot in the same period.

Although the main business in both areas of the country was agricultural, industry in the North grew by leaps and bounds compared to that of the South. In 1860, in the year ending 1 June, the value of steam engines and machinery in the 'middle states' of New York, Pennsylvania, New Jersey, Delaware, Maryland, and

▼John Brown had ridden against slavery in the fighting in Kansas prior to the Civil War, ending up hanged since he tried to start a slave insurrection in western Virginia. His raid on Harper's Ferry terrified the south and prompted the raising of hundreds of volunteer militia companies.

▶ While most of the South's wealth lay in its agriculture, the shift to industry, with its accompanying large cities, had already happened in the north. This scene of Broadway in New York City shows but a part of the bustling largest city in the United States in 1861.

the District of Columbia was $14,755,224. That of the 13 states that made up the Confederacy was only $883,284. In terms of the tonnage of ships and boats built, the Confederate states produced 18,309 tons; Maine, Massachusetts, New York, and Pennsylvania alone floated 144,878 tons of shipping that year. There were 266 banks and branches with a net capitalization of $104,884.0 million in the Confederate states; the rest of the country had 1,376 banks and branches with a net capitalization of $317,314.9 million. There were 21,276,840 miles of railroad tracks in the states that did not form the Confederacy; there were only 9,516,850 miles in the Confederacy. All of these numbers would greatly, and adversely, affect the ability of the Southern states to wage a war against the rest of the country.

The South certainly led in the production of cotton, with 5,197,538 bales of the white stuff produced in the year ending 1 June. Of the non-Confederate states, only Illinois had any production, and it was a measly six bales. But, this cotton went north and abroad to be processed. In total, Southern mills produced $9,303,921 worth of cotton goods in the year ending 1 June, while the 'middle states' alone produced $18,357,219 worth of the same type of goods.

Southern leaders, however, did not want to change their way of life to try to compete with Northern industry and agriculture. They wanted to keep their 3,200,364 slaves in the U.S. in 1860 to work their fields. At the same time, public opinion in the rest of the country – indeed, in the world – began to turn against the concept of human slavery. Northern states banned slavery, and individuals helped fleeing slaves. Only a handful escaped; in 1860 in Maryland, close to freedom over the Pennsylvania border, only 279 slaves escaped out of a slave population of 90,368. Still, those in the South, even those who didn't own slaves, began to feel their way of life threatened. Fighting broke out in territories as the nation expanded west and pioneers had to decide if they wanted to live in a slave or free society. A mad abolitionist, John Brown from Kansas, actually invaded a small Virginia town, Harper's Ferry, intending to spark a slave revolt that would end the entire system of slavery. Caught and hanged, he nonetheless caused real fear about a Northern threat throughout the South. Thousands of men joined new militia companies on both sides of the country. As the nation began to get ready to vote to elect a new President, many believed that war was inevitable.

▼ Although three of these African-American workers on a plantation on Edisto Island, North Carolina, wear items of cast-off Union army uniform that mark the photograph as being very late war or immediately post war, the scene is typical of earlier slavery days.

CONSTANCE CARY HARRISON, VIRGINIA CITIZEN

Our homestead was in Fairfax County, at some distance from the theater of that tragic episode (John Brown's execution); and, belonging as we did to a family among the first in the State to manumit slaves – our grandfather having set free those that came to him by inheritance, and the people who served us being hired from their owners and remaining in our employ through years of kindliest relations – there seemed to be no especial reason for us to share in the apprehension of an uprising of the blacks. But there was fear-unspoken, or pooh-poohed at by the men who were mouth-pieces for our community – dark, boding, oppressive, and altogether hateful.

THE CONFEDERACY IS FORMED

Up to 1860, the American government functioned because there were basically only two parties, one slightly liberal and one slightly conservative. Both sides respected each other and worked to form a consensus. By 1860 this was ending. One party, the old Whig party, had virtually dissolved, with many of its members going into a more radical Republican party. The Democratic Party, the old party of Virginian and slaveholder Thomas Jefferson, was the first to hold its convention to nominate a President. The *New York Times* reported on 26 April 1860 that, 'The Platform Committee are in trouble. They want to please all sides, but they cannot do it. Trouble in the camp is certain, unless they embody the Slave code, and defeat is certain in November if they do.' Finally Senator Stephen Douglas of Illinois was nominated the party's candidate for President.

The Republican Party's convention took place the following month in Chicago, and resulted in the nomination of Abraham Lincoln, also of Illinois. Douglas was familiar to Lincoln, with whom he'd held a famous series of debates in which Douglas made it clear how he felt about slavery. He'd been quoted in the first debate saying that he hated slavery 'because it deprives our republican example of its just influence in the world – enables the enemies of free institutions, with plausibility, to taunt us as hypocrites – causes the real friends of freedom to doubt our sincerity, and especially because it forces so many good men amongst ourselves into an open war with the very fundamental principles of civil liberty – criticizing the Declaration of Independence, and insisting that there is no right principle of action but self-interest.'

By June, however, the quest for a simple election fell apart. Die-hard Southerners doubted the sincerity of Douglas and his wing of the Democratic party in the battle for slavery. They nominated their own candidate, John Breckinridge of Kentucky, for the office of President. As the old Whigs fell behind Lincoln, the split virtually guaranteed that neither Douglas nor Breckinridge would get enough Democratic votes to win. To ensure a Republican victory, a number of moderates formed a Constitutional Union party, with John Bell of Tennessee as its candidate. In November, with a minority of votes nationally, but sufficient to win, Abraham Lincoln was elected the 16th President of the United States. His term would begin as tradition dictated, in March, 1861. However, it was clear that Southern states no longer controlled the political destiny of the country.

Unfortunately, it was a time when the cool-headed pragmatists of the previous decades, who had cobbled together compromise after compromise to keep the country going, no longer led events. Extremists were now in charge, and Southern extremists were determined to declare void the results of a popular election that did not please them. Long before the new President's plans of any sort were known, the Governor of Alabama, only a few days after the election, suggested forming a 'Southern Confederacy' to defend 'the religious institution of slavery'. Following these sorts of calls, South Carolina's leaders met in December to declare themselves independent and no longer liable to the rule of the nation's majority.

Other slave-states quickly held their own conventions of secession, with Florida, Mississippi, Alabama, Georgia, Louisiana, and Texas declaring their own independence in January. One of those who fomented this series of events, Robert B. Rhett, Snr., a South Carolina newspaper owner, suggested holding a convention to discuss forming a Southern nation should be held in February in Montgomery, Alabama, and state officials agreed.

But the "fire-eaters" like Rhett, who were essentially, as all extremists are, destroyers and not creators, were largely left in the dust when Southern state representatives gathered to create a new government. Instead, members of this, the first provisional Congress of the Confederate States of America, selected a Mississippi graduate of the U.S. Military Academy and latterly a U.S. Senator, Jefferson Davis, as its first President. Davis had been one of the last Southern senators to leave the Senate, sad to do so, but in accordance with his state's lead. The Confederate Congress also adopted a provisional constitution, virtually the same as the U.S. Constitution with minor differences that spelled out the right to hold slaves and forbid taxes on imports to promote industry – something that had always irritated the agricultural exporters of cotton whose taxes were used to develop Northern industry.

While this was going on, Southern militiamen spread out and seized U.S. Government property such as arsenals and forts throughout the south. The garrison of one such fort, Fort Moultrie, part of the defences of Charleston, South Carolina, quickly abandoned its easily captured fort and took refuge in another of the city's forts, one out in the harbour where it could not easily be captured, Fort Sumter.

▼► The 16th President of the United States, Abraham Lincoln of Illinois (below), was unprepared for the crisis that faced him. The highest elected office he had held was that of congressman. His rival, Stephen A. Douglas, held his hat at his inauguration (right) in March 1861.

▲► The 1st President of the Confederate States, Jefferson Davis (above), had been educated at Transylvania College and the United States Military Academy, serving as a regimental commander in the Mexican War, the U.S. Secretary of War, and Senator from Mississippi. He was as prepared for the office of president as any man could be. He was introduced at his inauguration in February 1861 (right) with the words, 'The man and the hour have met'.

▲ This typical northern political cartoon shows southern states chasing 'the butterfly of secession' while not seeing that they are headed for a cliff and disaster. By the time it was published in January 1861 South Carolina had already dived off that cliff.

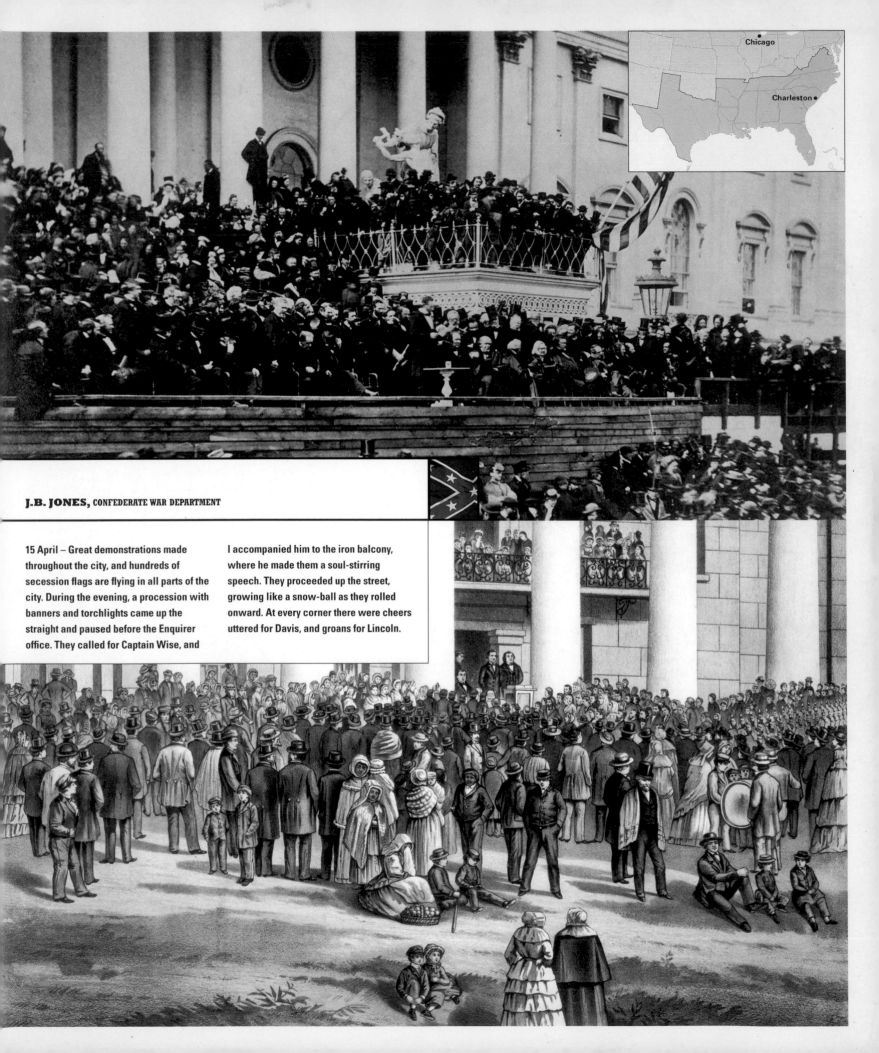

J.B. JONES, CONFEDERATE WAR DEPARTMENT

15 April – Great demonstrations made throughout the city, and hundreds of secession flags are flying in all parts of the city. During the evening, a procession with banners and torchlights came up the straight and paused before the Enquirer office. They called for Captain Wise, and I accompanied him to the iron balcony, where he made them a soul-stirring speech. They proceeded up the street, growing like a snow-ball as they rolled onward. At every corner there were cheers uttered for Davis, and groans for Lincoln.

FORT SUMTER

Fort Sumter, surrounded by the waters of Charleston Harbor, with guns that frowned on the harbour entrances, was like an irritating splinter in the eye of the Confederacy. Southern representatives went to Washington to negotiate with the outgoing President, James Buchanan, and his officials to have it turned over to them. Easygoing, slow to take action, in this case Buchanan decided to maintain his oath to preserve and protect the Constitution. With the advice of his commanding general, the aged Winfield Scott, he authorized sending supplies and a reinforcement of some 250 troops to the small garrison at Fort Sumter. Scott advised, however, that this shipment should not go on a U.S. Navy vessel, which would provoke the Carolinians, but on a merchant ship, the *Star of the West*.

On 5 January, the *Star of the West* set sail, arriving off the bar of Charleston Harbor around midnight on 8 January. As she made her way across the black waters, rockets and signal lights fired off in front of her. Carolinian gunners dashed to the guns they'd set up in a masked battery and on Fort Moultrie. Untrained, they did little damage to the ship, although a ricochet struck the ship's fore-chains, but they managed to turn the ship back.

On Sumter, the commander, Kentuckian and professional soldier Colonel Richard Anderson, forbade his men from giving covering fire to the ship. He was determined not to fire a shot that would start the Civil War. He sent a protest to the governor of South Carolina, who responded that the arrival of such a ship was considered a hostile act. Although the situation smouldered war had not yet been declared.

On 18 February, Jefferson Davis was inaugurated President of the Confederate States of America, and took over the position he regarded as most important, that of Commander-in-Chief of the South's armed forces. He assumed responsibility for defending the country, including removing the annoying garrison from Fort Sumter. His first attempt was diplomatic, sending three Confederate officials to Washington to negotiate for independence, as well as possession of the fort. On 1 March he named Confederate general, P.G.T. Beauregard, to command the area.

Things were getting desperate for the Federal garrison. Anderson told Washington officials on 1 March that he would soon have to either evacuate or would need reinforcements. While that

▲ Fort Sumter stood still uncompleted, one of a chain of brick fortresses designed to defend America's ports against foreign aggression. In December 1861 only a handful of workmen were in her until the U.S. Army garrison at Fort Moultrie moved to its safer walls.

message was being considered, Abraham Lincoln was sworn in, on 4 March, as President. The first problem the new President would face was that of Fort Sumter. Lincoln decided to reinforce the fort, as to do less would be to betray his oath of office, and ordered an expedition readied.

On 6 April, Lincoln informed South Carolina's governor that a relief expedition was to arrive at Fort Sumter with provisions, rather than men. If this was not fired on, he would not send men later; the clear threat was that if resistance were offered, U.S. soldiers would be sent and a war would be on. The reaction of state and Confederate officials, when they learned this, was to order their troops to man their battle stations. On 11 April, they sent word to Anderson that an immediate surrender was required. Anderson declined to surrender, but purposely let slip the fact that if they did not open fire on his men, he would be forced by lack of food to leave in a few days.

When they learned of this, the central government in Montgomery told its representatives in Charleston that they did not want to open fire, but only wanted to know when Anderson's men would leave. The officials made the trip across the choppy harbour again, and Anderson told them that they would leave by the 15th if not restocked and that he would not fire unless fired upon. This reply was not satisfactory to the Confederates who knew a supply ship was on its way. They replied that they would open fire on the unfinished fort that night, the 12th.

At 4.30 the signal gun was fired and Southern batteries concentrated on the brick walls of the fort. Around dawn Fort Sumter's guns began to reply, but the guns on the top of the ramparts were too exposed to Southern fire to use, so only part of the fort's 48 guns could reply. Charleston's citizens rushed to the rooftops to watch shells arcing through the night sky. Three times the wooden barracks in the fort caught fire, and black smoke filled the morning sky, lasting into evening. Finally, after 34 hours of bombardment, the Federal ships arrived off the bar of the harbour, but they could only watch, since they were not able to withstand the fire they would face.

The bombardment continued a second day, with surprisingly no casualties. Nonetheless, Anderson's men were out of every essential, and seeing that they would not be reinforced, finally struck their flag.

▲ Confederate batteries at Fort Moultrie fire on an already burning Fort Sumter. Despite the long bombardment, no U.S. soldier was injured until after the bombardment when a soldier was injured when a gun burst while firing a salute to the lowered American flag.

CAPTAIN ABNER DOUBLEDAY, 1ST U.S. ARTILLERY REGIMENT

By 11 a.m. the conflagration was terrible and disastrous. One-fifth of the fort was on fire, and the wind drove the smoke in dense masses into the angle where we had all taken refuge. It seemed impossible to escape suffocation. Some lay down close to the ground, with handkerchiefs over their mouths, and others posted themselves near the embrasures, where the smoke was somewhat lessened by the draught of air. Every one suffered severely. I crawled out of one of these openings, and sat on the outer edge; but Ripley made it lively for me there with his case-shot, which spattered all around.

WAR BEGINS

With the firing on Fort Sumter, the reality of war set in on both sides. Farm boys heard the news in the fields as they ploughed, shouted to them from horsemen, and they quit their jobs to flock into their nearby towns to join on either side. Huge patriotic meetings were held by daylight and torchlight, with speakers promising a quick war. Local leaders began recruiting volunteer companies, for the nation's traditional defence had not been its small regular armed forces, but the hordes of volunteers flocking to the colours for the duration of the war. These volunteers then elected their officers. Colonels and other field officers were appointed by state governors, largely on the strength of volunteers recruited, political importance, or prior military service. Retired soldiers such as the tanner's shop assistant Sam Grant in Illinois, who had seen service in Mexico or, better yet, had a military academy education, applied for, and were usually granted, state volunteer commissions.

In Washington, on 14 April, the day Sumter officially surrendered, Congress approved a call for 75,000 militia for 90 days' service. The telegraph wires buzzed with offers from state governors for volunteer infantry, cavalry, and artillery. In Montgomery, Davis worried that separation was not yet given. But it looked certain that many of the slave states still in the Union would not abandon their Southern sisters. Governors of Kentucky, Virginia, and North Carolina flatly refused to send troops to support Lincoln's war. Indeed, North Carolina troops quickly took over the unmanned Forts Macon, Caswell, and Johnston, in the name of the state. Virginia, the most populated and industrialized of all the slave states, now took the lead, holding a state convention that voted on 17 April to leave the Union.

Both sides looked immediately to the large Southern coastline and the business of Northern shippers. In Montgomery, Davis began authorizing letters-of-marque, allowing privateering, which had been abolished by international law among the European powers. Lincoln responded by declaring a blockade of the Southern ports. He had earlier thought to declare the ports closed, but this action would have meant that European ships already in these ports would have not been allowed to leave. As the great powers of Britain and France would not stand for such an action, he changed his declaration to one of blockade, which would give ships in such ports a certain time limit in which they would still be allowed to come and go.

However, the tiny U.S. Navy, with so many of its ships in ports ranging from Singapore to Rio, would be many months in making this blockade a reality. In the meantime, shipping continued to come and go as if there were no war at all. Had Southern leaders been more farsighted they might have predicted that this would be their best chance to gather all the cotton they could, ship it to European warehouses, and then sell it slowly for the equipment they would need to run a war. European weapons, accoutrements, and even uniforms from large manufacturers such as Ireland's Peter Tait, would play a major role in keeping Confederate soldiers and sailors in action, especially since the South's industrial capacity was so slight. Instead, however, they decided to forbid the export of cotton, reckoning that British and French cotton-goods manufacturers would demand that their government force their way through the Union blockade to get the raw material they needed. 'Cotton is king', was the conventional way of thinking. In fact, however, with a good supply of cotton already on hand in Europe, there

► In every small town leading citizens at rallies spoke to create excitement in getting young men into the town's company or regiments. Women added to the rush into the ranks by ignoring men who declined to serve.

► At first Union and Confederate regiments were recruited for less than a year, as the poster for the 36th New York (near right) indicates. Later Union recruits signed on for three years, and, as the war dragged on, large bounties, as shown in this illustration from Frank Leslie's *Illustrated Newspaper* of 19 March 1864 shows. Both sides also resorted to the draft to fill their ranks.

▼ Various propaganda
was used to fill the ranks.
This music sheet shows
'Yankee volunteers
marching into Dixie'
dressed as 'Uncle Sam', a
national representational
figure dating back to the
War of 1812.

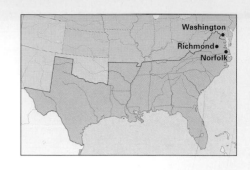

was no desire to break through - especially in the early years when the blockade was more a paper blockade than an actual one.

In the meantime, the U.S. Navy was forced to evacuate its dockyard in Norfolk, Virginia, partly burning it down, although much of its valuable equipment survived. The scuttled hull of the USS *Merrimac*, complete with its engines, would become the framework for the first Confederate Navy ironclad. Guns left at the dockyard would see service in Southern forts all along the coast. Even the bunting left behind would be used as battle flags in the Southern army protecting Virginia.

This army, based around Virginia's own militia, grew as North Carolina, Arkansas and Tennessee joined the new Confederacy. In May the Confederate government moved to the larger city of Richmond, then capital of Virginia. This city boasted the largest iron works in the south, and was a ship-building and cloth-making centre. Moreover, this move guaranteed attention would be given to Virginia's defence, as the strongest Federal attacks would doubtless strike this state from the Washington D.C. area. Troops began to flow into both capitals at a great rate, and the scene was set for the war's first battles.

CAPTAIN JULIAN W. HINKLEY, 3RD WISCONSIN VOLUNTEER INFANTRY

The preparations for departure were soon completed, and on July 12, 1861, we shouldered our knapsacks, strapped on our haversacks, containing several days' rations, and boarded the railroad cars for the seat of war in Virginia. The train of twenty-four coaches pulled out of the station amid the cheers and farewells of our many friends, who had gathered to see us off. All were in the best of spirits. It seemed to us as though we were setting out on a grand pleasure excursion. No thought of death or disaster appeared to cross the mind of anyone. And yet how many were saying farewell, never to return!

FIGHTING BEGINS

Both sides threw forces into Virginia and, eventually, small actions took place between them. In early June, Federal forces under Major-General George B. McClellan, based in Ohio, entered the western part of the state of Virginia, where pro-Union feelings ran strong. His troops made their way through rain and darkness along mountain trails until they were in position. At daylight on 3 June, his artillery opened fire on Virginian troops camped at Philippi. The unprepared Confederates, without any artillery of their own, immediately retreated, leaving several flags, as well as piles of baggage and munitions. This bloodless victory, called the 'Philippi Races', caught the imagination of a North hungry for a quick victory, and elevated McClellan to a high point in popular opinion.

To reverse the results of Philippi, officials in Richmond sent Brigadier-General Robert S. Garnett to command the Confederates in north-western Virginia. Garnett, with some 4,600 troops in his command, fortified the two strategic turnpike passes through the mountainous area, one at Laurel Hill and the other at Rich Mountain. McClellan, moving slowly as he would always prove to do, on 7 July sent a diversionary force against Laurel Hill, while moving his main force in an attempt to flank the Confederates on Rich Mountain. By the 8th, the diversionary force attacked. The Federals, working their way around Rich Mountain to the rear of the Confederates, reached there by 11 July, when they were discovered.

Garnett decided to retreat, leaving Laurel Hill and heading back to Monterey under cover of darkness. The Federals discovered the retreat in the morning, advancing into the camp where Garnett had left his tents standing to fool the enemy. Federals were sent to follow Garnett's retreating forces.

The Federals caught up with Garnett at Corricks Ford, a spot where the Confederates set up a defensive line, with artillery on a high hill that overlooked one of the two fords at the location. Unable to force the position with a direct assault, the Federals flanked the Southern position, forcing the Confederates to fall back with the loss of one of their three cannon. At the second ford Garnett himself was mortally wounded, the first general officer to fall in the Civil War. Survivors managed to escape back to Monterey to regroup under a new general, Robert E. Lee, commander of all of Virginia's forces. Lee himself would arrive on 1 August.

On the eastern side of Virginia, the Union army sent a brigade of seven regiments from Fort Monroe to attack a Confederate position near Bethel Church, also known as Big Bethel. Many of the Union troops were dressed in grey, and ended up firing on each other in a confused assault that saw a total of 76 Union losses and 8 Confederate casualties. Small in size, and unskilled in execution, this was, nonetheless, the first battle that reached the newspapers of both sides. Southerners were greatly encouraged by the easy victory, while Northerners tried to reassure themselves with the news of the victories on the other side of the state.

And news there was good for the North. The Confederates evacuated Harper's Ferry, Western Virginia, on 15 June, taking valuable musket- and rifle-making machinery with them. Musket machinery and parts would end up in the Richmond Armory, while rifle equipment went to the arsenal in Fayetteville, North Carolina. Both production sites would be the main long-arms manufacturing sites in the Confederacy and do valuable work for their side.

Western Virginia was falling into Union hands. Its population, largely not slave-holding, was mostly against secession, and on 19 June, Francis H. Pierpoint was named provisional Governor of Virginia under Federal command. This would eventually split away from the state to become the new state of West Virginia.

On 24 July, the Confederates at Tyler Mountain in that area had to retreat again as an Ohio force under Brigadier General Jacob D. Cox appeared at their rear. Under Brigadier General Henry A. Wise, the Confederates, fell back towards Gauley Bridge. Cox's men followed, reaching the Gauley Bridge area by 30 July. From this point on in West Virginia, however, there were mostly only skirmishes

▼ With a heavy heart, Colonel Robert E. Lee, who had just been offered field command of the U.S. Army, wrote this resignation from the U.S. Army to follow the fortunes of his native state, Virginia. Afterwards he said he felt the south would lose from the start.

▶ Senior officers from both sides tended to be graduates of the U.S. Military Academy at West Point, New York. These members of the Class of 1864 will see little action, however, before the war is over.

▼ Major-General George B. McClellan was one of the stars of the U.S. Army before the war, touring Europe in the Crimean War as an observer. He was president of a railroad before volunteering at the war's outbreak.

▼ *Left:* General Robert E. Lee was quickly commissioned as one of the Confederacy's five top generals, but his early performance was lacklustre and he ended up in largely advisory and inspection roles until 1862.

▼ Men of the 13th Indiana Infantry Regiment capture a Confederate cannon at the Battle of Rich Mountain, 11 July 1861. This was early in the war, when they wore makeshift sky blue uniforms and black slouch hats.

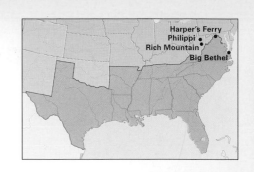

through the summer, with both sides digging in where they were.

In September, however, the action became larger-scaled. On the 10th, Federals attacked Canifix Ferry. The Confederates held, but were forced to withdraw as it was obvious that their position was weak. The next day, Lee began his Cheat Mountain campaign, a campaign with a Confederate army reinforced by such regiments as the 1st Tennessee Infantry. His plan called for five columns, mutually supportive, advancing through narrow mountain roads. This would have been difficult enough, but the weather was against them as the men slogged through cold, heavy rains. The Federals were ready and waiting. Lee, seeing that he had lost the element of surprise and realizing that the morale of his weary men was poor, decided to withdraw. On the 15th, they pulled back, permanently abandoning West Virginia to Federal law. Lee's first command had proved a failure.

PRIVATE SAM R. WATKINS, 1ST TENNESSEE INFANTRY REGIMENT

After the fighting was over, where, O where was all the fine rigging heretofore on our officers? They could not be seen. Corporals, sergeants, lieutenants, captain, all had torn all the fine lace off their clothing. I noticed that at the time and was surprised and hurt. I asked several of them why they had torn off the insignia of their rank, and they always answered, "Humph, you think that I was going to be a target for the Yankees to shoot at?"

FIRST BULL RUN

The taking of West Virginia was all very well, but it failed to satisfy a public that wanted the Federal army to go 'on to Richmond'. By early spring, a large number of regiments had reached the Washington D.C. area and began their training. Their overall commander, Major General Irwin McDowell, realized that it took much time and practice to get the officers and men, who were little more than armed civilians in uniform, to learn the details of company and battalion drill.

Lincoln, however, felt the longer he allowed the Southerners to exist as an independent state, the harder it would be to get them back into the Union. He ordered an immediate advance directly overland from Washington to Richmond. McDowell pleaded for time, as his troops were still green. Lincoln replied that the Confederates were equally green, and now was the time.

In mid-July, McDowell put his troops, aided by a brigade of marines (and almost as many Washington socialites and politicians who came in carriages to view the battle) on the road. The Confederates, who had dug in at Centreville, quickly fell back, abandoning their earthworks and a signal tower. Local residents told Federal scouts that the Confederates headed back towards Bull Run, a run being a local name for a creek or small river. On 18 July, the Federals found Confederates dug in at Blackburn's Ford on that run, and opened fire with artillery. Then the 1st Massachusetts advanced and were quickly driven back. Another advance was also driven back and then the Confederates, under Major-General James Longstreet, counterattacked. But the lack of training now showed, as both sides fell apart in confusion, the strict lines called for in battalion drill dissolving into loose clumps of men unable to budge each other.

McDowell rode to the sound of the guns and, upset a battle had begun that could spoil his plans, ordered the Federals to stop fighting and dig in where they were. He then returned to his main forces, and the Federals, disobeying his orders, followed him. Losses in the first skirmish of the battle were small, some 83 Union and 68 Confederates.

McDowell's plan was to turn the Confederate left flank along the Bull Run. Little did he know that the Confederate commander, Beauregard, up from his recent success at Fort Sumter, planned to turn McDowell's left flank at the same time. In the early morning of 21 July, McDowell had his flanking units on the march, while his diversionary attack on the Confederate centre began to fire at about 5.00 a.m. Meanwhile, the flanking column, believing itself hidden by the green woods through which they marched, reached a ford over the run.

Unknown to them, however, they met one of the first innovations of the Civil War. Before the war a U.S. Army doctor devised a system of signalling over long distances with signal flags, and his assistant, who had gone south at the war's outbreak, organized a small Signal Corps for Confederate service. These signalmen now spotted the Federals and signalled back to the Confederate headquarters, 'Look to your left. You are turned.' At the same time, Confederate troops began to arrive who were supposedly pinned down miles away in the Valley of Virginia. They had slipped away and taken a train, in one of the first military uses of this modern machine, to join Beauregard's troops.

The Federals pushed forward, smashing through troops from Alabama and South Carolina. A brigade of Virginia infantry fresh from the Valley, including the 33rd Virginia Infantry under eccentric schoolteacher Brigadier General Thomas J. Jackson, arrived and formed a line behind where other Confederates struggled on Henry Hill. 'There stands Jackson like a stone wall,' Brigadier-General Bernard Bee, commander of the other troops pointed out, adding they should 'rally behind the Virginians'. Bee fell, and his troops dashed back, many to reform around the Virginia Brigade.

The Federals placed two Regular Army batteries on Henry Hill, supported by a regiment of New York City firemen. The 33rd, battered by their fire, launched an attack on them, one that succeeded because confusion about the two armies' flags, which looked similar, and the uniforms of the 33rd, which caused the Federals to hold their fire until the 33rd was amongst them. The 33rd took the guns, but were quickly driven out. Then the 1st Virginia Cavalry charged into the New Yorkers, and sent them flying. McDowell's green troops, hot in new wool uniforms and exhausted from unaccustomed long marches, were just about finished.

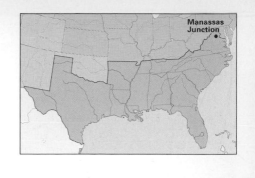

▼ Men, especially those from the losing army, were buried where they fell. If they could be identified their graves were often marked by crude boards like these, with names and units.

PRIVATE JOHN O. CASLER, 33RD VOLUNTEER VIRGINIA INFANTRY REGIMENT

I then took a stroll over the battlefield, to see who of my comrades were dead or wounded, and saw my friend, William I. Blue, lying on his face, dead. I turned him over to see where he was shot. He must have been shot through the heart, the place where he wanted to be shot, if shot at all. He must have been killed instantly, for he was in the act of loading his gun. One hand was grasped around his gun, in the other he held a cartridge, with one end of it in his mouth, in the act of tearing if off. I sat down by him and took a hearty cry, and then, thinks I, 'It does not look well for a soldier to cry,' but I could not help it.

► General P.G.T. Beauregard held field command at First Bull Run, although he was ranked by General Joseph Johnston who relinquished command because Beauregard was more familiar with the area and troop dispositions when Johnston's men arrived on the scene.

Finally, at about 4.00 p.m., the Confederates launched an attack on McDowell's right flank. Slowly at first the Federals began to retire. A stray Confederate shell destroyed a wagon on the bridge over the run, and many volunteers began to panic. While the Regular Army brigade withdrew in good order, volunteers began throwing away their arms and equipment. Their retreat didn't stop until they reached the outskirts of Washington. Many civilians, including a New York congressman who came to witness the great victory, became Confederate prisoners.

Jefferson Davis, unwilling to remain in Richmond, arrived in the hour of victory. Begged to order an advance on Washington, he refused. But because the green Confederates were as exhausted and disorganized in victory as the Federals were in defeat, the Confederates were content with their tactical victory.

THE BATTLE OF BALL'S BLUFF

McDowell was replaced, indeed many of his own men considered him to have deliberately lost the battle of First Bull Run, signalling his movements to the enemy with his oddly shaped hat. His replacement was the hero of West Virginia, George B. McClellan. Lincoln this time didn't argue about the necessity of keeping the army in its camps around Washington until it could be adequately supplied and drilled. At the same time, the terms of the regiments enlisted for 90 days expired – indeed some even expired on the way to Bull Run and the regiments refused to go any further. Lincoln called for more men to be recruited for the term of three years or the duration of the war, whichever was shorter. Volunteers came in such numbers that some had to be turned away; in Pennsylvania, the Governor, Andrew Curtin, created a Reserve Corps for the potential use of volunteer regiments who were too many for U.S. Government requirements.

Soon a belt of camps grew around Washington, extending into the city's Virginia suburbs. The Confederates drew up their lines around these, extending west along the Potomac River. The two sides skirmished, but neither side – and especially McClellan, who was drawing up his own secret plans that had nothing to do with this area – wanted to get into a real battle.

McClellan posted a division west of Washington, near Poolesville, Maryland, to protect the fords that crossed the upper Potomac. Southern scouts, spies, and carriers of needed materials, such as medicines, crossed these fords freely, and the Federals intended to stop this commerce. Brigadier-General Charles P. Stone, an old Regular Army officer, commanded the division. Across the river from Stone's division was a smaller Confederate command under Brigadier-General Nathan G. 'Shanks' Evans, a man reputed to favour the bottle from time to time. Evans' command was posted around the town of Leesburg, Virginia.

McClellan posted another Union division, commanded by Brigadier General George A. McCall, south of Leesburg, near Dranesville, Virginia. McCall's job was to force Evans to retire from Leesburg, and he asked Stone to help by making a 'slight demonstration' against the Confederates on his front. Stone authorized a reconnaissance and several officers crossed the Potomac, coming up on Leesburg from the south. Just outside Leesburg they spotted,

▼ *Left:* **Retreating Union soldiers carry the body of their dead leader, Colonel Edwin D. Baker, down the steep hillside to the Potomac River at the Battle of Ball's Bluff as victorious Confederates follow them. A minor battle, Ball's Bluff caught the national interest because of the famous Union commander and the lack of other military action at the time.**

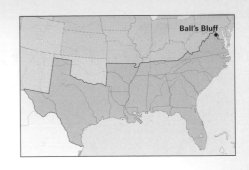

in the darkness, what appeared to be a line of tents, and returned to report that the Confederates had pitched an advance camp that could be easily taken, with fast-moving Federals returning quickly to their side of the Potomac after the raid.

Command of the brigade for this job went to Colonel Edward D. Baker, a U.S. Senator from Oregon and personal friend of Abraham Lincoln, but a military novice. He ordered a Massachusetts regiment to cross the river and take the camp on 21 October. The place picked for the crossing was cut by an island, Harrison's Island, in the middle of the river, and a steep bluff on the Virginia side of the river. Baker botched the operation from the beginning. He failed to make sure there were adequate boats to transport all the troops quickly and when he arrived on the scene, instead of going across first to be able to react immediately to events, he stayed at the crossing, playing the part of a river traffic policeman rather than that of a brigade commander. Moreover, the attack was not kept secret and Evans was therefore able to organize his troops to defend his position.

The first regiment went across and moved to where the tents had been seen. When they got there, however, it turned out what were believed to be tents were not tents at all. Moreover, Confederate infantry poured volley after volley into them, and they fell back through the woods and across the clearing to a position at the top of the bluff. In the meantime, Baker's other regiments and a couple of small cannon had crossed the river and formed a line along the top of the bluff. A semi-circular clearing stood as open ground between them and where the Confederates, hidden in the woods, had followed the retreating Federals and now continued to fire at their open targets. Only their poor marksmanship, not unusual in period armies, where marksmanship training was not practised, saved the Federals from worse losses. One Massachusetts regiment hung up their grey overcoats on tree limbs over their heads, only to have the overcoats torn to pieces by Confederate musketry.

Baker gave no commands. At one point he helped with one of the cannon. Finally, when he was on one flank, a Confederate advanced out of the woods and mortally wounded the would-be soldier. The cause of the Union had a notable martyr. Some Federals attacked the Confederate left, trying to work their way west along the river to a crossing. Others plunged down the bluff to escape, swamping boats and throwing away equipment in an attempt to swim to Harrison's Island. Many were shot in the water; others drowned; and many were captured on the Bluff. Stone was arrested and imprisoned without a trial for 189 days in the controversy that followed. Eventually freed, his career was nonetheless over.

▼ During the Battle of Ball's Bluff Baker strolled along the battle lines, not thinking to give orders necessary to save his force, until he was killed as a Confederate soldier darted from the woods line to gun him down. This is a contemporary print of that event.

◄ Senator Edward D. Baker, a pre-war friend of Abraham Lincoln, had seen military service in the Mexican War, but was no soldier when he was made colonel of the 1st 'California' Regiment, an infantry unit raised largely in Philadelphia at the war's outbreak.

◄ Brigadier-General Charles P. Stone, a career military officer with a distinguished record, became a scapegoat for Baker's rash and amateurish actions after Ball's Bluff. He was imprisoned without a hearing, but eventually was exonerated and reinstated in the U.S. Army.

COLONEL CHARLES DEVENS, JNR., 15TH MASSACHUSETTS VOLUNTEER INFANTRY

When we were fairly down upon this plateau, and moving along in the direction, Colonel Cogswell said to me, 'We shall all be destroyed here; we must do something to try to retard them.' I said, 'What shall we do?' He said, 'Deploy your regiment as skirmishers over the bank.' I gave the order, and the regiment pushed over this plateau over on to the abrupt bank of the river, and there behind the trees they fired up toward the bluff and towards the enemy, who were now crowding up towards the crest of the bluff in great force. It was obvious that resistance in that place was hopeless.

THE WESTERN THEATRE

◄ Confederates trapped a small force of Union troops in Lexington, Missouri, in September, 1861. The Union dug in on a school ground. After a short siege the Confederates attacked, using soaked cotton bales for protection, and captured the garrison and the gold it protected.

Out West things were generally going a bit better for the Union cause. On 12 September in the divided slave state of Missouri, Southern sympathizers under Major-General Sterling Price trapped a Federal force led by Illinois politician Colonel James Mulligan in Lexington. There, cut off from the river and after a short siege, Mulligan's men surrendered to Confederates who had advanced under fire, rolling soaked cotton bales before them. But he had bought time for Federal reinforcements to arrive in Missouri, which would never actually be wholly in the Confederate camp. Indeed, Lexington itself was recaptured by 16 October.

The important slave state of Kentucky, the birth state of both Lincoln and Davis, tried at first to be neutral, saying it would fight against either side that crossed its borders. Such a declaration favoured the South, since it created an artificial defensive line that protected its vital state of Tennessee from invasion. Since official Confederate government policy was to defend every inch of border, such a block released thousands of troops for defensive purpose elsewhere.

Unfortunately, the Southern commanders on the field failed to realize this, and on 18 September, Confederate forces occupied Bowling Green, Kentucky, a clear violation of the state's neutrality. There was no going back now, and the Confederates set up a defensive line based on the strong points of Columbus, Bowling Green, and the area around the Cumberland Gap. The Federals replied by scouting towards Columbus and then, on 25 September, setting up their own post in Smithland, Kentucky. As with Missourians, Kentuckians would serve on both sides in the war, and both Confederate and Union governments for both states would exist. And, in a hint of what was to come, Federal gunboats, operating from the naval base in Cairo, Illinois, sailed down to engage shore batteries near Columbus on 7 October.

Cairo was home to Brigadier-General Ulysses S. Grant, who was to be of great importance. Named a regimental colonel when

▲ A failed career soldier, driven to resign or face charges due to drinking, failed farmer, and insignificant store clerk when the war began, Ulysses S. Grant was given command of an Illinois regiment due to his U.S. Military Academy education and friendship with a state congressman. He would prove to be the Union's leading general.

the war began, he was quickly commissioned a brigadier-general of volunteers and posted to this Southern Illinois town. He was itching for a fight, something that would be true of him throughout the war. He was never happy when he was forced to remain still, but spent all his time plotting how to use whatever force he had on hand to win the war.

Grant devised a plan to use the ships available in Cairo to transport him and his troops down river to Belmont, Missouri, on what essentially would be a raid and a training mission under fire for his troops. On 7 November, the expedition took off and quickly landed just north of Belmont, which was opposite the bluffs at Columbus. Confederates on guard there were quickly driven back to their camps. Excited Federals stopped to loot their tents while the Confederates, reinforced by troops from across the Missouri River, reorganized within the woods outside their camp and returned to counter-attack the Federals. Many of them were greatly alarmed at seeing the revitalized Confederates and suggested that they should surrender. Grant would hear none of this and, stiffening their resolve, got his troops back to their ships and reboarded – himself being the last person to set foot on the gangway before they set sail.

Losses were surprisingly heavy for such a small affair. Federals lost some 607 casualties out of 3,000 engaged, while Confederates lost some 641 out of 5,000 participants. The skirmish itself was fairly meaningless, save that it did give Grant and his men valuable combat experience. But Lincoln was delighted to see one of his generals with a desire to take on and destroy the enemy, and thereafter kept his eye on the western leader.

On the Southern side, it became clear that superior Union naval power made the rivers running south, such as the Mississippi, daggers that plunged deep into the heart of the Confederacy. General Albert Sidney Johnson, a well known pre-war U.S. Army officer who had led the force into Utah to put down a potential Mormon rebellion just before the war, was given overall command of the theatre. His command called for 10,000 Mississippi volun-

teers, as well as the construction of forts along the river, especially Forts Henry and Donelson on the Tennessee and Cumberland rivers. Federals would continue to send reconnaissance parties in both Missouri and Kentucky, towards Milford and Mount Zion Church in Missouri, and to Mill Springs and Sacramento in Kentucky. Further out west, Native American tribes loyal to one side or the other clashed on 16 December at Chustenahlah, Indian Territory. The pro-Union Creeks were badly beaten and many of them failed to get through winter snows to safety in Kansas. The major fighting in 1861 was, however, all over.

▲ Colonel James Mulligan, who raised a regiment known as 'The Irish Brigade' in Chicago at the war's beginning, oversees the unsuccessful defence of Lexington, Missouri. Colonel Mulligan is standing left, centre, behind the cannon, pointing towards the attacking Confederates.

◄ Major-General Sterling Price of Missouri was not notably for secession when the war began, but was named leader of that state's pro-southern militia in 1861 and thereafter received a Confederate commission. However, he was not an outstanding general.

BRIGADIER-GENERAL U.S. GRANT, U.S. ARMY

About this time, too, the men we had driven over the bank were seen in line up the river between us and our transports. The alarm 'surrounded' was given. The guns of the enemy and the report of being surrounded, brought officers and men completely under control. At first some of the officers seemed to think that to be surrounded was to be placed in a hopeless position, where there was nothing to do but surrender. But when I announced that we had cut our way in and could cut our way out just as well, it seemed a new revelation to officers and soldiers.

THE NORTH CAROLINA COAST

Back on the east coast, McClellan kept his steadily improving army in its camps, as was traditional over winter months. Yet the war effort continued, as Lincoln pressed for a strategy of threatening the Confederates, who had avowed to defend every inch of their borders, 'with superior forces at different points, at the same time'. Federals profited from this approach when on 7 November a naval squadron sailed into Port Royal Sound, pounding two defending Confederate forts to pieces and driving off a small Confederate naval force. Landing parties secured Hilton Head Island, South Carolina, and a 12,000-man Army force landed to garrison the post. The post became an important point for refuelling Navy blockaders, as well as being a starting point for raids on the Confederate shore-line from Savannah, Georgia, to Charleston, South Carolina.

What planners in Washington now came up with was a joint Army-Navy plan for the biggest amphibious operation since allied forces had slogged ashore in the Crimea the previous decade. Approximately 100 vessels, under the command of Commodore Louis M. Goldsborough, set sail from Hampton Roads, Virginia, carrying some 15,000 soldiers, including the famed New York Zouave regiment, the 9th New York, or Hawkins' Zouaves, under Major-General Ambrose E. Burnside. Their destination was the coast of North Carolina, with its thousands of islands and inlets that made it ideal for blockade runners and privateers.

The force reached Hatteras Inlet on 13 January 1862, but poor staff work found the soldiers lacking the landing craft they needed to disembark with their artillery, horses, and wagons. Burnside, nevertheless, assumed command of the Department of North Carolina. On shore, state and Confederate officials scrambled to put together a defending force, but the troops simply weren't there. Three days later, Union Navy craft gave the coastal Confederates another scare by docking in the harbour of Cedar Keys, Florida, where they landed parties which burned seven small vessels, some railway carriages and a pier. Superior Federal Navy resources were already beginning to tell on Southern defence.

Finally, by 25 January, equipment for landing arrived, and Burnside's men began crossing the shallow bar into Pamlico Sound, Hatteras Inlet. Their movement was unopposed as no Confederate troops were available for local defence. On 8 February, Burnside was confident enough to send 7,500 of his troops against a fortified force of some 2,000 Confederates dug in on Roanoke Island, the site of the first British colony in the New World almost two centuries earlier. The battle itself was minor; the Confederates were unable to dig into the sandy soil well enough to make up for the overwhelming odds, and a quick charge easily overran the Southern position. The Confederates swiftly surrendered, along with the 30 cannon they had on the island.

While not much in terms of casualties (the Confederates had some 75 casualties, while the Federals had some 264), the result

▼ Union troops assault Fort Huger on Roanoke Island, North Carolina, in this contemporary print. The Confederate government, which had interior lines it could have used advantageously, instead tried to defend every inch of its states, deploying its forces in penny packets that could be easily picked off by concentrated Union forces.

▶ Colonel Rush Hawkins raised the 9th New York Volunteer Infantry, 'Hawkins' Zouaves', at the beginning of the war. To encourage morale he had them dressed in imitations of French Algerian Zouave units, which were then considered the finest soldiers in the world. His cap is a French-style kepi.

COLONEL RUSH HAWKINS, 9TH NEW YORK VOLUNTEER INFANTRY REGIMENT

Nearly two companies had succeeded in getting into the clearing immediately in front of the earth-work, where the mud was more than ankle-deep, and where they were receiving the undivided attention of the enemy's three pieces of artillery, and getting a shot now and then from the infantry. It was at this point that Colonel De Monteil was killed. Seeing that it would be almost impossible to get through the deep mud, I had made up my mind to face to the front and make an effort to charge the work, and after a moment's consultation with Lieutenant-Colonel Betts and Captain Jardine, who commanded the right company, I ordered my bugler to sound the charge.

▲ Rhode Island inventor and businessman A.E. Burnside gained early recognition by leading successful expeditions along the Carolina coast. He would prove less of a success in his roles as commander of the Army of the Potomac and IX Corps commander.

was shocking for the Southern cause. Command of Pamlico Sound not only cut off routes to the open sea for North Carolina shipping, it also secured the island for the Federals. Their base on the island threatened the heart of North Carolina, especially its coastal towns. A superior Union Navy ensured that the Confederates could not cross the waters in enough strength to regain the position, so it would remain safely and unthreatened in Federal hands from then on.

Burnside proved the value of Roanoke Island when, on 13 March, he moved troops to the North Carolina mainland, the goal being the town of New Berne. The town was defended by a small force of some 4,000 men commanded by Brigadier-General Lawrence O. Branch, who had placed his fortifications some six miles below the city, one flank resting on the Neuse River. Burnside's men landed six miles from this line of defence, and began advancing as Branch pulled his own men back closer to the town.

Driving rain and muddy roads, less of a problem in North Carolina's coastal sandy soil than in the thick mud of Virginia, did not slow down the Federals as they attacked Branch's lines. The Confederates fought well, holding their lines for several hours until finally their centre gave, and the Federals streamed through. Some

Southern troops managed to flee, crossing the Trent River and burning the bridge behind them. Others fought where they were, and eventually surrendered. Federal gunboats followed and shelled Confederates who stopped in New Berne.

Branch, realizing his troops could not hold, gathered as many as he could and fled by rail to Kinston. It would be almost a week until he managed to reconstitute his force in anything like the numbers he started out with, although his casualties were only some 600 including prisoners. On 14 March, Burnside entered New Berne, a town the Federals would hold, although once threatened in 1864, through to the war's end.

▲ The U.S. Navy proved a major factor in winning a war against the South, which had little shipbuilding capacity or naval tradition. Here Union ships commanded by Flag Officer Samual DuPont pound Confederate defences at Port Royal, South Carolina.

FORTS HENRY AND DONELSON

There was no winter rest for the Western armies. On 19 January 1861, Confederate forces under Brigadier-General Felix K. Zollicoffer attacked a Federal force near Mill Springs, Kentucky in a battle of the same name, also known as Fishing Creek, Logan's Cross Roads, Somerset, and Beech Grove. The Federals, having information beforehand of the attack, began moving towards the Confederates through the darkness and rain. Zollicoffer was very short-sighted and, in the dark, rode up to identify a formation. They were Federals, and their volley brought down the Confederate general, who had been wearing a white raincoat. Although devastated by Zollicoffer's death, the Confederates managed to rally and hold until Federal reinforcements broke their left, when they fled, abandoning their position at Cumberland.

At the same time, Federal army and navy units began probing Confederate defences at Fort Henry, defending the Tennessee River south. They found the fort badly positioned, on low-lying ground that allowed the river to flow across its mud walls. Moreover, work on Fort Heiman, another position across the river which would aid Henry's defence, had hardly begun.

On 3 February 1862, General U.S. Grant therefore had his troops at Cairo, Illinois loaded on to transports and they pushed off down a river swollen by heavy rains and melting snows. Ironclad gun boats preceded them. The next day Grant's troops began to land, and the Confederates quickly abandoned Fort Heiman, which still had no guns in place, and pulled some 3,000 men into Fort Henry. Federal forces quickly moved into Fort Heiman.

Much of Fort Henry was actually under water when, on 6 February, Federal gunboats began to bombard its soggy walls. The Confederate commander, Brigadier-General Tilghman decided with so much of the fort's walls impossible to defend, it would be best to get most of his infantry away, down the road to nearby Fort Donelson. In the meantime, those artillery who remained manned their guns gallantly against the four ironclad and three wooden gunboats. But it was a lost cause. The fort's big guns were soon put out of action, although they had done good work in inflicting considerable damage upon some of their attackers. The boiler of the *Essex* was pierced, scalding 28 officers and men and forcing it to retire.

▲ A serving naval officer later sketched this explosion of a gun on board the Union gunboat *Carondelet* during the attack on Fort Donelson. That fort's heavier guns and less exposed position allowed the Confederates again to prove that 'ships can't sink forts.'

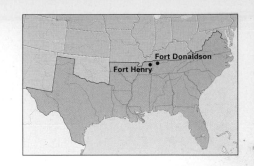

Nonetheless, the battle was one-sided and before Federal infantrymen even got in position to attack, the fort's flag was struck. The fort was so flooded that the ship's boat sent to receive the surrender actually rowed across its riverside walls.

Fort Henry secured, Grant himself went over the next day to reconnoitre Fort Donelson, whose guns covered the Cumberland River near Dover, Tennessee. He liked what he saw, and he brought up his troops to dig in and take the fort. On 13 February he attacked, but the fort, now under command of inept Major-General John B. Floyd who had arrived before the attack with reinforcements, held, as sleet fell and temperatures dropped. The Federals, most of whom were without overcoats, suffered in the trenches they had dug with their bayonets and tin cups.

In the meantime, the Navy gunboats arrived off Donelson's walls. But Donelson was no Henry. Her guns were better positioned and there were more of them. An over-confident Navy, expecting to repeat its Fort Henry success, began its bombardment only to be met with counter-battery fire that shot away the steering mechanisms on two of the gunboats and even wounded the Navy commander, Flag Officer Andrew Foote. The Federal gunboats, unable to overcome the fort's defences, withdrew in some confusion. The Army would have to do the job.

The Confederates, in the meantime, trapped with no way of escape from the river, decided to attack and break out through the Federal lines. Just before dawn on 15 February, the men, equipped for a long fight and march thereafter, hit the Federal positions, breaking through the line on the Federal right. They had an open road to Nashville and safety. But Floyd, for reasons unknown, had simply had enough and ordered his men to return to their own

lines. The last chance for escape was gone. Grant ordered his men to close the gap and by that evening both sides were virtually where they were when the attack had begun.

That night the Confederate generals held a council of war, and they decided, with the exception of cavalry commander Nathan B. Forrest, to surrender. Floyd, who had been Secretary of War in Washington before the war and had been accused of stuffing Southern arsenals with equipment in preparation, feared capture, as did Major-General Gideon Pillow, the second in command, and they turned over command to an old friend of Grant's, Simon Buckner. Then the two senior Southern commanders fled in boats, while Forrest led his command through snow and freezing water, along a route so rough that no Federal infantry bothered to guard it. In a short time, Forrest's men would be in Nashville, as would Floyd and Pillow neither of whom would hold further Confederate commands.

Buckner sent to ask Grant's surrender terms and was shocked to receive word that Grant would accept nothing less than unconditional surrender. Nonetheless, he did surrender his garrison on 18 February and Grant, now known throughout the country as 'Unconditional Surrender Grant', became a household name.

▼ Union gunboats engage the water battery at Fort Donelson in this post-war print. After suffering severe damage, the gunboats were forced to withdraw, leaving the army to besiege the fort until it surrendered.

▲ Brigadier-General Lloyd Tilghman saw that it was pointless to defend a fort that was so flooded. He withdrew his infantry, from Fort Henry to Fort Donelson which was supposedly much more defendable.

► Andrew H. Foote, here shown wearing the pre-war U.S. Navy dress uniform of a captain, was one of the Union navy's better officers. He received the thanks of Congress for his actions patrolling rivers in Confederate-held territories.

COMMANDER HENRY WALKE, U.S. NAVY

The firing from the armored vessels was rapid and well sustained from the beginning of the attack, and seemingly accurate, as we could occasionally see the earth thrown in great heaps over the enemy's guns. Nor was the fire of the Confederates to be despised; their heavy shot broke and scattered our iron-plaiting [sic] as if it had been putty, and often passed completely through the casemates. But our old men-of-war's men, captains of the guns, proud to show their worth in battle, inspired life and courage into their young comrades.

THE DEFENCE OF TENNESSEE

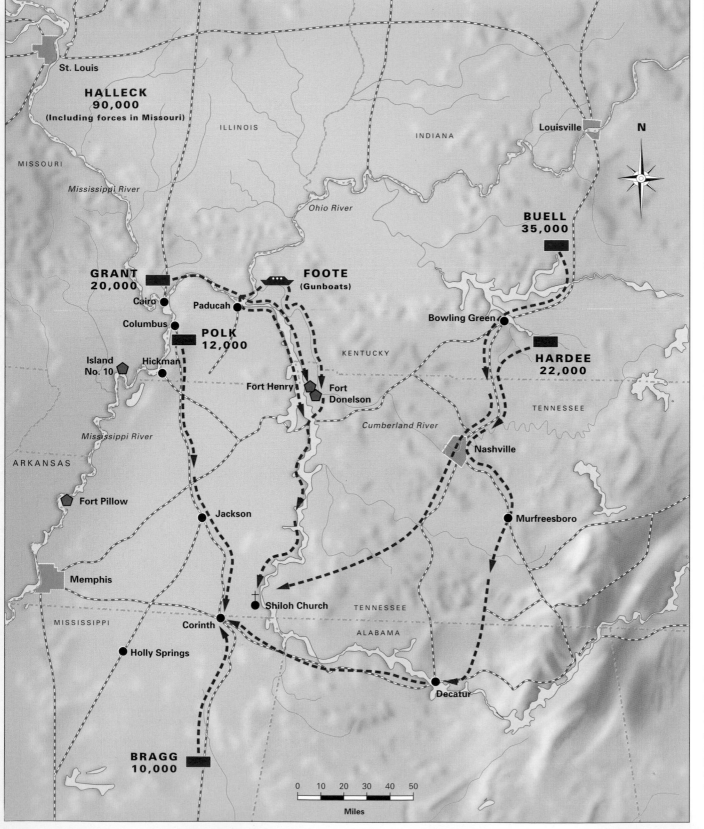

St. Louis

**HALLECK
90,000**
(Including forces in Missouri)

MISSOURI

ILLINOIS

Mississippi River

INDIANA

Louisville

N

Ohio River

**BUELL
35,000**

**GRANT
20,000**

FOOTE
(Gunboats)

Cairo

Paducah

Bowling Green

Columbus

**POLK
12,000**

KENTUCKY

**HARDEE
22,000**

Island
No. 10

Hickman

Fort Henry

Fort
Donelson

TENNESSEE

Cumberland River

Mississippi River

Nashville

ARKANSAS

Fort Pillow

Jackson

Murfreesboro

Memphis

Shiloh Church

TENNESSEE

MISSISSIPPI

Corinth

ALABAMA

Holly Springs

Decatur

**BRAGG
10,000**

0 10 20 30 40 50

Miles

▲ Brigadier-General
Simon B. Buckner, shown
here in the pre-war
uniform of a general of
Kentucky State Guard,
was disappointed that
Grant, a pre-war friend to
whom he'd loaned money
in a time of need, offered
nothing less than
unconditional surrender at
Fort Donelson.

◄ A.S. Johnson divided
his forces defending
Tennessee, with Bragg's
men in reserve. He had to
rapidly shift Hardee's
troops to aid Polk as
Grant came down to
Belmont and showed
how the Union could use
the Western rivers to
their benefit.

THE INVASION OF NEW MEXICO

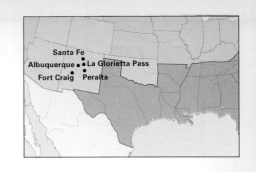

At the outbreak of the Civil War, most of the nation's small armed forces were spread across the West, safeguarding settlers from hostile Native American tribes and making sure land recently obtained from Mexico remained in American hands. After Fort Sumter was fired on, the government hastily recalled most of its combat troops to the eastern theatre, where the main war was to be fought. Defence in the West was left in the hands of locally-raised volunteer units with little or no combat experience.

At the same time, the west provided much of America's riches. Gold mines dotted California, while silver mines were bored into hillsides in Nevada and Colorado. Southern soldier, Henry H. Sibley, who had seen extensive service in the West before the war broke out, decided that the stage was set for a Confederate invasion which could take both silver mines in Colorado and gold mines in California to produce riches to sustain a prolonged war. Jefferson Davis accepted his plan for the invasion with a single brigade of Texans and sent him west with a brigadier-general's commission in June 1861.

Sibley's men were poorly supplied, armed largely with civilian weapons and Colt revolvers, and clad in a variety of dress that rarely matched the plates shown in the official Army Regulations. Nonetheless, with a great deal of enthusiasm, Sibley got his brigade organized and by January 1862 moved them out of Texas, heading for Fort Craig, New Mexico. By 21 February, they were camped across the Rio Grande from Fort Craig, but they had already begun to run short of food. Sibley's plan called for resupply from captured Federal posts, so the quick capture of each garrison was essential for the campaign to succeed.

Sibley advanced across the river at the Valverde Ford, where Union troops who had earlier left the fort, were waiting for them. Initially the Federals were successful, driving the Confederates back to a desperate position. A Confederate counterattack on the Federal battery, during which a limber chest exploded, disheartened the Federals, who fell back and were pursued to Fort Craig's walls. The one bright point for the Federals in the action occurred when a group of New Mexican militiamen came across some 30 of Sibley's supply wagons, four miles from the battle, and burned them, costing the Texans vital supplies.

Rather than besiege Fort Craig, which would take supplies the Texans didn't have, Sibley decided to bypass the post and head straight to the two largest towns in the area, Santa Fe and Albuquerque. On 7 March the first Confederates entered the latter,

only to find the burnt remains of what had been the largest Federal supply depot in the area. Some civilian stores remained and another depot at nearby Cuberco had survived, so the Confederates were able to replenish their supplies. This represented only a fraction of the supplies they needed however.

Still they pressed on to the territorial capital, Santa Fe, where they found a deserted town as Northern officials fled to Las Vegas or Fort Union. Sibley realized he had to capture Fort Union intact with its supplies. He marched his men out and by 25 March reached La Glorietta Pass, also known as Apache Cañon, the way through the Sangre de Cristo Mountains to Fort Union. Federal troops under a Colorado volunteer officer, Major John Chivington, prepared to defend this pass and on the 26th they fought to a stand-off. The two sides were reinforced on the 27th and moved into the pass to fight. The Confederates forced the Federals in the pass to retreat by nightfall, but a second, smaller, Federal column passed over the mountains to fall on the Confederate supplies left behind and destroy them, as well as the 500 - 600 mules and horses used to pull the wagons and artillery.

Lacking food and even sufficient clothing for the cold desert nights, Sibley's men fell back to the barren city of Santa Fe. The Federals received further reinforcements and headed after them, so Sibley had to pull back to Albuquerque, a miserable march in a cold rain. By 11 April, Sibley's survivors were back there. Sibley considered taking the offensive again, but realized his ill-supplied troops were unable to overcome the stronger, better equipped Federal forces. On 12 April, he sent his first troops towards El Paso, Texas, with the rest following the next day. They left many of their guns buried behind them.

Each man was allowed to carry only a blanket, eating utensils, and the clothes he was wearing. The march, through some of the worst country on the continent, with little water and less to eat, was a brutal one. Men died on the way and were left half buried in the sand. On 24 April, the survivors of this ill-prepared campaign finally reached friendly territory on the Alamosa River. Never again would Confederates threaten the West.

▼ Brigadier-General Henry H. Sibley had a good plan to take the silver fields of Colorado and gold fields of California. But his lack of attention to the logistics needed to make the plan work, compounded by his continuous heavy drinking, caused its ultimate failure.

PRIVATE OVANDO J. HOLLISTER, 1ST REGIMENT OF COLORADO VOLUNTEERS

Lowe's horse fell with and partly on him, badly wrenching his knee, in the ditch just around the corner where the fire was hottest. Hastily disengaging himself from his horse, he jumped over a bank to gain some shelter. He was confronted by a stalward Texan captain, who, with a cocked pistol bearing on him, 'guessed Lowe was his prisoner.' Lowe sprang on him like a cat, and after a violent struggle disarmed and marched him to the rear.

THE BATTLE OF PEA RIDGE

Missouri was a deeply-divided slave state with a large population of Germans, especially in the St. Louis area, who were against slavery. The state, one of the largest of the border states, was important for both sides. St. Louis, besides being home to a U.S. Army arsenal, was also known as the 'gateway to the west'.

Missouri's governor, Claiborne F. Jackson, was pro-Southern and he called for a state convention, which he believed would also be pro-Southern, to keep the state in the Southern camp. In fact, however, the state's voters picked a pro-Union body which named former Governor Sterling Price, who was a moderate, and up until that point had been pro-Union, as its president. In the spring of 1861, Jackson also authorized a pro-Southern State Guard which was organized near St. Louis, home of a large pro-Union majority. Price, who was lining up for an agreement with Jackson, became commander of the State Militia. By June, the government was firmly split, with a pro-Confederate state government set up in Jefferson City and a pro-Union government in St. Louis.

In November 1861 the Confederate Congress officially recognized Jackson's government and admitted Missouri to the Confederacy. At the same time, previously elected Missouri representatives and senators remained in Washington, declaring the state was, as it had always been, a part of the United States. Price moved against the Federal forces in the state, winning a battle at Wilson's Creek and then capturing Lexington by siege.

Although there were not a great deal of resources available for Federal troops in the area, Lincoln felt that retaking Missouri was important and was willing to authorize a rare winter campaign to do so. On 10 February 1862, Major General Samuel R. Curtis set off with a small army of some 11,000 men to drive Price's troops and Jackson's state government out of Missouri. While Jefferson Davis also felt Missouri was important, he was unable to reinforce Price to the same strength as Curtis, and Price withdrew his 8,000-man-strong Missouri force out of the state, into north-western Arkansas.

Once in Arkansas, Price was joined by a small force under Brigadier-General Ben McClulloch, which included pro-Southern Cherokee troops. The group fell back through Fayetteville, home of the state's university, and, by order of the overall Trans-Mississippi Department commander, Major-General Earl Van Dorn, halted just south of there in the rugged Ozarks. The force now numbered some 17,000 men. Van Dorn, eager for glory, decided to

▲ Brigadier-General Ben McClulloch was fatally wounded in the breast by a Union sharpshooter while directing the right wing of the Confederate army on March 7 at Pea Ridge. He had been a U.S. Marshal in Texas before the war.

go on the offensive himself. He sent his command north, through narrow roads in wet, heavy snow, towards Curtis's troops.

Curtis, learning of Van Dorn's advance, pulled his four infantry divisions back to a defensive position near Elkhorn Tavern, along the Sugar Creek. On 6 March, Van Dorn's men arrived in the area and the general, who was too ill to ride and spent the day in an ambulance, having learned the whereabouts of the Federal lines, decided to avoid a frontal attack. Instead his men would march around the Federal position at night. The next morning he would attack from the north at Pea Ridge, with McCulloch and the Cherokees under Albert Pike demonstrating against the Federal right, while the main attack from Price's men would fall on the Federal left near Elkhorn Tavern.

The night was bitterly cold, but the snow had stopped and the day was clear as Van Dorn's columns passed around the Federal position. Behind them they left camp fires burning to fool the Federals. On the morning of the 7th, the Confederates were in position. The plan would have succeeded had it been as originally ordered, for the Federals were not expecting an attack in that direction. However, Price's men were slow off the mark, and did not launch their attack against the Federals until around 10.30. By this time, Curtis had swung his army around and prepared to meet the Southern assault.

Even so, a third assault on the Federal left was successful, pushing the Federals beyond the tavern. Cherokees on the right took Federal artillery, and then seemingly ground to a halt. McClulloch fell, mortally wounded, as did another Confederate

general on the right. Van Dorn pulled some of his troops out of the attack on the right to reinforce Price's stalled assaults and by evening the Federals had been pushed back quite a distance but also reinforced. Night brought an end to the fighting.

Curtis decided overnight that the Confederates must have left much of their supply train behind and would be low on ammunition. Therefore, he decided to launch a counter-attack. First thing in the morning, he sent two divisions under Brigadier-General Franz Sigel against Price's troops and another division, under Colonel Eugene Carr, against the Confederate left. He was right. Although they fought stubbornly, the Confederates first on the right and then on the left, were forced back, past the Elkhorn Tavern. His line broken all along its front, Van Dorn ordered his men to fall back to Huntsville, on the Arkansas River, and then to Van Buren, Arkansas. The Confederacy would never again threaten Missouri, which remained firmly in Union hands.

▼ In the final stages of Pea Ridge, shown here, the Union troops drove the Confederates past Elkhorn Tavern. The northern name for the battle was Pea Ridge, as they usually named battles after geographic sites, while the Confederates called it Elkhorn Tavern, as they preferred man-made sites for their battle names.

▲ Major-General Earl Van Dorn, who was fatally shot on May 7, 1863 at his headquarters by a local doctor who claimed that Van Dorn has 'violated the sanctity of his home.'

◄ Union troops under Curtis were initially driven back by the Confederates at Pea Ridge, but regrouped overnight and returned to the attack the next day. Here they mass for their counterattack that will clear the north-west corner of Arkansas.

FIRST SERGEANT WILLIAM WATSON, 3RD LOUISIANA INFANTRY

The battery was soon silenced, and a loud hurrah showed the guns had been captured by the Indians, and our astonishment was still greater when we saw the whole battery with limber waggons and caissons of ammunition in flames. It seemed that the Indians had a great horror of artillery, and being commanded by their own chief (Standwattie, I think was his name) when they got possession of the guns, they determined, like the old woman at Oakhill, to "burn the pesky things." So, gathering the wheat straw they piled it round the gun carriages and set fire to it, and thus the carriages, ammunition chests, and everything of wood was burned, the guns falling useless on the ground, while the explosions of the ammunition and bursting of the shells made the Indians clear off, thinking the things were possessed by the Evil One, and that even fire would not destroy them.

THE MONITOR AND THE VIRGINIA

From the beginning the South had some basic problems. It had a long coast to defend; it needed to ship cotton abroad to pay for the arms and equipment it could not easily manufacture itself; and it had very limited shipbuilding facilities. Nevertheless, one of the first departments the new Confederate Government created was a Department of the Navy. In one of Davis's more inspired selections, he placed at its head a Floridian, Stephen R. Mallory, who had been head of the U.S. Senate's committee that oversaw naval operations.

Mallory was not only a capable administrator, but also selected top talent to oversee the Confederate Navy's departments, and he had an open mind. He knew the batteries with iron walls used by the French in the Crimean War, and decided that if he could not overcome the U.S. Navy with numbers, he would have to depend on the latest technology. Therefore he told a joint Confederate Congressional committee as early as June 1861 that their navy

would have to depend on iron-clad ships to defend their shores and keep the shipping lanes open.

The question was, where to begin? Luckily for Mallory and his aides, an answer presented itself almost immediately. When the U.S. Navy abandoned its dockyard at Norfolk, Virginia, its men attempted to destroy anything of use there. They failed. They both scuttled and burned one of their better frigates, the USS *Merrimac*, which was having engine work done on it. The burning removed the superstructure, while scuttling it meant that the hull and precious engines simply sunk beneath the waters, quenching the fire. The idea, then, was to raise this hull and engines – engines Southern manufacturing plants would have a very difficult time duplicating – and tow them into one of the dry docks the northern Navy had failed to destroy. From there an iron-clad super-structure could be built on her.

▲ The CSS *Virginia* and the USS *Monitor* engage in this first ever battle between metal vessels. The USS *Minnesota*, the frigate the *Monitor* showed up to protect after the *Virginia*'s victory over the *Cumberland* and the *Congress*, is in the background.

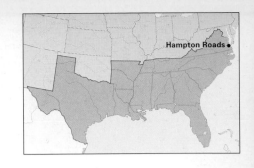

Operations began right away. She was made to mount four guns on each side, poking through sloped iron walls, with a bow gun and an aft gun on a pivot that could be fired through any one of three ports. A heavy iron ram was mounted on her bow, with the idea of ramming enemy ships. Her pilot house was mounted just above the bow gun.

Although her building was kept as secret as possible, word did leak out, and the U.S. Navy Department learned of the threat to its ships off Port Comfort. U.S. Navy Secretary Gideon Welles organized a panel to determine the best type of iron-clad vessel possible and order it to be built. The panel looked over a number of types of ships, mostly simply ships of ordinary design with iron plating over their wood walls. But one, designed by a Swede named John Ericsson, who had earlier designed naval ordnance, was a radical departure. It called for a ship with a very shallow draught, a low freeboard, and essentially no superstructure except for a pilot house of iron bars towards the bow and a single cylindrical turret mounting two guns on the centre of the deck. The turret would revolve, bringing the guns to bear in any direction, as no stacks would be built to obstruct its fields of fire. Unusually, it could be built rapidly as parts would be farmed out to different manufacturers and then assembled in a very modern manner. The panel picked this ship, as well as two others. By October 1861 the keel of this ship, named the USS *Monitor*, was laid, and it was ready to be launched by January 1862.

This was just in time as the CSS *Virginia*, as the Southern iron-clad was named, was sent on its first tests in March 1862. Her engines proved sluggish and undependable, and her draught was deep. Nonetheless, on 8 March, under Flag Officer Franklin Buchanan, she set off against the Federal ships in Hampton Roads. There she first attacked the USS *Cumberland*, ramming her, raking her decks with gunfire and sinking her, whilst receiving little damage. The *Virginia* then turned to the USS *Congress*, setting fire to her before retiring as darkness fell.

That night the *Monitor*, worse for wear after fighting heavy seas, arrived and put in near the remaining major Federal warship, the USS *Minnesota*. Soon the *Virginia* appeared and the *Monitor* was put between her and the *Minnesota*. For some hours the two fought, balls bouncing off both of them. For fear of the Federal ship's guns exploding inside the turret, her gunners were authorized to use only smaller charges than usual; had this not been so it is likely the *Virginia*'s sides would have been pierced. Even so, her stack was riddled with shot, making her already balky engines draw badly. Attempts by the *Virginia* to ram the nimble Federal ship failed and, Buchanan wounded, she finally withdrew, leaving the small, epoch-making *Monitor* in command of the area. Never again would the two meet in combat and the Confederates finally blew up their first iron-clad when her berth was threatened by advancing Federal soldiers. The *Monitor*, not a very sea-worthy ship, sunk while being towed south past Cape Hatteras, North Carolina.

▼ Sailors on the USS *Monitor* wait as a meal is cooked. A hot sun beating on metal decks and an inadequate ventilation system made life below decks miserable in southern climates and most men spent as much time as possible on deck, even sleeping on the wooden topped turret.

▶ The CSS *Virginia* was built on the hull of the old USS *Merrimac*, using that sunken ship's engines, at the Gosport Navy Yard. Her design became a standard for southern-made `ironclads,' as such boats could be built by house carpenters.

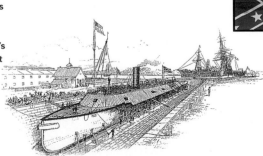

CAPTAIN WILLIAM H. PARKER, C.S.N.

Much has been written and more said about this celebrated fight – the first encounter between iron-clads in the world's history. Viewing it as I did at a distance of more than a mile, I will state that my impression at the time was that, after hammering away at each other for three hours, and finding that the men were wearied out, without making much impression on either side, both vessels had simultaneously drawn off, and decided to consider it a drawn battle.

OPENING THE VALLEY CAMPAIGN

The Valley of Virginia is a rich land of farms, producing so much that it could almost support the population of the state as well as the Confederate Army in Virginia. It runs north and south, the upper valley being in the south, with Harper's Ferry at one end and Staunton at the other. The Shenandoah River wanders lazily through it, flowing from south to north, where it empties into the Potomac River at Harper's Ferry. On the west it is bordered by the Allegheny Mountains, while the Blue Ridge Mountains separate it from eastern Virginia. There are few gaps in the Blue Ridge Mountains that allow easy passage from the Valley to the east; from the north they are Manassas Gap near Front Royal, Thorton's Gap near Luray, Swift Run Gap near Conrad's Store, Brown's Gap near Port Republic, and Rockfish Gap near Staunton. Defending the Valley was vital if the Confederates were to keep eating.

In November 1861 an eccentric professor from the Virginia Military Academy named Thomas Jonathan Jackson was assigned to command the 17,000 Confederates defending the Valley. Jackson was an oddity, prone to riding around with his left arm in the air 'to improve the circulation', and sucking on lemons. Deeply religious – he had taught a Presbyterian Sunday School for African Americans before the war – he was also secretive to an extreme, not sharing his plans with even his nearest subordinates. Moreover, although a West Point graduate, he had not been tried at an independent command level, although his performance at First Bull Run, or the first battle of

Manassas as it was called in the South, where he had gained the nickname 'Stonewall,' was excellent.

Odds were against him. Directly north was an army of some 38,000 men under Major General Nathaniel Prentiss Banks. Banks was not a professional soldier; indeed he held his commission because he was a leading Democratic Party leader, one-time Governor of Massachusetts and Speaker of the U.S. House of Representatives. In order to assure the country that the war was a non-partisan affair, that it was just not a military action of one political party against another, a number of leading politicians such as Banks and a fellow Massachusetts Democrat, Benjamin Butler, received high-level commands in the volunteer U.S. Army. Some of these men worked out; most did not.

Lincoln ordered an overall advance of all Federal forces to begin on the birthday of the country's first President, Virginian George Washington, which fell in February. Therefore, in February, Banks took his men across the Potomac and into the Valley. By 12 March they had reached Winchester, Virginia, the first major town in the Valley. Jackson's men fell back. On the 19th, however, Banks was ordered to give up two divisions of his force, who were to return to Washington to help defend it.

To make up for this loss, another 9,000-man Federal division, under Major-General James Shields, passed through the Manassas Gap from the east, heading towards Strasburg. Small Southern

▼ *Left:* Lieutenant General Thomas J. 'Stonewall' Jackson, in unaccustomed splendor as a Confederate general. He was careless about his personal appearance and at Slaughter Mountain attempted to draw his sabre from its scabbard to rally his troops only to find it rusted in place.

▼ The Battle of Kernstown, the first engagement in the famed 'Valley Campaign' of 1862, was the only battle Stonewall Jackson lost. Jackson's men moved so quickly up and down the Valley, engaging separated Union forces, that they became known as 'Jackson's Foot Cavalry'.

forces fought a brief delaying action there on 19 March. The next day, Shields, being threatened by Jackson's force, headed north towards Winchester. Jackson's men followed closely. Banks advanced to the small town of Kernstown, just south of Winchester.

Encouraged by reports about the weakening of Banks's force, Jackson ordered his 4,000-odd infantry to attack the positions at Kernstown. Shields, however, had deployed his larger force well. On 23 March, Jackson sent two brigades to flank a Federal brigade posted along a ridge, while the cavalry was to hold the right. The Federals hurled a brigade against the Confederate infantry. The exchange lasted two hours and at the end the Confederates withdrew with a loss of 718. The defenders lost some 590.

Although Jackson lost, leaving Shields to boast that he was the only Federal general to ever beat Old Stonewall in battle, the confrontation began a chain of events that would clear the Valley of Federals. Lincoln ordered Banks to return to the Valley to defend Harper's Ferry, an important post because of the railway line that ran east and west through it. Moreover, he withheld an entire corps of troops in the Washington area, where they could defend against any possible attack from the west. And, although beaten in this particular battle, Jackson and his men were far from beaten. True, he was forced to withdraw up the Valley, but he was already planning new offensives. Shields slowly followed in Jackson's wake, finally halting at Strasburg. Action was over for March.

▼ Major General James Shields, shown here in a typically heroic period print, claimed correctly that he was the only Union general ever to have beaten Stonewall Jackson in battle. His career, however, was otherwise quite undistinguished.

▼ Major-General Nathaniel Prentiss Banks may have looked like a dashing soldier in his regulation uniform, but he was actually a politician from Massachusetts whose party support Lincoln needed more as he was embarrassed by the poor soldier Banks actually was.

COLONEL RICHARD TAYLOR, LOUISIANA BRIGADE

I rode down to the river's brink to get a better look at the enemy through a field-glass, when my horse, heated by the march, stepped into the water to drink. Instantly a brisk fire was opened on me, bullets striking all around and raising a little shower-bath. Like many a foolish fellow, I found it easier to get into than out of a difficulty. I had not yet led my command into action, and, remembering that one must "strut" one's little part to the best advantage, sat my horse with all the composure I could muster. A provident camel, on the even of a desert journey, would not have laid in a greater supply of water than did my thoughtless beast. At last he raised his head, looked placidly around, turned, and walked up the bank.

REGAINING THE VALLEY

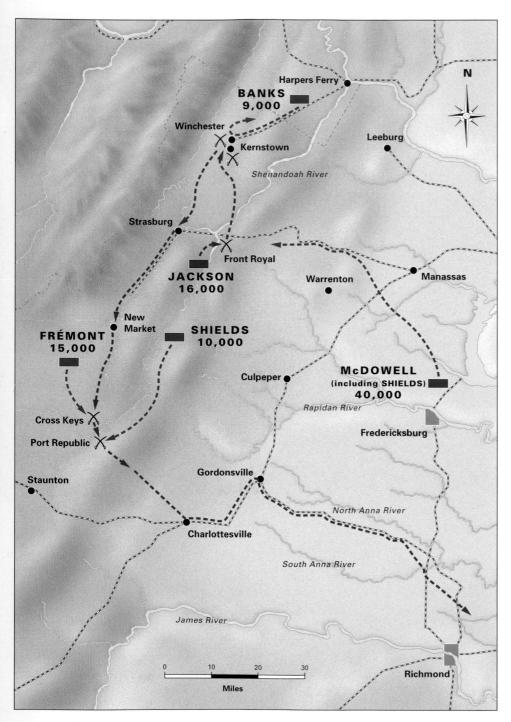

Although threatened by Federals driving towards Richmond, the Confederates recognized the importance of the Valley. In April, the War Department therefore ordered a 8,500-man division under Major-General Richard Ewell to join Jackson's force. This was all Jackson needed. On 30 April, leaving Ewell's division to watch Banks, he took his brigades from Elk Run, along with troops he had left to guard the passes on the Allegheny Mountains to Staunton. The Confederates reached Staunton on 6 May.

Banks, learning of Jackson's reinforcements, fell back towards New Market, passing through the town and reaching Strasburg on 13 May. But Jackson was not after Banks; he aimed his men west towards troops under Major-General John Charles Fremont, who were in a position to link up with Banks's force and again present overwhelming odds. On 8 May, the 10,000 Confederates under Jackson ran into some 3,000 men from Fremont's command who rashly attacked the Southerners. Jackson, who had the advantage of numbers and ground, deployed his troops in a semi-circle on the military crest of Sitlington's Hill, near the Bull Pasture River, east of McDowell. Again and again the Federals attacked, but each time they were forced back, eventually losing 256 men, while Jackson lost 498. The Federals withdrew towards Franklin, in Western Virginia, getting there by 13 May, thus essentially being taken out of the remaining Valley battles.

Jackson, barely waiting to pick up the wounded, headed his men back north towards where Banks's force was waiting in Strasburg. Banks, not having any idea of Jackson's plans, decided to cover the Valley at any point where the Southern troops could appear. He sent a detachment of 1,100 troops under Marylander John Kenley to Front Royal, just east of Strasburg. Jackson in the meantime advanced straight towards Banks's main force, but at the last minute swung east at New Market, crossing the Massanutten Mountain to Luray. He then marched his weary troops, now known as 'Stonewall's Foot Cavalry', north-east again. He ordered Ewell's men to join this force, which now reached some 16,000 men with 48 cannon. Were this force able to get north of Strasburg, he would have caught Banks unable to retreat and could force his surrender.

On 23 May, Jackson's men reached Front Royal, quickly attacking and capturing all but 200 of Kenley's men. By mid-morning of the 24th, an alarmed Banks ordered his men quickly north, towards Winchester. Jackson pushed his men, and advance parties of Southern troops ran into Northern cavalry from Maine and Vermont, skirmishing the next day at Berryville, Strasburg, Middletown, where they captured many Federals from the rear of Banks's column, and elsewhere in the Valley. While it was a close call, eventually Banks did manage to get his men away safely, reaching Winchester, where he ordered his wagon trains even further north, to Williamsport on the Potomac River.

The morning of 25th May found Banks at Winchester, while Jackson's equally weary men prepared for the day's obvious com-

▲ Three Union armies, under Fremont, Banks, and McDowell, threatened the lush Valley of Virginia. Jackson dashed his famed "foot cavalry" up and down its dusty roads to defeat each force separately in a lightning campaign.

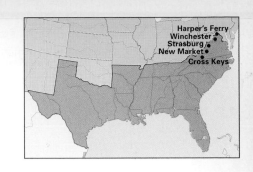

ing attack. It was a Sunday, a day on which Jackson did not like to fight, but he didn't want to wait for Federal reinforcements to arrive.

Banks drew up his defensive lines just south of the town itself, and Jackson's old brigade, the Stonewall Brigade, led the attack in the centre of the line. Under heavy assault, the Federal line finally caved in, the blue-clad men running for their lives through the streets of Winchester as civilians braved the bullets to cheer their men on. Banks and his troops fled 35 miles, finally resting along the Potomac River. Losses would have been heavier for the Federals, but the Confederate cavalry had been sent earlier after another Federal detachment and was unavailable for the pursuit.

By the 27th, the survivors of Banks' army were in Williamsport while Jackson led his men north again, this time towards Harper's Ferry. Lincoln now ordered Fremont, possibly the brightest of his generals, with 15,000 men to cross the Allegheny Mountains to block Jackson's path, while another 20,000 men under Major-General Irwin McDowell was to cross the Blue Ridge from Washington to Strasburg, and Banks' 5,000 men would return to the attack from the north. These forces should be capable of trapping Jackson and clearing the Valley.

Jackson gave his men no rest. Marching over muddy roads he hurried south of Winchester and slipped between McDowell and Fremont. Federals did find Confederates near Front Royal and there was some skirmishing on 31 May, with other skirmishes on 2 June at Strasburg and Woodstock, but essentially Jackson had escaped. By 6 June, Jackson was at Port Republic, sending his troops on 8 June against Fremont's men, who were still not united with McDowell's troops, at Cross Keys. A single brigade there drove off a Federal division, paralysing Fremont into total inaction. Then the next day Jackson swung around and struck Federals at Port Republic, forcing them to retire to Mount Jackson and Luray. Lincoln ordered McDowell back to Fredericksburg and Fremont to halt at Harrisonburg. The campaign was over. From 22 March, Jackson's men travelled 676 miles in 48 marching days, fought five battles, and kept the Federals largely out of the Valley.

▼ Union troops under Fremont who have obviously outstripped their sources of supply attempt to trap Jackson's forces in the Valley. The quick-marching Confederate infantry moved too rapidly for them, however, and Jackson was able to avoid all such attempts.

▲ Major-General Richard ('Dear Dick') Stoddard Ewell lost a leg during the Second Manassas campaign but returned to service in the Army of Northern Virginia with a wooden leg. He commanded the first Confederate troops to be on the field at Gettysburg.

▲ Major-General John Charles Fremont was the first candidate for president on the Republican Party ticket, while Lincoln was the second. His premature emancipation proclamation in the west embarrassed Lincoln, while his military activities were inept.

CHAPLAIN HENRY R. PYNE, 1ST NEW JERSEY CAVALRY REGIMENT

While the rebel battery continued to fire, the first battalion took a wider sweep, and now came toward the road in its rear, while a portion of the third, under Haines and Janeway, strove to take it more in front. As our men set up their wild cheer, the supporting rebel cavalry broke and retreated in disorder, leaving the guns without protection. The artillerists and drivers began to waver and look behind them, but by each gun sat the officer of the piece with his pistol in his hand. Deserted by their supports, our troopers coming on, and their pistol-shots whistling over them, these gallant fellows forced their gunners to limber up as accurately as if on drill; and then, at a gallop, the pieces were whirled along to the rear.

THE WAR GETS BLOODIER

1 APRIL **1862** The Army of the Potomac sends troops to the Peninsula, advancing on Richmond from the east.

6 APRIL The Battle of Shiloh begins – Grant's army barely turns back a major Confederate assault.

7 APRIL Island No. 10 captured – Federals open the way down the Mississippi River to Memphis.

25 APRIL The U.S. Navy captures New Orleans – A fleet under Rear Admiral David Farragut receives the surrender of the South's second most important city.

3 MAY Confederates evacuate Yorktown, Virginia – Federals prepare a formal siege of the first defence line on the Peninsula, but the Confederates fall back before it can begin.

5 MAY Battle of Williamsburg, Virginia – Federals engage a Confederate rearguard operation.

1 JUNE Battle of Seven Pines – The Army of the Potomac (A.o.P.) withstands a Confederate counterattack outside Richmond.

25 JUNE Beginning of The Seven Days – The Army of Northern Virginia (A.N.V.) forces the A.o.P. to withdraw ending its drive on Richmond.

9 AUG Battle of Cedar Mountain – Lee sends Jackson to turn back a Federal threat from Washington.

26 AUG Second Manassas campaign opens – Jackson and Longstreet fool Federals under John Pope and nearly destroy his army.

14 SEPT Battle of South Mountain – Federals reacting to a captured Confederate orders rush to trap the A.N.V. as it moves into Maryland.

17 SEPT Battle of Antietam – The A.N.V. stops the A.o.P. in the bloodiest single day of the war.

22 SEPT Emancipation Proclamation – Lincoln frees slaves living in seceded states.

3 OCT Battle of Corinth, Mississippi – A Confederate attempt to retake Corinth fails.

8 OCT Battle of Perryville, Kentucky – An attempt to bring Kentucky into the Confederacy fails.

7 DEC Battle of Prairie Grove – Federals retain control of northwest Arkansas.

13 DEC Battle of Fredericksburg, Virginia – An attempt to break through the A.N.V. and take Richmond is turned back in a one-sided battle.

31 DEC Battle of Stone's River, Tennessee – Both sides run into each other and the Confederates eventually withdraw although the battle was essentially a draw.

23 JAN **1863** The Mud March – The A.o.P. gets stuck as it tries to flank the A.N.V. in the rain.

APR 7 Naval attack on Charleston. S.C. – An attempt to bombard Southern forts with iron-clads fails.

MAY 1 Battle of Chancellorsville – The A.o.P. tries to turn the A.N.V. flank at Fredericksburg, but an audacious Confederate attack ends in victory.

MAY 1 Battle of Port Gibson – Grant's army continues a move against the major Southern stronghold on the Mississippi, Vicksburg.

MAY 16 Battle of Champion's Hill – An attempt to halt Grant's steady march fails.

MAY 12 Siege of Port Hudson, Louisiana – A Federal army besieges another city on the Mississippi.

While there had been fighting, the battles, even the largest of them, had been relatively small affairs, not much larger than the public was used to from the Mexican-American War of 1846–48. This would not last long. In 1862 huge battles with losses larger than all of America's previous armies would be fought. In the east, little more would result from all these than stalemate, with the Army of Northern Virginia turning back attempt after attempt to capture the south's leading industrial centre, Richmond. In the west, too, no key locations would be taken by northern troops, nor any whole southern armies captured. At the end, however, the result would be the continued chipping away of the Confederate States of America.

SHILOH

Grant wasn't one to rest on his laurels, and he moved on down the Tennessee River into enemy territory. While one Federal army under Major General Don Carlos Buell took Nashville, Tennessee, Grant's forces ended up at the small riverside town of Pittsburg Landing. Some 23 miles away at Corinth, Mississippi, Confederate General Albert Sidney Johnson, seconded by General P.G.T. Beauregard, gathered an army and drew up a plan to destroy Grant's army before it could be reinforced and capture Corinth.

Johnson's 44,000 men were inexperienced and not fully armed. However, they outnumbered Grant's men by 5,000. This would not be the case once Buell's 36,000 men joined Grant. So Johnson, widely believed to be the best general in the Confederacy, had to move quickly if his plan was to succeed.

On 3 April, the Southerners started off. The weather was against them, rain turning roads into mud. In all, it took three days to get into position. Grant, never one to bother his mind greatly about what his opponent's forces were doing, discounted any potential Confederate attack. His men were drawn up in their unfortified camps, with their left on the river. Two Federal gunboats, the *Lexington* and *Tyler*, added their cannon to the defence of the Union left.

Just before dawn on 5 April, the Confederates were finally in position. The plan called for an attack that would be heaviest on the Federal left, driving them away from the river and trapping them. Poor staff work, and vague plans, however, caused the Confederate attacking force to be fairly evenly spread across the entire front, ensuring the plan would fail.

The orders were given to advance without drum or bugle so as not to warn sleeping Federals, and the Southern troops moved out. At about 5.00 a.m. they first made contact with Federal pickets in the heavily wooded area. More Federals were awakened or dropped their coffee cups, formed up, and entered the battle until a full brigade was in action. As a result it was three hours until the first Confederate wave actually hit the main camp of Brigadier-General William T. Sherman. Despite the warning of the firing, many of Sherman's men were caught unawares and fled. The Confederates next hit divisions commanded by Brigadier-General Benjamin M. Prentiss and Major-General John A. McClernand. For a time, the Federals rallied and held, but after three hours of fierce fighting, they fell back. Many ran to hide behind the bluffs of Pittsburg Landing.

Many of Prentiss' men rallied in a heavily wooded area in the centre of the line, later known as 'The Hornet's Nest'. There they withstood as many as a dozen attacks, tearing great holes in the Confederate ranks. While the stubborn Federals bought Grant

▼ *Bottom:* The Confederate plan called for the main assault on the Union left, next to the river. The gunboats *Lexington*, shown here, and *Tyler*, however, kept up a stream of cannon fire that, while it did not cause many casualties, did stop the Confederates by intimidation.

▼ Heavy artillery, in this case 24-pounder guns normally used for sieges and fortifications, formed the last line of defence for the Union army at Shiloh. These guns would see considerably more action at Vicksburg.

▶ Major-General John Alexander McClernand, an Illinois politician whose support Lincoln needed, had virtually no military service before his appointment as a general. A bombastic individual who rubbed Grant and other professionals the wrong way, he was sent home during the siege of Vicksburg.

time, he drew up a new line of defence along the ridge overlooking Pittsburg Landing. At around 2.30 p.m., a stray shot struck Johnson in the leg, passing through his tall boot. He disregarded the injury, instead pressing his men on to the attack. However, his boot soon began to fill with blood and, wavering, he fell from his horse. By the time his wound was discovered, he had bled to death and Beauregard assumed command.

Attacks on the Hornet's Nest continued, the Confederates bringing up some 62 pieces of cannon to rake the Federal position. Finally, at about 5.30 p.m., Prentiss saw that his men were not capable of resisting further. He surrendered about 2,000 survivors who had bought a great deal of time to allow the Federals to build up the rest of their line.

On the Confederate right, where the main blow was to come, the Federal gunboats fired into attacking troops, driving them further inland and making disrupting their attack.

By twilight the Confederates were in possession of much of what had been Federal camps. But many hungry Southerners had left their ranks to go through stuffed Union haversacks for food and to hunt through tents for blankets, clothes, and ammunition. By twilight it was obvious that the puff had gone from the Confederate attack, and Beauregard decided to suspend operations. He nonetheless planned to press on the next day.

During the night, however, Grant was heavily reinforced by both a division of his own army which had taken a circuitous route, only arriving after, and by most of Buell's army. Grant decided to strike himself. At 7.30 the next morning, a greatly revived Federal army attacked across the entire front. Although the Confederates fell back slowly, the Federals had the upper hand. Finally, by late afternoon, Beauregard called off the battle and ordered a withdrawal. Although the Federals prevailed, even Grant did not feel

strong enough to pursue the Confederates back to Corinth, where Beauregard's weary troops finally halted.

The result of the two days' of gruelling fighting appalled everyone. Beauregard's morning reports showed 1,723 men had lost their lives, 8,012 wounded, and 959 missing. Corinth was a charnel house of wounded Confederate soldiers. Grant lost 1,754 killed, 8,408 wounded, and 2,885 captured, mostly from Prentiss' command.

PRIVATE LUCIUS W. BARBER, 15TH ILLINOIS VOLUNTEER INFANTRY

Our camp was situated three miles from where the fighting began, and it was not until after sunrise that the tide of battle surged upon us. I heard the distant rattling of musketry and first thought it was something else. I was writing a letter home at the time. But soon the long roll was sounded and then I knew that there was work for us to do. Throwing my unfinished letter to Milton, who was sick, I told him to finish it and tell where I was, then hastily putting on my accoutrements, gun in hand, took my place in the company. In less than five minutes from the time the bugle was sounded, the regiment was on the march to the scene of conflict.

▶ A Union battery holds its position in the well-named 'Hornet's Nest'. The time spent by the Confederates there allowed Grant to draw up a second line of defence while Union reinforcements hurried to his support.

OPENING THE PENINSULA CAMPAIGN

Major-General George B. McClellan, fresh from his victories in Western Virginia, was brought to Washington to replace ageing war hero and General-in-Chief of the U.S. Army, Winfield Scott. McClellan produced a plan to take Richmond and end the war. He would move south all the forces from the Washington area, using the overwhelming Federal Naval might, and land by sea on the end of the Peninsula separating the James and York Rivers that flowed east from around Richmond. Then he would move up the Peninsula and take the city.

The plan had advantages. First, it made use of the U.S. Navy, both to protect the Army's flanks and to ensure quick resupply. Even the wounded could be evacuated more quickly and easily by ship than overland. Second, Fort Monroe, at the tip of the Peninsula, was already in Union hands. But, the plan also had disadvantages. It would require a great deal of trust from political officials that their capital city was safe with only a minimal force around it. It would limit the front of the Federal Army so that at any given fight, the Confederates could meet the Federals equally man for man. This latter fact did not seem to be a problem to McClellan. Using a civilian detective, Alan Pinkerton, who sent operatives into Richmond to spy, McClellan already believed – or said he did – that the Confederates had vastly more troops than they actually did.

At any rate, McClellan's fame and success record gave him the upper hand and Lincoln reluctantly agreed to this plan. In March 1862, McClellan began loading his troops and equipment onto a fleet of ships and headed south. In all he brought 105,000 men to attempt to overcome a Confederate force of some 17,000 Confederates under Major-General John B. Magruder, a pre-war professional U.S. Army soldier. Magruder had drawn up a line of defence that included ponds and works first used by British and American forces in the War of American Independence near Yorktown, Virginia.

McClellan's problems began the first day his troops landed and he took advantage of every problem to avoid having to fight tough battles. His information was that the land was sandy so that rain would quickly drain away and roads would be easily passable. This was wrong, and thick Virginia mud slowed him down greatly. Moreover, Lincoln, concerned about the success of Jackson's Valley campaign, detained some of the forces McClellan had expected would be assigned to his army.

So it was that a cautious McClellan arrived outside Magruder's works and decided they were too strong to take by assault. Magruder helped him to reach this decision by passing the same troops again and again within view so McClellan's scouts thought the Confederates had a much larger force than they had. McClellan, a military engineer by training, decided on a formal siege and sent for siege guns and began building works. On 5 May, he prepared for a grand assault, only to be notified by his scouts that Magruder's men had already pulled out.

General Joseph Johnston arrived on the Peninsula with reinforcements and took over command from Magruder. The rearguard of the retreating Confederates was caught in a fierce fight near Williamsburg, colonial capital of Virginia, by advancing Federals.

▼ Right: **Major-General John Bankhead Magruder's engineers laid down a carefully designed series of fortifications around Yorktown that took maximum advantage of geographic areas such as swamps to aid the defenders. This was the 'water battery,' the strongest of their forts.**

◄ Allan Pinkerton, left, was McClellan's chief source of information about the Confederates facing him. A railroad detective before the war, Pinkerton's operatives proved inept, fuelling McClellan's mistaken ideas that the Confederates greatly outnumbered his own army.

► McClellan had seen the Siege of Sevastapol during the Crimean War and produced his own copy of allied lines outside the greatly outnumbered Confederate forces near Yorktown. These great guns were never to fire a shot in anger from these lines.

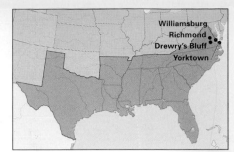

▼ McClellan originally planned to land his force at Urbana, closer to Washington, and dash into Richmond before Johnston could react. Fear of the CSS *Virginia* made his switch to Fort Monroe, a fortress the Confederates never took.

However, they managed to retreat. Norfolk then fell to the Federals on 9 May. Unable to bring the CSS *Virginia* with its deep draught further up-river to safety the Confederate Navy had no choice but to destroy the ship. The Federal Navy took advantage of this, bringing its ships to Drewry's Bluff, a point on a bend in the James River only seven miles below Richmond. There, Confederate sailors, marines and soldiers used heavy guns and employed underwater mines, called 'torpedoes', which scattered the Federal flotilla.

McClellan's troops drew near enough to Richmond to see the spire of St. Peter's Episcopal Church and hear its bells call to worship on Sunday. Davis grew as impatient with Johnston's constant retreating as Lincoln had with McClellan's failure to advance. But McClellan then made an error. He separated his army, putting two corps south of the Chickahominy River, a swampy creek that ran across the Peninsula, and three corps north of it. With the rains that arrived in late May the Chickahominy turned into a raging torrent.

Johnston then turned and, on 31 May, struck the Federal III and IV Corps. Unfortunately for the Confederates, imprecise orders passed on by untrained and uncertain staff officers caused the Confederate corps to become entangled on the narrow roads and the attack to be delayed. In the rough fighting that followed, Federal command control and troops outperformed that of their enemies, and ended in a Federal tactical victory. Moreover, Johnston, who seemed to attract enemy bullets, was wounded and taken from the field. Command passed to an adviser of Jefferson Davis, Robert E. Lee.

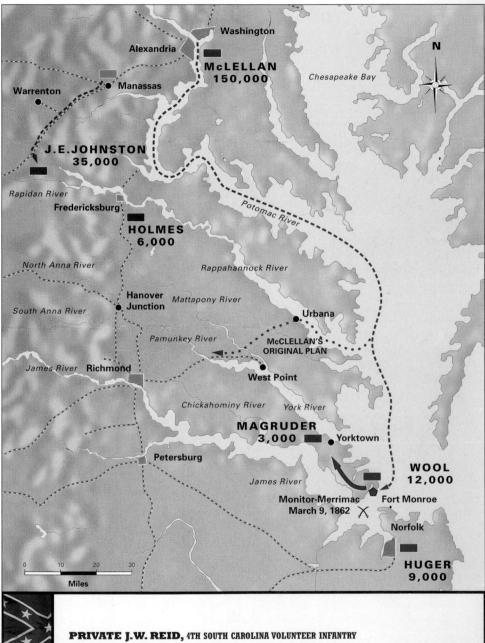

PRIVATE J.W. REID, 4TH SOUTH CAROLINA VOLUNTEER INFANTRY

A little after daylight they appeared in large numbers and soon attacked. We held our ground as long as possible, giving them as good as they sent, until about 7 o'clock, when they came in such overwhelming numbers as to force us back on our main lines, a distance of about six hundred yards, with the loss of several of our men. I lost all my clothing and blankets. In falling back we had a slanting hill to go down and when we got to the foot of it our artillery opened fire on the enemy over our heads. This stopped them from following us.

THE SEVEN DAYS' CAMPAIGN

▲ The 5th U.S. Cavalry
Regiment charges at
Gaines Mill. The famed
cavalry charge was largely
a thing of the past,
rendered obsolete by the
rifled musket. Most
cavalry fought dismounted
with their carbines more
like light infantry than
traditional cavalry.

► Major-General J.E.B.
Stuart led his cavalry in a
ride around McClellan's
Army of the Potomac to
reconnoitre before Lee's
attacks on that army
during the Seven Days.
Stuart lost only one man
and one cannon in the
three-day ride.

McClellan, shocked by the furious assault on his two corps, even though he had driven the Confederates off, and concerned by the artificially inflated assessment of the enemy he and his intelligence operatives made, decided to use siege tactics again to overcome the fortifications facing him outside Richmond. On the other side, Lee assumed command, on the wounding of Johnston on 1 June 1862, of the force he now named the Army of Northern Virginia. Lee, known to his new command as 'Granny Lee' and 'The King of Spades', organised the digging in around the city while he took time to visit each subordinate command to learn about its men and leaders.

Lee, however, was not of a defensive mind. He wanted to strike the Federals at any opportunity. Soon one would arise. McClellan decided to change his base to the south side of the Chickahominy where his army could be easily supported by the Navy. Soon he had the bulk of the Army of the Potomac, 70,000 men, on that side of the

swampy creek. A veteran general, Major-General Fitz John Porter, commanded this force, a reinforced V Corps. At the same time he left some 30,000 men north of the Chickahominy to link up with another corps he expected to join his army. This new corps would be marching overland from Washington, past Fredericksburg, and around to join McClellan's force. Once again his force would be divided.

Lee, desperate for intelligence of McClellan's forces and positions, sent his cavalry under Major General J.E.B. Stuart, to reconnoitre his left flank. Stuart was authorized, if his way back was cut off, to continue around the entire Federal army, rejoining Lee on the right. On 12 June the cavalry, accompanied by horse artillery, set off. In a three-day ride, with the loss of only one man, Stuart reached the right flank and safety. In the process the cavalry had done a great deal of damage to Federal supplies, burning a boat, and, even more important, had learned that the Federal northern flank was open to attack.

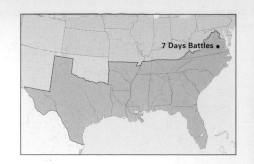

7 Days Battles •

The decision to attack was simple. To lull the Federals facing him while adding to concerns in Washington and in the Valley, he made a great deal of noise about sending a division west to the Shenandoah Valley where Jackson had defeated the separated Union forces. At the same time, however, he secretly had Jackson's army leave the Valley and join the main army outside Richmond. Then he moved the bulk of his army north of the Chickahominy, leaving only some 25,000 men south of the river. He had already taken his measure of McClellan and reasoned that the chances of McClellan suddenly assaulting his lines in force there were minimal.

After a meeting with his generals, including the unusually weary Jackson, Lee picked 26 June as the day to hit Porter's troops. That morning most of Lee's troops were in position, but Jackson's men were strangely missing. An impatient Major-General A.P. Hill, who always showed his lack of respect for reconnoitring his front before bounding into action, finally gave up waiting for Jackson, and opened the attack at Mechanicsville without proper support. Heavy artillery and small arms fire broke up this attack. A second attack by a cousin, Major-General D.H. Hill, also failed. In all, 1,484 Confederates were lost, compared to 361 Federals.

Porter withdrew to Gaines' Mill, where, under orders from McClellan, he drew up a strong semicircle of lines. The next morning Lee sent his men against this position, in another series of failed attacks. Confederate losses were 8,751 compared to Union losses of 6,837. Many of these, 2,836, were lost when the position was abandoned. Porter continued his skilled withdrawal, unfortunately losing the wounded at hospitals around Gaines' Mill, to rejoin McClellan's main army.

Lee, however, felt that it was his attacks that were driving Porter's men back, unaware that McClellan had previously ordered the eventual withdrawal. Lee believed it was he who had the initiative and continued to press the attacks. In fact, most of his attacks continued to fail, victim not only of his basic incorrect belief, but

The day being clear and warm, the men soon began to realize the difficulty of transporting large amounts of clothing and camp equipage on their shoulders, and the roadsides were strewn with blankets and overcoats, dress coats and pants. The bushes and trees for miles along the route were thickly hung with articles of clothing, mostly new, and all good. Soldiers who had put on their marching suit would fall out of the ranks, the knapsack would quickly disgorge a new coat and pants, the wearers would as quickly divest themselves of the soiled garments and replace them with the new ones, the others being left on the ground.

also of poor staff work that led to uncoordinated assaults and misdirected troops. The two forces clashed on 29 June at the Peach Orchard and Savage Station, and at White Oak Swamp and Glendale the next day. Finally, McClellan had all his troops together on a ridge protecting his base Malvern Hill on the James River. It was ringed with Federal artillery – artillery which Confederates acknowledged was superior to their own. Despite the strength of the Federal position, Lee ordered a final series of assaults that were bloody failures. The result of the last three days' action was losses of over 9,000 Confederates and almost 5,000 Federals. For an army with a significantly smaller population than the Federals, Lee's campaign was a disaster. In the short term, however, it appeared to be a success, as McClellan never again attempted a drive on Richmond. That threat was over.

▲ Union artillery was quickly recognized by both sides as vastly superior to Confederate artillery. Here Union artillery checks the advance of Confederate infantry during the Battle of White Oak Swamp. Lee's attempts to destroy McClellan's army were in vain as McClellan had already begun his retreat as Lee attacked.

BATTLE OF CEDAR MOUNTAIN

From his vantage point in Washington, Lincoln saw the fighting around Richmond during the Seven Days' Campaign and decided that the bulk of Confederate forces had to be engaged in this fierce fighting. He therefore brought east a Western hero, Major-General John Pope, who had overseen the capture of Island No. 10. He assigned him a hodgepodge of forces in Northern Virginia and Maryland, dignified by the name Army of Virginia. Pope was ordered to strike overland towards Richmond.

Pope took some time to organize his widely spread forces and in that interval, as fighting had died around Richmond, Lee reacted to the new threat. One of the first things Pope had done when he assumed command of the new army was to issue a proclamation stating that he'd come from the West, where they did not entertain lines of retreat and were used to seeing the backs of their enemies. He promised to have his 'headquarters in the saddle' until Richmond fell and Lee was beaten. Lee took Pope's bombast rather personally, and, once he was convinced he'd so bloodied

McClellan that 'Little Mac' was no longer a threat, dispatched Jackson's corps north to meet this new threat.

Jackson's 17,000 men reached Orange Court House on the evening of 7 August, moving a few miles further north the next day. Again bad staff work worked against the Confederates, as A.P. Hill's division had not been notified about the next day's march and the bulk of Jackson's men became separated from them.

Pope was also on the move and by 8 August had learned Jackson's men were in the area. His lead troops, a corps of some 8,000 strong, were commanded by General Banks, then placed at Cedar Run, eight miles south of Culpeper. Jackson, without waiting for proper reconnaissance, decided to hit Banks's II Corps. It was late in the afternoon of August 9 before the Confederates were in position to attack. The Federal left was drawn up in open fields, but their right was masked by heavy woods. A turnpike ran up the centre, dividing the two flanks, while much of the Confederate artillery was posted on Cedar Mountain itself, a high, wooded hill slightly to the rear of the Confederate right.

The Confederates advanced across the wide front, entering the woods where some commands became separated and lost. Worse, the commander on the extreme Confederate left, Brigadier-General Charles S. Winder, late commander of Jackson's old 'Stonewall Brigade', was struck by a shell fragment and mortally wounded. The lead unit, the 1st Virginia 'Irish' Battalion, was stopped dead by a heavy Union volley. As the Confederate attack in the woods stalled, Brigadier-General Samuel Crawford's brigade of 1,700 Federals hidden in the woods launched a massive counter-attack, sweeping through the Confederate line and breaking it up totally. Even the famed Stonewall Brigade fled, many of its troops out of the battle for the remainder of the fighting.

Jackson himself, waving his sword, which had been rusted into its scabbard, rode among his troops to rally them. Reinforcements in the form of A.P. Hill's division arrived and dashed into battle. Officers waved their regimental colours to give their troops points to fall back to. Eventually the Confederates were able to stabilize their position.

On the Confederate right the situation was less desperate. The men fell back slowly and in good order, never having been broken under the weight of Banks's attack. As the sun was setting, Jackson ordered a counter-attack all along his lines. The larger numbers of

▶ Brigadier-General Samuel White Crawford had been the regular army surgeon in the Fort Sumter garrison at the war's beginning. He rapidly switched to a combat command and proved to be a very adequate general as well as a doctor.

KEY
1 McCELLAN
2 LEE
3 POPE
4 JACKSON
5 HEINTZELMAN
& RENO
6 LONGSTREET

◀ No longer fearing McClellan, Lee sent Jackson and then Longstreet to stop John Pope's Army of Virginia. Jackson first clashed with Union troops at Cedar Mountain, then pushed on to decisively beat Pope at the Second Manassas.

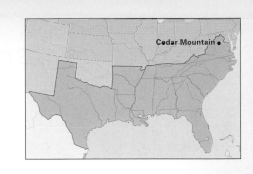

CAPTAIN JULIAN W. HINKLEY, 3RD WISCONSIN VOLUNTEER INFANTRY

Suddenly, from the side of the slope and from the bushes and rocks on our front, arose the Confederate infantry, and poured into our ranks the most destructive musketry fire that I have ever experienced.

Lieutenant-Colonel Crane was killed, and fell from his horse at the first volley. Major Scott was wounded, being carried off by his horse. Captain Hawley, of the company on our right, was wounded, and a third of his

men were killed or wounded at the same time. The right began to fall back, some of the men helping off wounded comrades, others loading and firing at the enemy as they slowly retreated to the woods.

▲ A contemporary print of Union troops charging Confederates at Cedar Mountain shows the regulation way of advancing. The front rank is at the position of 'charge bayonets', while the second rank hold their muskets at 'right shoulder shift'. In reality, combat was a great deal more informal than this.

Confederate troops now told, and the Federals in their turn began to fall back. A desperate Federal cavalry charge down the turnpike in the centre of the line failed to make a dent in the Confederate advance. Still, the advance was slow as the Federals, encouraged by their initial success, gave way only slowly. Nonetheless, at the end Jackson's men drove Banks completely off the field, Banks himself narrowly avoiding capture in the process.

In all Banks had lost 2,200 men, while Jackson had lost some 1,300 – and both generals had made some serious mistakes. Jackson failed to obtain accurate information of the actual enemy

numbers and positions. Banks also failed to learn his enemy's numbers and, even when it was obvious that his troops were badly outnumbered, failed to send back to Pope for reinforcements or to disengage. Moreover, he failed to keep a reserve to stem the final Confederate counterattack.

Both sides picked up valuable intelligence from this fight. Pope learned that Jackson's corps was now in his area, separated, he figured, from Lee's main force and vulnerable. The Confederates learned that Pope was advancing south aggressively and had best be taken seriously.

SECOND BULL RUN

Now that it was clear that McClellan's campaign was going nowhere, Lincoln ordered his troops withdrawn from the Peninsula, to be brought by ship north and then to join Pope's army. The last of McClellan's men left Harrison's Landing on the James River on 16 August. Two days later Pope pulled his men back along the Rappahannock to await the arrival of these reinforcements. For several days Confederates skirmished with Pope's men, convincing the western general that he had time for more troops to arrive before launching his offensive.

But the Confederates were on the move. Stuart's cavalry raided Catlett's Station, capturing Pope's baggage wagons complete with his best uniform coat, as well as important papers. And, on 25 August, Jackson set his men in motion, aiming for Manassas Junction and its vital rail supplies. The next day, Confederate cavalry captured this centre, with Jackson's men following by that evening.

What they found astonished the hungry Confederates, who picked through crates of delicacies such as canned oysters, jams, and, most important to them, bottles of Champagne and whiskey. There being few Confederates of German origin, they largely ignored the barrels of lager brought south for the many Federal Germans.

Large numbers of the poorly clad Southern troops were now seen in nice new blue trousers, overcoats, caps, and even jackets—although this could prove dangerous in combat. What the men did not put on or eat, they burned and a pillar of smoke could be seen for miles as packed railway carriages went up in flames.

Pope reacted quickly. Within two days his troops located Jackson's force, as, to draw them into his web, Jackson had struck a Union division near Groveton in a skirmish known as Brawner's Farm. From a hidden position just north of the Warrenton Turnpike, once one brigade had passed, he hit another on the march. Fierce fighting, with the battle lines at times only 75 yds apart, produced many casualties, about 1,300 on each side, but little results. By nightfall, the Federals were forced to withdraw, but the Confederates were too exhausted to pursue. They remained there with their main line of defence along the Stony Ridge, using an unfinished railway line for trenches.

Pope now believed he had Jackson in check. He concentrated his troops on this line, on the same battleground as First Bull Run had been fought just over a year earlier. His attack, however, was not concentrated, but piecemeal. As each unit reached the field he

▼ *Left:* **This contemporary Currier & Ives print shows a Union assault during Second Bull Run. Such prints were printed and coloured cheaply to be sold widely and hung up in parlours all over America as an early mass medium.**

▼ **Lieutenant B.S. Calef, 2d U.S. Sharpshooters, shows the typical informal wear of Union officers in the field. Recruits in the two regiments of sharpshooters had to pass a shooting test and thereafter wore special dark green uniforms and carried breech-loading Sharps rifles.**

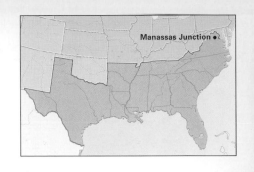

ordered them forward, but the Confederates were able to beat each unit back in turn. Federals in the centre of the line actually reached the top of the Confederate line. However, their line held and the Federals fell back.

As Pope's men pressed on, the second army corps in the Army of Northern Virginia, led by Lieutenant General James Longstreet, believed by Pope to be far away, crossed through the passes to the field and took its position on the Confederate right. That's where Pope then hurled troops under Fitz John Porter. But the unexpected presence of fresh Confederates was more than they could handle. Federal attacks on the Confederate right were broken up. For the first time in action Confederates massed their artillery and did to the Federal infantry what Federal artillery had done to Confederate infantry at Malvern Hill.

Porter was then ordered to renew his attacks, but simply ignored the order. Although the move saved thousands of Northern lives, it cost Porter his career. Pope, suspecting him of being a political ally of McClellan had Porter brought before a court martial. Porter was removed from the army, although years later his rank was restored.

That night Federal scouts reported that the Confederates were retreating. In fact they were just shortening and strengthening their lines, but Pope wanted to believe otherwise. He ordered Porter to attack again, which his men did three different times. Each time they were beaten back, the Southern troops so short of ammunition that they resorted to throwing rocks at the advancing enemy. Federal reinforcements also failed to budge the solid Southern line.

When it was obvious that the Federals had nothing left, Longstreet ordered his entire line forward. As the famed 'Rebel Yell', a fearsome battle cry, echoed over the field, the Federal line, hit on its left, rolled up and disappeared. Jackson's men joined in the attack as entire Federal units disintegrated. Some managed to pull themselves together and join in a valiant defence of Henry Hill, where fighting had been fiercest a year before. They managed to buy time for the rest to escape. By nightfall Pope's entire Army of Virginia was in retreat to Centerville.

▼ **Stonewall Jackson's men virtually destroyed the important Union supply depot at Manassas Junction, Virginia, drawing Pope's army after him. Even so, the U.S. military was so well organized that the depot and rail lines were running smoothly again within a matter of days.**

PRIVATE JOHN O. CASLER, 33RD VIRGINIA INFANTRY

We then sallied forth in quest of more plunder, and went to the captured trains of cars. They were loaded with everything belonging to an army-such as ammunition for infantry and artillery, harness, tents, blankets, clothing, hospital stores, and several loads of coffins for officers to be sent home in (we didn't want them), and one car was loaded with medical stores in boxes. Here we found something we did want, for each box had stored in it from four to eight bottles of fine brandy and whiskey. We soon commenced tearing them to pieces, throwing the medicine around in every direction in search of bottles.

THE BATTLE OF CHANTILLY, VIRGINIA

On Sunday, 31 August, Pope's army was gathered along the heights of Centreville, where they were reinforced by two corps from McClellan's Army of the Potomac. While the Federals spent the day reorganizing, taking care of the wounded, and getting fresh food and supplies to its veterans, the Confederates continued their aggressive scouting. Lee saw the Federals on the ropes, ready for the one knock-out punch he always anticipated scoring. Now he thought he had a chance to destroy Pope's Army of Virginia, plus whatever troops from the Army of the Potomac had reached him before they could retire to the safety of the ring of forts around Washington. He sent the cavalry under Stuart, who had, after the Peninsula ride around McClellan been given overall cavalry command of the Army of Northern Virginia, to scout the Union right. Jackson and Longstreet, meanwhile, moved their corps to Chantilly, towards that position.

Jackson's men were in the lead, crossing Bull Run at Sudley Ford on the 31st and heading towards Fairfax Court House. That night a heavy rain slowed down the men, many of whom were

clad in new U.S. Army issue boots captured at Manassas Junction and not yet broken in. Still, the foot soldiers outpaced their supply wagons, making slow progress over the muddy roads, and by evening Jackson's Foot Cavalry slept in the rain, without tents or food along the turnpike in Pleasant Valley.

The rain let up towards the morning of the 31st, but dark clouds in the west promised more rain as the Confederates rose, assembled and marched off again, heading towards Chantilly, a plantation mansion house. Federal cavalry vedettes spotted the advancing Confederates, and notified Pope. He hurried men to Chantilly. There the Confederates would find Federals, units commanded by Brigadier-General Isaac I. Stevens and Major-General Philip Kearny. Kearny was a grizzled veteran of many actions, one sleeve pinned up from where he had lost an arm in Africa in the service of France as a soldier of fortune. One of the army's most popular generals, he had ordered his men to wear a red square on their caps so they could be easily identified after he'd mistaken some stragglers as coming from one of his units.

▲ *Left:* Major-General Philip Kearny was one of the Union's more aggressive generals. Independently wealthy, he served in both the U.S. and French armies, seeing action at Magenta and Solferino as well as in the Mexican War. His death was a blow to his men.

▲ Brigadier-General Isaac Ingalls Stevens had been a congressman before the war. He organized the 79th New York ('Highlanders') in 1861 and reached division command when he was shot in the temple at Chantilly.

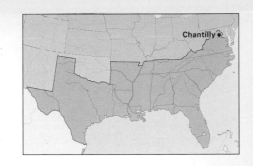

Jackson saw the Federals in position and deployed his artillery on the turnpike leading to the position, with his divisions drawn up south of the artillery. As his men were manoeuvring into position, the rains finally came, with heavy peals of thunder and lightening flashes in the sky like faraway artillery. The rain drove heavily into the Confederates faces, and onto the backs of their enemies, as the order to advance was given. Two brigades under A.P. Hill on the right of the turnpike charged over a cultivated field and into the woods were the Federals awaited. There they were stopped by a heavy volley, and the two sides halted to exchange fire.

Hill sent in a brigade to strengthen his line. By then the fierce rain, coupled with the spattering of musketry and roar of artillery, made passing and receiving orders difficult. The advancing Confederates in the open bent their heads down and shut their eyes as they moved to the front. This one brigade was not enough, and Hill sent in two more. But his attack was getting nowhere.

On the Confederate left the attack by that division also was stopped, and Jackson's line was becoming bent backward as the Federals counter-attacked. They were stopped in turn, and the Confederates tried another counter-attack, which also failed. Fighting in the swirling rains lasted until Stevens fell, killed in action. Kearny, riding into a unit he thought in the poor visibility of rain and increasing darkness was a Union one, was also shot. Greatly respected by both sides, his body was later returned under a flag of truce.

With the deaths of the two important Union leaders, the Federal troops withdrew, but Jackson's men, between hunger and weariness, were unable to pursue. Pope, also because of the rain, was unable to reinforce Stevens' and Kearny's forces with troops from two nearby corps, saving the Confederates from a serious defeat. But Pope was able to withdraw and end in stalemate Lee's attempt to crush his army. At the end, between Second Bull Run and Chantilly, the Federals lost some 16,000 men out of 76,000 engaged. Confederate losses were some 9,000 out of 49,000 engaged. Moreover, after the boastful proclamation Pope had issued on arriving in Washington, his career where there was heavy fighting was over. He was sent west, to do excellent service in the Sioux Uprising in Minnesota the following year, but never to regain any leading combat role in the war against the Confederacy.

PRIVATE EDWARD N. MOORE, ROCKBRIDGE ARTILLERY, ARMY OF NORTHERN VIRGINIA

Soon after this, our attention was attracted by the approach, along the road in our front, of ten or twelve horsemen, riding leisurely towards us, one of whom bore a banner of unusually large size. As they passed, the most conspicuous figure in the party was a Federal officer in new uniform, and several other prisoners, escorted by a guard of our cavalry. The banner was the flag of New York State, with the field of white satin emblazoned with the coat-of-arms of the Empire State, and all elaborately decorated with flowing cords and tassels.

◄◄ *Far left:* Lieutenant-General Ambrose Powell Hill, a professional soldier although sickly all his life from time to time, was one of Lee's most trusted lieutenants. He would be killed when scouting in front of his lines only days before the surrender at Appomattox.

◄ Major-General John Pope came east from a successful career in the west but so annoyed all those under him that he never had the full confidence of his new command. After Second Bull Run he was sent back west to fight Indians.

▲ Kearny's death was an accident as he rode into Confederate lines by mistake. Called on to surrender, he spun his horse around and spurred it towards Union lines. He couldn't outrun a bullet. His body was returned to his own army by equally grieving Confederates.

THE BATTLE OF SOUTH MOUNTAIN

▼ McClellan, having discovered Lee's plans for Maryland's invasion, moved towards his splintered forces. Burnside took his corps through a northern pass, while Franklin's men passed to the south. Southern troops held them up at South Mountain.

On 2 September 2 1862, a thoroughly disgraced John Pope lost his command as George B. McClellan was restored to command all the forces in Virginia. The Federal soldiers of all ranks, thoroughly disgusted with Pope and having considered McClellan their friend, were delighted at the change, and morale instantly improved. Knowing McClellan's lack of speed, Lee decided that chances were quite good that the Northern leader would take his time in getting the forces back together. He therefore got permission to take the war north, into Maryland. This slave state, he was assured, would

provide many recruits and supplies to his needy army. At the same time, taking the war off Virginia's soil would allow farmers to get their crops in and prepare for the approaching winter.

On 4 September, his army began crossing the Potomac onto Maryland's soil. By 6 September, Jackson's men were in Frederick, in the centre of the state, a town that had been previously evacuated by Federal troops. There Southern hopes for a popular pro-Southern uprising were apparently dashed. While the story of Barbara Fritchie hanging out a U.S. flag before Stonewall Jackson may be false, no Southern flags hung in front of the shuttered shops that dotted the town's streets. The residents did not appear wildly pleased to see Confederate troops, whom many described as being the dirtiest men they'd ever seen. It was a low point in Southern fortunes of all sorts. Moreover, many Confederate enlisted men stopped along the Potomac, feeling that they had joined to defend the south rather than invade the north. Straggling was at its worst of any point during the war, and these men were not replaced by Marylanders.

Federal troops skirmished with Confederates sent to screen their forces as Lee split his army into several wings. Jackson, in Special Orders No. 191, dated 9 September, was sent to Harper's Ferry, while many of Longstreet's Corps were ordered to Boonsborough, and other troops to Crampton's Gap. These orders were sent to senior field commanders, with apparently two copies for the attention of D.H. Hill. Hill's set of the orders, wrapped around three cigars, was lost. Several Federal soldiers found the orders, recognized their importance, and immediately forwarded them to their commander. The orders passed through the chain of command, with the signature of Lee's assistant adjutant general being recognized at the highest level as being authentic. Such was the intimacy of war when both sides knew and served with each other before the war began.

Armed with knowledge of Lee's plans, McClellan saw a chance to destroy the Southern army piecemeal. 'Here is a paper with

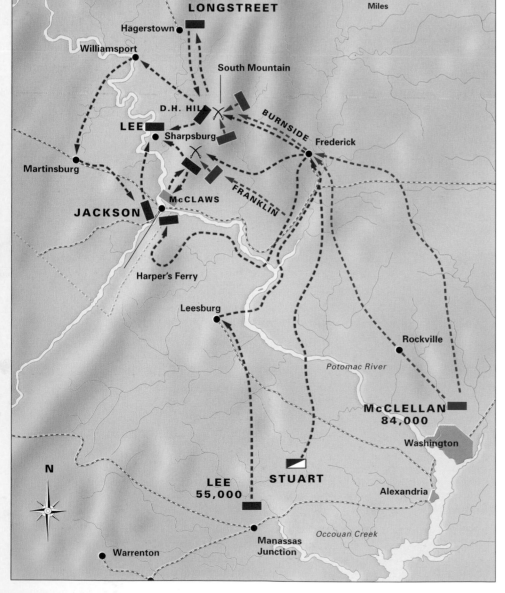

◄ After Pope's failure, Lincoln felt forced to return to George McClellan as the only general the eastern army felt any confidence in. He gave the 'young Napoleon' a second chance by giving him overall command again. McClellan would fail that second chance.

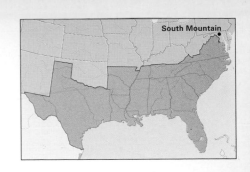

▼ Harper's Ferry was a vital point, mostly because the Baltimore & Ohio Railroad ran east to west through it. Yet, as one sees in this photograph, it is hard to defend since it is at the bottom of a number of tall hills all around it.

which if I cannot whip Bobbie Lee I will be willing to go home,' McClellan gloated to a subordinate. He then acted with surprising and uncharacteristic speed, gathering his army and placing it on the march immediately. Major-General William B. Franklin took his left wing of the Union army towards Crampton's Gap, in a move designed to relieve Harper's Ferry and trap the Confederates besieging that point. On 14 September Franklin's troops assaulted the thin line holding that pass. Confederate reinforcements arrived, but were pushed back, and by that evening Federals were in Pleasant Valley. There they saw a larger Confederate battle line, and Franklin decided to end his attack. As a result Harper's Ferry was doomed.

Indeed, Jackson's men quickly grabbed the heights overlooking the troops garrisoning the town. Trapped inside the town, some 1,300 cavalry, managed to slip through the Confederate lines at a point that had been carelessly left open. However, the 12,000 Federal infantry who did not follow the cavalry had no chance against a stronger force that held the heights around them. On the 15th, the garrison surrendered.

While this was going on, the right wing of McClellan's army, some 30,000-strong, aimed at South Mountain, held by only one Confederate brigade. Federal cavalry first engaged this brigade, giving the Confederates time to bring up four more brigades. Federal infantry joined the attacking force, but their attack was stalled by noon. The broken terrain and wooded areas helped the defenders, who were holding ground against an enemy attacking up a hillside. A lull fell over the battlefield as both sides brought up more troops. But it was the Confederates who brought the first troops onto the

scene, consisting of the divisions of Major-General David R. Jones and Brigadier-General John B. Hood, as well as brigades under Brigadier-Generals George B. Anderson and Robert E. Rodes.

By mid-afternoon the Federals had reorganized and again pressed their attack. Major-General Joseph Hooker's I Corps assaulted the main Confederate position across the National Road. The Confederates fell back slowly, even counterattacking at points. It was well into darkness, around ten at night, when the Federals finally captured the high ground overlooking Turner's Gap. The Confederates fell back to where Lee, now aware of his lost orders falling into McClellan's hands, was concentrating his forces in the small town of Sharpsburg.

▲ Major-General William B. Franklin graduated first in the same West Point class in which Grant finished 21st. He was an excellent corps commander, but Burnside's claim that he performed poorly at Fredericksburg effectively finished his career.

ADJUTANT FREDERICK L. HITCHCOCK,
132ND PENNSYLVANIA VOLUNTEER INFANTRY

Another shell incident occurred during this artillery duel that looked very funny, though it was anything but funny to the poor fellow who suffered. He, with others, had been up near our battery, on the knoll just above us, witnessing the firing, when one of those rebel shells came ricochetting along the ground towards him as he evidently thought, for he started to run down the hill thinking to get away from it, but in fact running exactly in front of the shell, which carried away one heel. He continued down the hill at greatly accelerated speed, but now hopping on one foot.

THE BATTLE OF ANTIETAM

The Confederates fell back to where Lee had drawn up his lines in a semi-circle, with the small town of Sharpsburg just behind his centre, his right drawn along the shallow Antietam Creek. (Confederates named their battles after population centres, while Federals used geographic sites for their battles names; hence, the battle that followed was called Antietam in the North and Sharpsburg in the South.) On Lee's left lay a mixture of woods and farmed land, now high with American corn. His rear was blocked by the Potomac River, normally an exceptionally bad defensive position, but one that left Lee unconcerned as he had so much confidence in his own army and so little in his opponent.

Lee had only some 40,000 men at hand, many of his men having been left straggling on the roads of Virginia and Maryland while others were besieging Harper's Ferry. Against him McClellan brought almost 75,000 men through the gaps and down the roads leading to where Lee's men were waiting.

McClellan's plan was to strike at both flanks and then, when Lee's army was weakened, he would hit at the centre and destroy the entire Southern force. But McClellan wasn't a battlefield leader. He, much like Lee, would bring an army to battle, define his

plans to his subordinates, and then leave the fighting to them. Before dawn on 17 September, Hooker led his I Corps through a cornfield against the Confederate left where Jackson's men, save for the troops of A.P. Hill at Harper's Ferry, waited. In a smashing assault with the famed Western 'Iron Brigade' hot in the fray, Hooker's men cleared the cornfield.

But behind that position were Texans and others of Hood's men who were sitting down to their first meal in days. Hurriedly called into line, having to pour coffee into fires and shove corn in their haversacks, the hungry and thoroughly irritated Confederates dashed towards where Hooker's men had reached the Dunkard Church. The weary Federals fought hard, but were forced back.

In the second of a series of what would be uncoordinated Federal assaults, the XII Corps passed through the East Woods, through the cornfield, and into the West Woods. Jackson's men held on. Men fell in virtual battle lines, in heaps, and clumps. The entire cornfield was flat to the ground, beaten down by bullets and charging troops. The XII Corps commander was killed and Hooker taken from the field wounded. The II Corps now hit the Confederate lines, but Lee pulled two divisions from his right,

▲ *Left:* A post-war impression of well-uniformed Union troops under Burnside who, having just crossed the Antietam Creek over Burnside's Bridge, now push Cobb's Georgia Brigade from the heights overlooking the creek.

▲ A detailed map of the battlefield of Antietam showing how Lee used terrain to his advantage, but still left the Antietam Creek in his back by which, had McClellan organized his attacks better, he would have been trapped.

SURGEON GEORGE STEVENS, 77TH NEW YORK VOLUNTEER INFANTRY

Our boys are almost on the road, when, at a distance of less than thirty yards, they find themselves confronted by overwhelming numbers, who pour a withering fire into their ranks. The Seventy-seventh receives the fire nobly, and, although far ahead of all the other regiments, stands its ground and returns the fire with spirit, although it is but death to remain thus in the advance. The brave color-bearer, Joseph Maurer, falls, shot though the head; but the colors scarcely touch the ground when they are seized and again flaunted in the face of the enemy.

which was not being pressured, and they reached the left at the right time. The line held. Indeed Jackson launched a doomed counterattack, but the essential positions were unchanged and two weary armies halted their firing.

The next attack came in the centre, where the Confederates held the line of the 'Sunken Road', virtually a trench with wood fences on its sides. Men of the II Corps hit this position in waves, the third wave including the famed 'Irish Brigade', made up of units from Northern states with large Irish populations. At this final attack, the Confederates made a mistake, leaving a gap in the centre of the line through which the Federals poured. McClellan's officers looked on and pleaded with the general to release the V Corps which he had in reserve. Porter, the Corps commander, reminded McClellan that his troops were the last reserve between Lee and Washington, and McClellan, always looking for a reason not to fight, declined to commit his reserves. The weary, battle-torn Federals in the Sunken Road were unable to take advantage of their luck.

On the left, Ambrose Burnside led his IX Corps against what was essentially little more than a single Georgia Brigade guarding

the heights over a stone bridge that crossed the Antietam. Burnside failed to reconnoitre the stream, an act which would have told him that the stream was easily forded. Instead, he aimed his full attack at crossing the bridge, and his attacks were turned back again and again. Finally, towards mid-afternoon, two of his regiments forced their way across the bridge. The Confederates fell back and finally a large force was in a position to roll up their lines.

But at this moment Lee's prayers were answered and, miraculously, A.P. Hill's division arrived on the field. Hill had force marched from Harper's Ferry and was understrength, a number of men having fallen out exhausted by the punishing pace. However, at the crucial point of the battle his division arrived on the left flank of Burnside's IX Corps and turned the tide in Lee's favour. The IX Corps was forced back to the stream as evening fell. McClellan's shot at winning the war in a day had ended. The next day he declined to attack, which was lucky for Lee as, although he remained on the field that day, he would have been hard pressed to repeat the previous day's work. The cost was huge, with over 12,000 Federals wounded, killed or missing, and 13,700 Confederate casualties. It had been the single bloodiest day of the war.

▲ A Union supply train crosses the Antietam Bridge, which was not the same as Burnside's Bridge, after the single bloodiest day of the war, the battle of Antietam, as it was known in the north, or Sharpsburg, as Southerners called it.

THE INVASION OF KENTUCKY

Lee's invasion of Maryland was one of two prongs of an overall Confederate attack on the North. As with Maryland, Kentucky was a slave state with divided pro-Southern and pro-Union feelings. In late August, Confederate troops invaded the state with a force lead by Major-General E. Kirby Smith, running into a brigade of Federals south of Richmond, Kentucky. The Confederates were driven back, while the Federals gathered around to defend Richmond.

On 30 August, Kirby Smith's men went back on the attack. In a fierce fight of see-sawing attack and counter-attack, the Federals fell back towards Louisville, losing some 1,000 men killed and wounded and over 4,000 captured or missing. The Confederates lost fewer than 500 men in an impressive beginning to the invasion. By 2 September, Kirby Smith's men occupied Lexington, while the Confederate Army of Tennessee, the South's second most powerful army, under Lieutenant-General Braxton Bragg was on the march north from Chattanooga, Tennessee.

Bragg was a career soldier who happened to have earned the friendship of Jefferson Davis when his artillery battery supported Davis's Mississippi volunteer infantry regiment at the Battle of

Buena Vista during the Mexican-American War. A humourless, by-the-book soldier, he was generally detested by his officers and men alike. During the Mexican-American War some of his soldiers rolled a live shell with a burning fuse under his tent flap. The destruction to the tent was major, but Bragg, lying on his cot at the time, was totally unhurt. Davis, however, was an individual to whom loyalty to friends, regardless of what others thought, was vital, and supported Bragg throughout the war.

While civilian militias drilled in Ohio and Northern Kentucky, the main Union defending force was commanded by Major-General Don Carlos Buell whose troops were at Murfreesboro and Nashville. Bragg and Smith, however, bypassed his positions on their way north. By 12 September they were in Glasgow, with Kirby Smith's men some 50 miles from Louisville, while Bragg was around a hundred miles south of that important city.

Buell quickly put his men on the road and by forced marches, reached Bowling Green, Kentucky by 14 September. Meantime, Southern troops were stopped by a thin line at Munfordville, a town on which Bragg opened a siege. By the next day men from

▲ **Union soldiers cross from Ohio into Kentucky on a temporary bridge made from planks and coal barges. The umbrella carried by one man and the top hat worn by another clearly indicates that these troops are militia called out because of the emergency.**

▶ *Near right:* **General Braxton Bragg, a personal friend of Jefferson Davis, was a by-the-book soldier who made no friends among his lieutenants. At one point Davis had to go west to attempt to straighten out the political problems between Bragg and his corps commanders.**

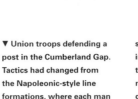

▼ Union troops defending a post in the Cumberland Gap. Tactics had changed from the Napoleonic-style line formations, where each man stood shoulder to shoulder in line of battle, to modern tactics where a rough line was made with each man finding cover as best he could.

Smith's force actually reached the Ohio river at a point where they could look across at Cincinnati, Ohio. Fearing that they were outnumbered and could be trapped, however, Smith pulled his men back after only a short time.

On 16 September the 4,000-man garrison of Munfordsville surrendered to Bragg's 30,000 troops. After several days to process the prisoners, refit, and rest, Bragg took to the road again on 21 September to Bardstown, where he planned to meet Kirby Smith's units. Buell, however, continued on his way and actually reached Louisville on the 25th before Bragg could. Moreover, Federal detachments also occupied Munfordsville less than a week after Bragg took it. Bragg's invasion had reached its high point.

Instead of going after Louisville, Bragg took time off to install a pro-Confederate governor, Richard Hawes, and his government at the state capital of Frankfort on 4 October. Then, on the 6th, he moved back towards Harrodsburg, followed closely by Buell's 50,000 Federals. Bragg divided his force in the face of this enemy, with Kirby Smith's units at Frankfort and others near Perryville, while Buell's men drew close to the latter town, mostly looking for water in the strangely hot autumn weather. Bragg had no idea that Buell would attack there, having been led to believe that he would attack either Frankfort or Versailles.

Bragg, figuring he had run into only a small part of Buell's army near Perryville, brought up troops there and ordered them to attack. They ran into a feisty young brigadier general, Philip Sheridan, who forced the Confederates back as fighting grew fiercer. Due to an unusual atmospheric condition, Buell, some miles in the rear, could not hear the sounds of cannon and musketry, and was not notified of the battle until late afternoon. He did not arrive on the field until after 4 p.m. Brave Confederate attacks stretched the Union line so that by the evening some sections had been shoved back a mile or so. Casualties were heavy, 3,500 Confederates and 4,200 Federals. However, the battle, known as Chaplin Hills by the Confederates, was not as large as it could have been as Bragg kept troops near Frankfort and Buell, unaware of the action, had not committed all of his troops.

Buell held his position through the night, ready to resume fighting the next day. Bragg, however, had had enough. He ordered a

retreat, falling back to Harrodsburg under cover of night. Two days later, Buell's men ran into Bragg's rearguard there as the main Confederate army continued to retreat southward, accompanied by the governor they had inaugurated. He would never serve in his native state, becoming more a government in exile. And by 19 October, the Army of Tennessee reached the Cumberland Gap, passing into Tennessee and out of harm's way four days later.

▶▶ *Far right:* General Edmund Kirby Smith was given command of the Trans-Mississippi Department. After the fall of Vicksburg he essentially became the overall Confederate commander in the South's western states, with his forces among the last to surrender.

PRIVATE SAM R. WATKINS, 1ST TENNESSEE INFANTRY REGIMENT

After the battle was over, John T. Tucker, Scott Stephens, A.S. Horsley and I were detailed to bring off our wounded that night, and we helped to bring off many a poor dying comrade – Joe Thompson, Billy Bond, Bryon Richardson, the two Allen boys-brothers, killed side by side – and Colonel Patterson, who was killed standing right by my side. He was first shot through the hand, and was wrapping his handkerchief around it, when another ball struck and killed him. I saw W.J. Whittorne, then a strippling boy of fifteen years of age, fall, shot through the neck and collar-bone. He fell apparently dead, when I saw him all at once jump up, grab his gun and commence loading and firing, and I heard him say, 'D-n 'em, I'll fight 'em as long as I live.'

THE BATTLE OF FREDERICKSBURG

Once the Confederates had been driven from the banks of the Potomac, McClellan fell back into his old lethargic ways. Lincoln despaired of getting the Army of the Potomac's favourite leader to move, as McClellan came up with excuse after excuse to stay in his camp.

On 26 October, McClellan moved his army across the Potomac into Virginia, but travelling so slowly that the Confederates had time to block its every move. Finally, on 5 November, Lincoln had had enough. He sent an order relieving McClellan and replacing him with one of the army's corps commanders, Ambrose Burnside. Trained as a soldier although he spent most of his life in inventing and business efforts, Burnside did not consider himself up to the task, but accepted the new assignment under some protest. The army's officers and men were angered and saddened at seeing Little Mac taken away a second time. McClellan, who was wholly self-centred and unable to look at anything from any other perspective but his own, was shocked at the development.

Burnside took over command of the army, then largely in the area of Warrenton, Virginia, on 9 November. A day later, McClellan, accepting his fate, staged a gigantic review of his old army and then rode away, taking with him Fitz John Porter who would face charges of wilful disobedience at the Second Bull Run. Porter's replacement was a self-confident West Pointer named Joseph Hooker.

Burnside came up with a plan to bring his army quickly to the left, passing around Lee's troops, to cross the Rappahannock at Fredericksburg, and then drive straight at Richmond. Lee, unable to concentrate in front of him, would be forced to follow. Lincoln approved the plan, as well as Burnside's reorganization of the Army of the Potomac that called for three 'grand divisions', one on the right, one on the left, and one in the centre. On 15 November he put the army in motion.

The Rappahannock at Fredericksburg was too deep and wide to be forded, although there were a number of fords several miles to the west. Several pontoon bridges would therefore have to be erected at the chosen site to allow Burnside's troops to pass. Word went back to the Engineer Depot in Washington to get pontoon bridge trains moving south. However, there was little urgency placed on these orders, and poor staff work meant they were assembled and moved too late to reach Burnside's troops when they first arrived at the riverside.

By 17 November, the Right Grand Division of the Army of the Potomac arrived across from Fredericksburg on the northern side of the Rappahannock. No pontoon bridges or trains were there when they arrived, nor were any expected in the near future. As the Federals waited, Lee moved his troops into Fredericksburg and, by 20 November began to fortify the area. It was not difficult; the town spread to the river banks, but behind it rose a ridge line, topped with roads and stone fences, that would force any attacking force to cross the river in plain view, form up on open fields, and charge up a hillside into entrenched defenders.

Burnside, towards the end of the month, called for the inhabitants of Fredericksburg to leave, threatening them with artillery, but beyond that, made no move to take the city or the heights beyond. On 25 November the pontoon bridges finally arrived, but by this point a strange lethargy seemed to have overtaken Burnside. His generals and engineer officers pleaded to get the bridges in the water and move, before Jackson's men, coming from the Valley, could add their weight to the Confederate line. But Burnside continued to wait, letting week after week pass.

▲ Union artillery pounds Fredericksburg in a vain attempt to drive off the Confederate infantry whose sharpshooters kept Union engineers from laying pontoon bridges across the Rappahannock River. The old Colonial town was badly damaged in the attempt.

COLONEL ST. CLAIR MULHOLLAND, 116TH PENNSYLVANIA VOLUNTEER INFANTRY

The Irish Brigade had reached a point within thirty yards of the stone wall and began firing. All the field and staff officers of the Regiment were wounded. The color sergeant, William H. Tyrrell, was down on one knee (his other leg being shattered), but still waving the flag on the crest. Five balls struck him in succession; a dozen pierced the colors; another broke the flag-staff, and the colors and the color sergeant fell together. The orders to retire passed down the line and the command began falling back.

▲ Union infantry piled into pontoon boats and used them as landing barges to cross the Rappahannock and secure the town by hand-to-hand fighting in the streets of Fredericksburg. Only after the town had been secured could Burnsides' assault commence.

By early December it was clear to many Federal officers that an attack at Fredericksburg could not succeed. Burnside, however, thought differently. He had come to believe that a road ran right along behind Lee's forces and if his men could just penetrate the Confederate line at any point they could take that road, turn left and right, and defeat the Army of Northern Virginia. No arguments could persuade him otherwise, and he ordered the pontoon bridges laid. On the morning of 11 December in the fog the first of two went into the water across from Fredericksburg. Confederate infantrymen hiding in the town's buildings picked off the volunteer and regular Army engineer troops, and several regiments of infantry used the pontoons as landing craft to row across the river and clear the town. Then the bridges were laid, with several more laid east of the town, and the army began to traverse the river. On 13 December, Burnside ordered a general advance. The right failed even to reach the stone wall of Marye's Heights, despite valiant efforts and tremendous losses of life, while the left did manage to make some headway, but was finally unable to fully penetrate the Confederate line. Burnside wanted to make another attack the following day leading his own IX Corps personally, but was talked out of it. In late January, he led his army to the west to cross the Rapphannock and try to turn Lee's flank. But extremely heavy rains washed out his 'mud march', and his army went into winter quarters.

▲ Infantry rushes to the support of Union engineers attempting to lay pontoon bridges under Confederate fire. This post-war print shows the men in their fatigue uniforms; in fact, most wore heavy light blue great coats in the bitter December cold.

THE BATTLE FOR ARKANSAS

On 20 August 1862, the Confederate Army set up its Department of the Trans-Mississippi, a command that included Arkansas, Missouri, the Indian Territory (now Oklahoma), Texas, and the parts of Louisiana west of the Mississippi River. Arkansas, a sparsely populated state just south of Missouri and east of the Indian Territory, was bound to be an important part of this new command. Major-General Thomas Hindman was the Confederate general on the scene, while the Federal forces, the Army of the Frontier, were led by Brigadier-General John M. Schofield.

On 18 October, Schofield's army entered into north-western Arkansas. In a few weeks, however, he fell back into Missouri, leaving a division under command of Brigadier-General James G. Blunt as the only field force in Arkansas. Hindman, at Fort Smith, south along the Indian Territory border, discovered how far apart the elements of the Army of the Frontier were. Despite being under pressure from authorities in Richmond to send reinforcements to Vicksburg, he decided to attack Blunt.

His lead troops were a cavalry force of some 2,000 men under Brigadier-General John S. Marmaduke. These poorly supplied troops crossed the Boston Mountains with the plan of screening Hindman's infantry advance as well as distracting Blunt. Blunt was distracted. He hurried a force of 30 cannon and 5,000 infantry to block Marmaduke, the two forces meeting at Cane Hill on 28 November. Superior numbers and weapons told the story, as the Federals forced the Confederates back from position to position. After a nine-hour fight, Marmaduke's men retired.

But Blunt had been drawn deeper into Arkansas. On 3 December the First Corps, Army of the Trans-Mississippi moved from Van Buren towards Blunt's position. Hindman had 11,000 men and 22 cannon under his command. But again numbers alone wouldn't be enough to win a Southern victory. Hindman's ill-trained men were poorly supplied, ragged, and equipped with a variety of long arms that included flintlock muskets. Most of the cannon were obsolete six-pounder smoothbores, and draft animals had to be used to haul them because of a lack of horses. Hindman had been able to rally only a handful of wagons, not enough to carry supplies to maintain an army in the field longer than a few days.

Still Hindman thought he had a chance if he could use Marmaduke's cavalry to move on Blunt's position from the south, while the main part of the First Corps would swing past Blunt to turn back on him from the north. Trapped, his only chance would be to flee through frontier woodlands, destroying his formations and cutting off his supplies.

▶ Major General James Blunt, a doctor by training, was an anti-slavery fighter in Kansas before the war. Appointed a brigadier general of volunteers in April 1862, his excellent service gave him the rank of major general a year later. He returned to a medical career in Kansas after the war.

▶ Fayetteville, Arkansas, was a sleepy little town in northwestern Arkansas, nestled in the Ozarks. It was, and still is, the site of the state university. It lies directly between Pea Ridge to the north and the important town of Fort Smith to the south.

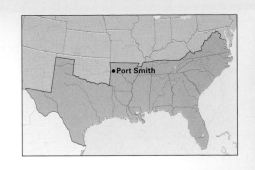

Blunt, however, learned that the First Corps was ready to move even before it did. On 3 December, he telegraphed back to Brigadier General Francis J. Herron in Missouri to move to his support. Herron wasted no time, but put his troops right on the road in unseasonably mild weather. Herron's men made a desperate march, covering an average of 35 miles a day, hundreds of his men wearing out their shoes on the march. As in all similar marches, straggling was a problem, but in this case the tremendous pace cut Herron's force of 7,000 almost in half by the time they reached Blunt.

On 6 December the Confederate cavalry found Federal cavalry near Reed's Mountain, while Hindman's main body moved to the east of Cane Hill. Movement was far slower than Hindman had wanted, due to bad roads, wagons that could not take the stress of moving over them, and horses and mules that were unable to perform. Moreover, that evening Hindman heard the news of Herron's approach.

This news changed Hindman's plans. He decided to move north to intercept Herron and beat him in detail. Then, despite his ordnance officers saying that they did not have enough ammunition for two battles, he would turn back and defeat Blunt. On the night of 6 December, Herron's men reached Fayetteville, moving on at sunrise when they ran into Confederate cavalry. As these bodies were fighting, those who had managed to make the entire First Corps march, only some 9,000 men, arrived on the field. There Hindman learned that Blunt was moving from his position at Cane Hill, and Hindman simply halted his troops at Prairie Grove to await developments.

The two Federal bodies drew towards each, with Blunt's troops on the right and Herron's on the left. At first Herron allowed his

COLONEL THOMAS SNEAD, STAFF, CONFEDERATE ARMY

Hindman sheltered his demoralized army behind the Arkansas, opposite Van Buren, and tried to reorganize it. It was still lying there when, on December 28th, Blunt dashed into Van Buren at the head of a small mounted force, and hastened the long-projected Confederate retreat to Little Rock, which place was reached toward the middle of January. During the long and dreary march thither the troops, who were not clad to withstand the snows and rains of winter, suffered severely. Sickness increased alarmingly; the men straggled at will; hundreds deserted; and Hindman's army faded away.

◄ Major General Thomas C. Hindman saw service in the Mexican War with the 2nd Missouri Infantry, serving as a lawyer and politician between that war and the Civil War. He was wounded so badly at Atlanta that he saw no further active service as a Confederate officer.

artillery to bombard the Confederate position for a couple of hours, smashing the Confederate artillery and driving the soldiers to the rear of the ridge on which they were posted. Seeing the field virtually empty, Herron then ordered his troops forward. The Confederates counter-attacked, but Blunt's men, marching to the sound of the guns, drove into their flank. Then superior Federal artillery again took over the fight, pushing back the Confederates. That night Hindman pulled back, reaching Van Buren on 10 December. Blunt and Herron followed, attacking the Confederates on 27 December, capturing most of their supplies and many of their men. The Confederate campaign for northwest Arkansas was over.

▲ A Windslow Homer sketch of a Union bugler, his uniform marked by the bars across his chest that indicate his musician status. Cavalry was extremely important in the largely rural west, both sides using it for raids into enemy territory, where it was more tied to infantry in the east.

FIGHTING ON THE MISSISSIPPI RIVER

At the outbreak of the war, one of the central points of the plan the army's commander Winfield Scott presented Lincoln to win the war was to clear the Mississippi River. This great river was a highway down which the products of the north flowed to be eventually shipped overseas from New Orleans. Lincoln had, as a young man, worked on a barge that travelled from Illinois to New Orleans where he had seen slavery first hand.

In fact by the 1860s, much of the real value of the river was historic, bound in memory rather than of real importance. Railways now carried agricultural products east, rather than south, to be shipped out of New York and Philadelphia, while other products went to the booming city of Chicago and thence across the Great Lakes. The Mississippi River was still a powerful symbol of nationhood. Moreover, it was still important to the Confederates because it was a dividing line between their eastern territory and the west, from where they drew men, horses and cattle, and supplies from Mexican border towns.

New Orleans, at the Mississippi's southern mouth, fell on 25 April 1862. As early as 19 May a small Federal force moved against Fort Pillow, Tennessee. The fall of Corinth, Mississippi led the Confederates to evacuate Fort Pillow on 3 June, the last river defence above Memphis, Tennessee.

The major advantage the Federals had in moving along the Mississippi was their overwhelming naval force. This included a number of iron-clad gunboats actually built under army supervision and commanded initially by an army officer, although absorbed into the U.S. Navy in the autumn of 1862. These were largely built in Cairo, Illinois, where there had long been boat-building capabilities. From the south the U.S. Navy was able to bring ships from its blue water navy.

▼ The U.S. fleet passes Forts Jackson and St. Phillip, as well as a Confederate Navy flotilla, on the Mississippi River. Once past this line of defence, New Orleans, the Confederacy's largest city and sea port, fell into Union hands easily.

BRIGADIER-GENERAL GEORGE W. MORGAN, U.S. VOLUNTEERS

A short time previous to this, while standing near Foster's 1st Wisconsin battery, I saw approaching from the enemy's right, about a mile away, a caisson, with gunners on the ammunition boxes, and a few horsemen in front. I asked Foster if he could blow up that caisson. He replied, 'I can try, sir.' He waited until the caisson came within fair range, and fired. The report of the gun and the explosion of the caisson seemed to be instantaneous; caisson and gunners were blown into the air; every man and horse was killed, and a shout went up from around Foster and his battery.

As a desperate move on 15 July the Confederate Navy sent its one almost-finished iron-clad boat on the river, the CSS *Arkansas*, past an overwhelming number of Federal ships above Vicksburg. Despite a severe battering, the crew brought her safely under protection of Vicksburg's guns where she added to the city's strength. Federal ships tried to sink her but failed. The bulk of the Federal Navy then retired to New Orleans, leaving a small force to defend between Baton Rouge and Vicksburg. The canal on which so many hopes had been pinned, was opened but low water made this plan yet another failure.

On 5 August, the Confederates unsuccessfully attacked Baton Rouge, retiring to fortify Port Hudson above. The *Arkansas*, part of that attack, suffered engine failure and had to be destroyed.

In December Major-General William T. Sherman mounted an expedition from Memphis to take Vicksburg overland from the north. On 29 December, his men tried to force a Confederate line near Chickasaw Bayou but were easily beaten off. At the end of the year, the Confederates still controlled the river from Port Hudson to Vicksburg.

▲ Courageously handled, the CSS *Arkansas* suffered from the same faulty engine problems most southern boats had. Finally, unable to move and under threat of Union attack, her acting captain had her beached on the riverbank and set afire as the men made their way to safety.

The Confederates, on the other hand, had few facilities, skilled craftsmen, or trained sailors to operate its small naval forces. The Confederate Navy Department authorized the building of several gunboats of its own, built largely on the design of the CSS *Virginia*, with sloping iron-clad walls to protect their few guns. The first one of these was built in New Orleans, but was not finished before the Federal Navy forced its way past Forts St. Phillip and Jackson below the city. Indeed, it had fought that battle without power, tied up as a floating battery near the forts, and had to be destroyed to prevent its capture after the city's fall.

On 6 June, a Federal flotilla of five iron-clads and four rams approached Memphis, defended by a small and poorly equipped Confederate flotilla of eight boats. In a short action the Confederate force was destroyed and the city, a major Southern manufacturing centre, taken. The Confederates began fortifying major points south along the Mississippi, in particular Vicksburg.

At the southern end of the river, Federals had passed Baton Rouge and on 20 June headed towards Vicksburg. The aim was to put a force on the west side of the Mississippi, which took a wide bend near the city, and build a canal to bypass Vicksburg altogether. In the meantime, Federal mortar boats, little more than barges, each with one large mortar, began bombarding Vicksburg, attempting to batter its defences so that the Federal Navy could pass north and join with the forces above the city. On 28 June, under cover of darkness, the Federal Navy did just that, escaping with little damage and few losses and proving that even on a river its ships could pass large land-based guns successfully. However, such a fleet by itself could not defeat well-fortified infantry and artillery. The Union army would also be needed.

▲ An angry mob met U.S. Navy Captain Theodorus Bailey and Lieutenant George H. Perkins as they landed at a New Orleans dock to receive the surrender of the city of New Orleans. Despite the threat the two brave sailors were unharmed.

HOOKER TAKES COMMAND

After Burnside's failure to turn Lee's flank around Fredericksburg, the demoralized general wrote to Lincoln saying that he no longer had his men's confidence. He should, he suggested, retire. On 25 January, Lincoln relieved Burnside, replacing him with one of the army's corps commanders, Joseph Hooker. Hooker, a brash and self-confident officer, had told Lincoln after First Bull Run that he was by far the best general on that field and he had continued his attempts to gain command of the Army of the Potomac thereafter. Lincoln, on writing to Hooker to tell him of his new command, admonished him for not supporting his superiors, but added that if Hooker produced victories he would tolerate the general's political manoeuvres.

Hooker now commanded a thoroughly beaten army, and he immediately set about improving its morale. He began by granting furloughs to deserving men to give them a chance to rest at home. He also got Lincoln to grant amnesty to soldiers who had deserted but returned by 1 April. He seized on an innovation begun by Philip Kearny in his old division of giving each member a unique division insignia so that he could tell his men from all the others. Hooker ordered that coloured, geometric cloth shapes should be worn on cap tops or sides – a circle for I Corps, a trefoil for II Corps and a diamond for III Corps etc. The colours would be red for 1st division, white for 2nd, blue for 3rd. He encouraged the building of warm and clean winter camps and began a series of drills and parades designed to give the demoralized men their confidence back. Slowly the Army of the Potomac began to resemble a serious fighting force again.

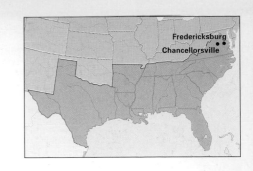

Lincoln, of course, wanted not just a confident army, he wanted a victorious army, and he pressed Hooker for a plan to beat Lee's Army. In Lincoln's mind, the emphasis of the Army of the Potomac's main goal had changed from being the capture of Richmond to being the destruction of the Army of Northern Virginia. He had begun to recognized that the Confederacy remained alive only on the points of its armies' bayonets.

Hooker began to test the capabilities of the newly rebuilt Army of the Potomac. On 17 March his cavalry struck at Kelly's Ford, one of the fords west of Fredericksburg along the Rappahannock. Where previously Federal cavalry, largely wasted as orderlies and headquarters guards, had been markedly inferior to their Confederate counterparts, in this little fight the Federals stood well, inflicting more casualties than they suffered. Hooker felt he had found a soft spot in Lee's defences, which still loomed large on the heights beyond Fredericksburg.

In early April, Lee detached one of his two orps, the one commanded by Lieutenant-General James Longstreet, which was sent to Suffolk, south of the James River. Hooker, who had created the army's first effective intelligence efforts, decided that this gave him a great opportunity to strike, and proposed to move around to his right, cross the Rappahannock to the west of Fredericksburg, and turn the Confederate army. At the same time, Federal cavalry would strike around the Confederates, severing links with Richmond. Lincoln approved the plan.

On 27 April, Hooker put his army in motion. Leaving a large force to pin down the Confederates at Fredericksburg, his troops were across the river and into a tangled mess of trees and low brush that made visibility impossible for any distance. Known to locals as 'the Wilderness', the area was cut up with narrow country roads that made moving large bodies of troops through it difficult at best. Confederate scouts, cavalry and signalmen, spotted the Federals and reported the threat, but were in such small numbers that they could do little more than slow the advance down slightly. By 30 April Hooker had set up his headquarters in the heart of this jungle at a home owned by the Chancellors, an area known as Chancellorsville.

An unfortunate part of his plan to send the bulk of his cavalry around Lee's army far south was that Hooker had very few scouts of his own. He was essentially blind in enemy territory, facing a capable force that knew the area better than he did. Nonetheless, he confidently telegraphed back to Washington that his troops had been extremely successful so far. He told his men that they were now in a position where the Army of Northern Virginia had no choice but to flee or attack the Army of the Potomac on ground of its own choosing.

Lee was the type of individual more apt to do the latter than the former. He hurriedly pulled troops out of the Fredericksburg line, back towards this new threat. At Fredericksburg he left a division under Major-General Jubal Early to hold against an entire Federal Corps, the VI Corps under Major-General John Sedgwick. Sedgwick, ordered to assault the Confederate position as a diversion, attacked the stone wall on Marye's Heights, and after several tries, his men smashed over the stone wall and cleared the heights that had blocked the Federal army for so long.

▼ **General Jubal A. Early was given the task of filling Stonewall Jackson's shoes in 1864 when he was sent by a desperate Lee down the Valley of Virginia and then to threaten Baltimore and Washington. Unfortunately for the south, Early was no Jackson.**

▶ **'Uncle' John Sedgewick, one of the best-loved Union corps commanders, was finally killed in 1864 when, some distance from Confederate lines, he disregarded advice to keep under cover, saying, 'They couldn't hit an elephant at this distance.' Those were his last words.**

COLONEL ST. CLAIR MULHOLLAND, 116TH PENNSYLVANIA VOLUNTEER INFANTRY

Many of the Regiment were wounded. Duffy, of Company A, was lying with a great piece of his skull crushed in. Another man lay besides him with his foot torn in a terrible manner. Dan Rodgers, a boy, had his shoulder-blade smashed; but still the men kept wonderfully calm. Captain Nowlen sat in the road, humming a tune, filled his pipe, lit it with a burning fuse of a Confederate shell, and began smoking. Corporal Emsley, of the color guard, was passing jokes with Abe Detwiler, the color sergeant; and one would suppose that the boys were listening to the church bells, on that sweet Sunday morning, instead of the rush and scream of the shells.

THE BATTLE OF CHANCELLORSVILLE

By the evening of 30 April, Lee's Army was pressed on two fronts. On the left, Hooker personally commanded a force of some 75,000 men, while Sedgwick sent another 40,000 men against the lines at Fredericksburg. Missing Longstreet's Corps, Lee's 60,000 men, as Hooker told his men, had either to retreat back towards Richmond or attack. Lee always chose attack over retreat.

By 1 May, Hooker, blind without his cavalry in the Wilderness, ran into troops identified as Jackson's Corps. He halted his men at that point, later admitting that he lost confidence in himself. He drew up his lines centred on Chancellorsville, his left extending to the Rappahannock, while his right lay exposed along the Plank Road. His right consisted largely of the XI Corps, made up of regiments raised among German immigrants. Many were experienced in European armies and had seen action in the 1848 liberal rebellions that swept central Europe then. But the rest of the Army of the Potomac distrusted the Germans, as native-born Americans then tended to mistrust all immigrants. Moreover, the corps commander was Major-General O.O. Howard, a strange man who would punish a man severely for the slightest offence and then visit him later in his tent to pray with him. He was generally not a popular officer.

Fighting continued throughout 1 May, but neither side, save for Sedgwick's attack at Fredericksburg that pushed Early off the heights, was committed to an all-out assault. Lee sent scouts from Stuart's cavalry to discover the shape of the Union lines. Stuart's men brought back word that the Federal right flank lay exposed. Lee sent his engineer officers to find the road network in that area and report back. As evening fell, Lee met up with Jackson. The two, sitting on biscuit boxes by a camp fire, decided to perform one of the war's most audacious actions. Lee's already split army, of which 10,000 were with Early, would be again split. Jackson would take his men and swing around the Federal right on the roads that the engineer and cavalry scouts found earlier, roads that would keep them hidden from Federal eyes. Then they would smash into the flank and roll up the Union line.

The roads Jackson's men would take amounted to 14 miles in length. Guided by the engineers and cavalry who had previously scouted them, Jackson's 32,000 combat troops took most of the day to get into position. In the meantime, Federal scouts had learned of Jackson's approach on their right and warned Army headquarters of it. Word went down to Howard, who ignored it,

► A dramatic, post-war illustration of Jackson, doffing his hat, and Lee meeting for the last time just before the two agreed that Jackson's corps would disappear from the Chancellorsville battle, march around the Union flank, and roll up Hooker's troops.

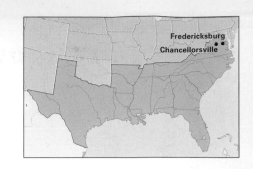

leaving his men lounging around camp fires, weapons stacked, and a minimal number of pickets placed. In the woods to their right Jackson deployed ten of his 15 brigades in three waves.

Shortly after 5.00 p.m. many of the Federals noticed small animals darting from the woods to the west. They were followed quickly by the first wave of grey-clad soldiers screaming their feared 'rebel yell'. Many Federals threw their weapons and accoutrements away in terror and fled back down the Plank Road towards Chancellorsville. Here and there handfuls resisted – one Ohio artillery battery commander, a veteran of European wars, held off much larger Confederate forces with a single cannon in the centre of the road which his men would pull back after each shot. But essentially the bulk of the XI Corps ceased to exist.

Darkness in that rough terrain put an end to the possibility of pursuit. The Federals took advantage of the time to pull back their lines, now L-shaped, with the Rapidan River anchoring the right, while the Rappahannock anchored the left. While men on both sides rested around camp fires, taking advantage of the relative peace to cook their rations over small fires, Jackson with other staff officers rode to the front to personally reconnoitre the enemy's new position. In the darkness, nervous Confederate infantrymen opened fire on Jackson's approach. Jackson was hit in the hand and arm.

The survivors gathered him in a blanket and carried him to the rear. Later he was taken to a small house where a surgeon amputated his wounded arm. Within days, however, he developed pneumonia and died.

Stuart received temporary command of Jackson's men and ordered the attack resumed the morning of 3 May. In one of the rare times they were able to do so, the Confederates massed their artillery, some 40 cannon, at the centre of the Federal line at Chancellorsville. Around 9.00 a.m. one of their shells struck a pillar of the Chancellor house near Hooker as he was observing the action. He was thrown to the ground and, dazed, turned his command over to one of his senior corps commander, Major-General Darius Couch. Then he left the field, without giving Couch any orders.

Seeing that Hooker's army was now frozen, Lee switched his troops back towards Sedgwick. This general, seeing his flanks and front threatened, recrossed the Rappahannock 4 May. The main army held on until 5 May, retiring to safety that night.

▼ Once they had been hurled back by Jackson's troops, the Union troops formed a new defensive line south of the Rappahannock and held it doggedly. After Jackson's death, J.E.B. Stuart was given the job of renewing the attacks, but Union troops, as here, held.

▲ Hooker sent his own cavalry, under Major-General George Stoneman, to circle Lee's army, far from the battlefield. This move deprived Hooker of scouted intelligence of the enemy when he needed it most. This period Currier & Ives print makes the best of Stoneman's raid.

PRIVATE EDWARD N. MOORE, ROCKBRIDGE ARTILLERY, ARMY OF NORTHERN VIRGINIA

It was now Sunday morning and there had been heavy firing for an hour or two about Fredericksburg, and thither the third and fourth pieces were ordered. As they were starting off, I saw Stuart bidding good-by to several friends, and I, not wishing to undergo a thing so suggestive, was quietly moving off. But he called out, 'Where is my partner?' and came to me, looking so jaded after his long night-march that his farewell made me rather serious. In half an hour he was dead. As he was going with his gun into position a case-shot exploded close to him and three balls passed through his body, any one of which would have been fatal.

THE VICKSBURG CAMPAIGN

On 30 January, one of Lincoln's favourite generals, one 'who fights', U.S. Grant, assumed command of troops involved in the overall assignment of taking Vicksburg. Operatins were bogged down there, with work still going on in an attempt to get the failed canal to succeed. If it had, it would have diverted the Mississippi River and left Vicksburg in the centre of a dry part of land. Ships could still pass the city – on 13 February the iron-clad *Indianola* passed the city safely – but the Confederates still held on inside the city.

Grant decided to move his men by boat down the Yazoo to the rear of the city and come to it from the east. His expedition got underway that February, making slow progress. The Confederates countered this approach with the construction of Fort Pemberton near Greenwood, 90 miles from Vicksburg. His access blocked, Grant was forced to retire on 16 March.

From the south, another Federal force under Banks worked its way towards Port Hudson. Navy ships passed this Confederate post on 14 March, but the city itself still held.

Now Grant decided to approach the city via Steele's Bayou, a route that would take his men some 200 miles through winding bayous to a point behind Fort Pemberton. As Federal ships slowly made their way, watching for natural obstacles that could poke holes in their wooden hulls, the men could hear the chopping of Confederate axemen felling trees across the narrow, swampy bayous to their front. Guerrillas fired at men on the decks from time to time, forcing them to stay mostly behind shelter. Federals fought minor battles on 21 March and again on 24 March, this time on Black Bayou. The Black Bayou skirmish marked the end of the expedition, as all concerned realized they could not take such a waterway to Vicksburg.

Grant was never a man to accept defeat, but kept on plugging until he succeeded. Another canal, the Duckport Canal, was started. On his return, Grant ordered troops led by Major-General John McClernand to come up from the south to New Carthage, below Vicksburg. They would be followed by troops under Sherman and McPherson. McClernand's men were in position by early April.

On 16 April, a major Union naval force of 12 vessels, led by Acting Rear Admiral David Porter, passed Vicksburg's guns safely, contributing to the Federal naval build-up below the city. Another flotilla of mostly supply ships passed the fortifications on 22 April with the loss of one transport and six barges. Grant led his forces overland from the north to south, bypassing Vicksburg to the west. The Confederates fortified their position at Grand Gulf on the Mississippi where Grant wanted to cross the river. Federal naval gunfire failed to clear the obstacles there, so Grant was forced to march southward. He would now cross at Bruinsburg. Naval ships also went south to the same place to ferry the soldiers across.

On 1 May, Grant's army crossed the Mississippi from its west bank to its east bank at Bruinsburg. The Confederate commander at Vicksburg, Pennsylvania-born Lieutenant-General John Pemberton, sent a detachment south to block Grant's approach. The Confederates drew up defensive lines just below Port Gibson where cane brakes and steep ravines lessened the force of superior numbers. The battle was marked by fierce attacks and counterattacks. Entire Confederate regiments disappeared in action. However, Grant's superior numbers were impossible to halt, and the Confederates fell back, through Port Gibson, burning a bridge along the road to Vicksburg. Grant had now established a secure foothold south of Vicksburg from which to attack the city itself.

Grant's troops did not halt at Port Gibson, but moved rapidly after the retreating Confederates. The Confederates were forced to evacuate Grand Gulf, now a useless position as it had been turned. By 4 May Grant's men were at the Big Black River, skirmishing their way across Hankinson's Ferry.

From Richmond, Mississippi native Jefferson Davis followed this march with alarm, telegraphing Pemberton: 'To hold both

▲ Rear Admiral David Dixon Porter came from a long line of U.S. Navy men. Extremely self confident, he started the war as a relatively young lieutenant and ended it as the second rear admiral ever appointed in the U.S. Navy.

◄ A main part of any Union overall strategy was to free the Mississippi River, the 'Father of All Waters'. Grant sent Sherman's men straight down the river to Vicksburg, while Banks went on his own further south of Baton Rouge.

Vicksburg and Port Hudson is necessary to our connection with Trans-Mississippi. You may expect whatever it is in my power to do for your aid.' One thing Davis thought to do was to name Joe Johnston overall commander of all Confederate troops in Mississippi and give him orders to prevent Vicksburg and Port Hudson from falling. This gives some idea of how concerned Davis was about the state's capture, as Davis personally disliked and mistrusted Johnston. Davis was the kind of man who took offence easily and never forgot a grudge; he held one against Johnston dating from First Bull Run. Johnston was just as prickly and the two never got on. Johnston, however, a senior officer of the pre-war U.S. Army, was one of the most respected generals in the south. Davis swallowed his pride and appointed him to this vital command. Johnston was, however, a cautious man and not given to dashing off immediately to the rescue. He would take time to organize and consider his options.

A.P. ADAMSON, 30TH GEORGIA VOLUNTEER INFANTRY REGIMENT

We were hastily formed in line of battle on the west of Jackson, and engaged the enemy in a slight skirmish for an hour or two, when we began our retreat. This was the first time that the regiment was under fire, but all behaved well. We marched for miles in a heavy rain and the roads soon became sloppy, so much so that the feet of the men sunk into the sticky mud over the tops of their shoes. The next morning our men were wet and muddy, some of them barefooted; hats and caps were drooped and appeared dilapidated.

THE FALL OF VICKSBURG

Grant's men not only moved north to Vicksburg, they also moved east to fend off any attempts to keep lines to the city open. On 12 May his advancing forces were attacked by a brigade of Confederates at Raymond, some 15 miles from Jackson, capital of the state of Mississippi. After a battle of several hours, the Confederates were hurled back towards Jackson. The battle drew Grant's normally fixed focus away from just Vicksburg to include Jackson. The next day he sent two corps of his men towards the city, held by some 12,000 men under Johnston.

On the morning of 14 May, in driving rain, Grant's troops approached Jackson. Johnston, who always preferred the strategic withdrawal to the attack, began to evacuate the city, leaving two brigades as a rear guard. After a short action, the two brigades were tossed aside, and the Federals entered Mississippi's capital. The next day, leaving troops to destroy Confederate war material in Jackson, Grant moved towards Edwards' Station where Pemberton's main force was drawn up. Pemberton, ever mindful of Davis' orders not to give up Vicksburg and promises that he would be reinforced, decided not to move east to join Johnston, but instead to retire west into the line of fortifications that ringed Vicksburg.

Johnston, however, sent Pemberton word that he should move north to link up with the main force there, even abandoning Vicksburg. Before the two could draw together, however, Grant raced his men to Champion's Hill where they could block a linkage.

On 16 May, the two sides clashed there and in attacks and counterattacks, Pemberton was forced back to Vicksburg. He'd lost almost 4,000 men, while Grant's losses were fewer than 2,500.

Pemberton fell back, burning bridges on the Big Black River that temporarily stopped Grant's advance west. Federal engineers supervised the rebridging of the Big Black River on the 17th, however, and the next day a formal siege of Vicksburg began. A frantic Davis called on local civilians to join Johnston's force, ordering Johnston, at the same time, to move to the relief of Pemberton. Johnston, however, did not move.

Grant was unsure whether Johnston would attack his besieging army, and on 19 May he ordered a sudden assault, hoping to hit the Confederate line before it was fully fortified. Unfortunately the Confederates were indeed ready and easily repelled each Federal assault with heavy casualties. Grant brought up mortars which began to pound the city.

Inside residents were driven from their homes as artillery plastered the city. Many fled to the bluffs that overlooked the city, digging caves to use as their homes during the siege.

Grant, never willing to sit around doing nothing, even if nothing was a siege, ordered a second assault on 20 May. His troops would advance hidden by deep ravines until close to the Confederate works, then attack. Here and there his troops were briefly successful but the Confederates soon retook the entire line

▼ *Left*: A post-war print of the siege of Vicksburg. Grant, bottom right, examines Confederate lines with his binoculars as the officer of the day, denoted by the sash, points out some enemy activity. The wicker baskets, called gabions, are filled with earth and used for protection.

▼ Grant and Pemberton, in the light coloured civilian clothes, meet for the formal surrender in front of Stone House on the morning of 4 July, U.S. Independence Day. Grant's move to parole the Confederates was a masterstroke as solved the prisoner of war problem and many paroled Confederates never returned to fight.

of works. Federal losses were again heavy, some 3,000 out of 45,000 in Grant's army. Never again would Grant try a frontal assault on Vicksburg.

As the siege of Vicksburg dragged on, life in the city became impossible. Food ran short; people resorted to catching and eating rats. Mule meat was considered a delicacy. Towards the end paper grew so rare that the local newspaper printed its editions on wallpaper. People looked to Johnston's friendly army, but this force never made a major attempt to relieve the city.

In the lines, soldiers made informal truces so they could stretch their legs. Otherwise, they spent time in improving their trenches, the Federals constantly rolling saps forward to dig new lines ever closer to the Confederate defences. Both sides lost sleep due to the constant crash of artillery fire, day and night, as well as the occasional popping of pickets' muskets. Finally, his supplies of all sorts running short and it becoming obvious that there would be no outside relief, Pemberton sent to Grant on 3 July to discuss surrender terms. Grant offered to parole Pemberton's men, an act that would allow them to return to their homes having signed a promise not to take up arms until properly exchanged, and the surrender was agreed to. The official surrender took place on Independence Day, 4 July.

Grant's plan to parole, rather than imprison, Pemberton's army was a brilliant one. Not only did it free the Federal army from the

problem of guarding and transporting tens of thousands of prisoners north where they would have to be fed, housed, and clothed, but it also took all those men out of the war. He correctly figured that a large percentage of the paroled prisoners, who signed pledges not to take up arms until officially exchanged, would simply go home and drop out of the war regardless of any later official exchange. He was correct. Pemberton's was one of the few armies on either side that was actually destroyed, and it was through parole rather than battle.

▲ H. Charles McBarron, a well known 20th Century military artist, did this painting of Union troops in an assault on Vicksburg's works for the U.S. Army. Despite some local successes, assault did not take the city; only starvation would do that.

PRIVATE LUCIUS W. BARBER, 15TH ILLINOIS VOLUNTEER INFANTRY

We now received orders to move farther to the right. We kept changing position every few days, gradually drawing nearer the rebel lines, fortifying as we advanced. One day we were on the skirmish and picket line and the next in the trenches. There was no rest for us, but labor, fight and dig was the order. Occasionally we would make a charge on the rebel picket to drive them back and secure a more eligible position for ourselves. From noon until night for days, weeks and months, the rattling of musketry and the heavy notes of artillery were heard.

FIGHTING TO A STALEMATE

9 JUNE **1863** Battle of Brandy Station – Federal cavalry proves it is the equal of Confederate cavalry.

14 JUNE Assault on Port Hudson – Another frontal attack fails.

1-3 JULY Battle of Gettysburg – Lee's second invasion fails.

4 JULY Vicksburg surrenders

8 JULY Port Hudson surrenders

10-11 JULY Attack on Battery Wagner – The Federals chip away at Charleston, South Carolina, defences.

13-15 JULY New York Draft Riots – Working class citizens revolt against an unpopular conscription act.

21 AUGUST Sacking of Lawrence, Kansas – Pro-Southern guerrillas burn a pro-Northern town.

19-20 SEPT Battle of Chickamauga – Confederates drive the Federals back into Chattanooga.

9 OCT Bristoe Station Campaign begins – Meade and Lee probe each other for weaknesses.

23-25 NOV Battle of Chattanooga – Grant breaks the siege and pushes the Confederates south.

26 NOV Mine Run Campaign begins – Meade tries to outmanoeuvre Lee again.

20 FEB **1864** Battle of Olustee, Florida – A Federal raid into Florida is defeated.

12 MARCH Red River Campaign begins – An unsuccessful raid towards Texas through Louisiana to obtain cotton.

12 APRIL Fort Pillow captured – Confederates recapture this post and massacre many of its African-American garrison.

4 MAY Army of the Potomac moves south – The beginning of the final campaign, which will not end until the Army of Northern Virginia surrenders.

5-6 MAY Battle of the Wilderness

7 MAY March to Atlanta begun – Sherman leads his men south from Tennessee.

8-19 MAY Battle of Spotsylvania Court House

11 MAY Battle of Yellow Tavern – J.E.B. Stuart is mortally wounded.

14-15 MAY Battle of Resaca, Georgia

23-26 MAY Battle of the North Anna

1-3 JUNE Battle of Cold Harbor

In the east, the Army of Northern Virginia was never more sure of itself, despite the fact that Stonewall Jackson, its brightest light, was no more. But Robert E. Lee and his trusted subordinates survived and the men they led felt certain of them. In the west and along the coasts, however, the Federals continued throughout 1862 and into early 1863 to nibble away. The Mississippi River, dividing east from west, was almost all in Federal hands. European recognition, once deemed possible, which would mean foreign assistance, seemed unlikely to most unbiased observers. The South could still win its war, but their chances were dimming.

THE BATTLE OF BRANDY STATION

▼ The Army of Northern Virginia moved north in June 1863, with Stuart's cavalry first screening the army well to the east before it became separated, depriving Lee of his 'eyes' in the field. Gettysburg, a major road junction, became the gathering spot.

Not only were Johnston and Pemberton under pressure from Davis to defend the posts on the Mississippi, Lee was, too. There was much talk in Richmond about detaching some of his Army of Northern Virginia troops and sending them west to relieve the threatened posts. Lee, however, kept his eye on Virginia. He argued that instead of sending troops west, he should take the army northward, over Maryland into the rich farmlands of Pennsylvania. From there he could threaten Washington, Baltimore, even New York.

After some discussion, Davis agreed. On 3 June the first elements of Lee's army left Fredericksburg heading west. The idea would be to use the mountains along the Valley of Virginia as a shield, depending on Stuart's Cavalry Corps to screen the Southern infantry and artillery.

Stuart's cavalry had always been markedly superior to Federal cavalry. Most Southerners were of rural upbringing, used to riding, while many Northern recruits came from big cities where they had little or no riding experience. It therefore took many more months of training to get Northern cavalry simply to ride as well as their Southern counterparts. On top of that, while the Confederates concentrated their cavalry into organizational combat units, adding horse artillery in which every man was mounted, Federal doctrine was to split its cavalry among divisions where the generals were free to use cavalry as they wanted. Many used cavalrymen as couriers and scouts, while others assigned the cavalry to headquarters to act as guards and provost marshals.

Hooker would change all that. As part of his reorganization of the Army of the Potomac, he also reorganized the cavalry, putting it under overall command of Major-General Alfred Pleasonton.

Union intelligence learned early on that Lee was on the move. But it didn't know where or with what strength. Therefore Hooker sent the VI Corps on a reconnaissance in force on 5 June at Franklin's Crossing. There Sedgwick, the corps commander, tried to force the Confederate infantry who were dug in on the other side of the river. The attempted crossing failed. Sedgwick then ordered an attack using pontoon boats, which succeeded in crossing the river quickly enough to seize the enemy trenches. Still, the strength of the enemy opposition convinced Sedgwick that Lee was still in his old position, and in force.

However, this reconnaissance did not convince Hooker who decided to send Pleasonton's cavalry on yet another probe of the Confederate lines. On 8 June Pleasonton's 11,000 men left Falmouth, moving along the Rappahannock. Little did he know that the place he planned to bring his blue-clad troopers was being used on 9 June as a concentration point for the Confederate cavalry, some 8,000 of them.

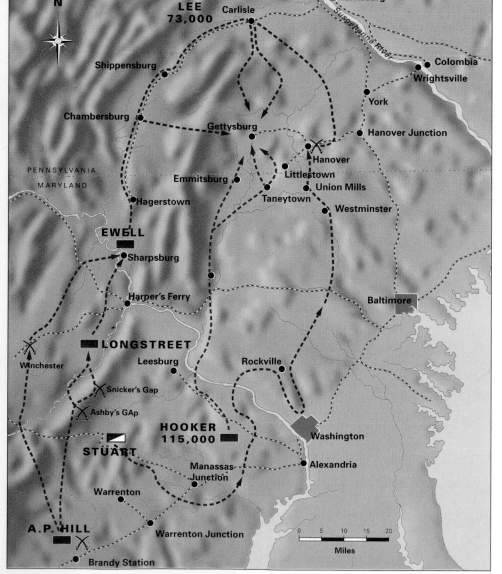

◄ Major General Alfred Pleasonton, a U.S. Military Academy graduate, was given command of the Army of the Potomac's Cavalry Corps in June 1863. Despite his successes, he was replaced by Grant's friend Philip Sheridan in March 1864 and sent west. He retired from the U.S. Army in 1888 as a major.

Map inset top right: Brandy Station

▲ A lone horseman, perhaps a dispatch carrier, pauses in the Hazel River near Brandy Station in 1863. Early in the war Union cavalry was wasted as couriers, headquarters guards, and videttes, but by 1863 the cavalry became massed and an effective fighting force.

PRIVATE T.E. BESSELLIEN, 2ND SOUTH CAROLINA CAVALRY

Within a few yards of the fence and not thirty steps from me was the whole force of the enemy, apparently a brigade at least, in column, quietly sitting on their horses and conversing as if with no apprehension of danger near. An officer, who was specially conspicuous from the gold lace on his coat, was directly in front of me, and I made up my mind to have one shot before I left. So I quickly got behind a large oak tree near and having carefully aimed my Sharps carbine at the breast of the officer, pulled the trigger. The cap exploded with a noise sufficient to startle the whole body of troops, but the gun did not go off. So with as little noise as possible I made all haste to put a greater amount of space between myself and the foe, expecting every moment a volley of musketry in my rear. What a run I had! for behold, when I reached the place where I left my friends they were gone!

It was dark and foggy at 4.00 a.m. as the first Federal cavalrymen crossed the fords. The Confederates were not expecting such a raid, and the Federals quickly overran the camp of a brigade commanded by Brigadier-General William Jones. Survivors regrouped and fell back towards Brandy Station. Another Federal cavalry brigade crossed at Kelly's Ford and joined the troops near Jones's camp.

Stuart learned right away of the Federal attack and hurried a brigade under Brigadier-General Wade Hampton to support Jones. Even with this reinforcement, the Confederates were being badly handled by the Federals who soon turned their right flank. In a short time Federal troopers galloped into Stuart's own headquarters on Fleetwood Hill, capturing his plumed slouch hat.

More and more cavalrymen on both sides poured into the fight, which became a traditional cavalry fight with pistols and sabres rather than carbines. This was highly unusual in the war, as in most fights the cavalry rode up to the front lines and dismounted. One out of every four men would lead the four horses back, while the three remaining cavalrymen would advance on foot, firing their short-barrelled carbines. Brandy Station, on the other hand, was a true cavalry battle in the Napoleonic tradition.

The battle ebbed and flowed as both sides attacked and were beaten back. Finally, however, Pleasonton, realizing he had done what was required, ordered the the Federals to fall back. They had lost almost 1,000 men, while the Confederates lost just over 500.

However, the Confederate cavalry of the Army of Northern Virginia had suffered a more serious loss than men: it had lost face. Used to being virtually unstoppable in fights with Federal cavalry, it now had met its match. Newspapers in the south indicated Stuart had been surprised and narrowly escaped defeat. For a person who lived and died by his personal publicity as Stuart did, this was an impossible situation. Indeed his attempt to relive his ride around the Union army in the Peninsula in the month that followed, an attempt that was a major cause of the Confederate defeat at Gettysburg, had its roots in Brandy Station.

THE ARMIES MEET AT GETTYSBURG

Despite the minor setback at Brandy Station, the Army of Northern Virginia headed north in June.

Almost immediately Lee's cavalry, which had screened the movement across Maryland, disappeared, heading their own way. Lee's infantry blundered about blindly, some men heading east into York and the Susquehanna River, while others headed to the small town of Gettysburg where shoes were said to be had and the only defenders were local militia.

On the contrary, ahead of the grey-clad troops marching towards Gettysburg there were two brigades of veteran Union cavalrymen under Brigadier-General John Buford. Learning of the Confederate advance, Buford immediately sent word to both Army of the Potomac commander Major-General George G. Meade and nearby I Corps commander Major-General John F. Reynolds. Reynolds got the message first and sent orders to the I and XI Corps to move into the town, and started his own infantry towards the town as well.

Meanwhile the blue cavalry waited. At around 8.00 a.m. the cavalrymen opened fire on the advancing Confederate infantry. Although the Federals fought bravely, two brigades of cavalry could not be expected to hold long against an entire infantry division. Soon they fell back to a second ridge that crossed the road down which the Confederates advanced. There, on McPherson's Ridge, the cavalrymen turned back attack after attack, holding for two hours until the I Corps' First Division arrived and deployed into line.

More Confederate infantry began to arrive from the north and east, as the XI Corps began to arrive from the south. Two divisions from XI Corps advanced to meet this new threat, but found little ground that was easy to defend. The Confederates continued their push and by mid-afternoon the Federals had fallen back from McPherson's Ridge, across the Seminary Ridge, on which the Lutheran seminary sat, and into the town of Gettysburg itself.

Confederates dashed into the town, taking many prisoners. Federals who escaped rallied outside of town on a rocky hill on their right called Culp's Hill and around a city cemetery built on a hill itself. Lee arrived on the field at about 2.00 p.m., determined not to have a large battle before his army could be reunited. But he saw the victories his men had gained and therefore suggested to Major-General Richard Ewell that his corps should continue to push the Federals. Ewell, however, did not have his entire corps together. Moreover the Federal position, its lines punctuated with regular artillery batteries and its infantry hidden by rocks and brush, looked very strong. He decided to postpone the assault until the morning.

Meade himself arrived at 2.00 a.m., when he rode along his line in the darkness and decided that it was good ground for a defensive fight. As fresh troops arrived, they were put along the ridge to the south, where the line ended at a small, brush-covered hill known as Little Round Top.

On the Confederate side two divisions commanded by Lieutenant-General James Longstreet arrived and were sent to the south to face newly arrived Federal forces. Longstreet himself met Lee during the night and suggested moving the entire army to the south, around the Union left flank, to get between the Federals and their capital city of Washington and to dig in for a defensive fight. Lee would have none of it.

Lee ordered an assault on the Federal left flank by Longstreet's two divisions which would be available in the morning, accompanied by a spoiling assault with Ewell's men against Culp's Hill on the Federal right. Neither Lee nor Longstreet could have anticipated that the Federals would be of assistance with an ill-advised move. In the early hours of the morning, the III Corps, under New York politician-turned-soldier Major-General Daniel Sickles, arrived at the very point Longstreet had been ordered to attack. Instead of halting on the ordered line between Cemetery Ridge and the Round Tops, Sickles decided to advance to a line along the Emmitsburg Road that led into Gettysburg in the middle of the valley between Cemetery and Seminary Ridges. Time was on his side as it was not until 4.00 p.m. that Longstreet was able to launch his attack.

Troops under Major-General John B. Hood hit the left flank of the Federal line. While Texas troops fought their way through huge boulders left by some pre-historic geological incident in an area known

▶ **Major-General George Gordon Meade, although born in Spain, was a Pennsylvania native and commanded the Army of the Potomac's V Corps before being given the army's command after Hooker was relieved. He commanded the army until the war's end.**

◀ **Meade made his Gettysburg headquarters in this unassuming, whitewashed farm building just over the ridge that would be the focal point for Pickett's Charge on 3 July. The building was badly damaged in the artillery barrage that preceeded the attack.**

Gettysburg •

as Devil's Den, troops from Longstreet's other division under Major-General Lafayette McLaws slammed into Dan Sickles' men in the Wheatfield and the Peach Orchard. Meanwhile, Alabama troops ran into stubborn Maine men who had only moments before rushed to the summit of the key position of Little Round Top. Although the Confederates pushed the Federals back in the hot July afternoon, the basic line was unbroken. The attacks had been turned back.

▲ Culp's Hill, the site of a major Confederate attack on 2 July, was broken up by huge boulders that made the Union defence easier than it otherwise should have been. The Confederate failure to secure this position on the evening of 1 July was a major cause of the eventual Confederate defeat.

BUGLER H.P. MOYER, 17TH REGIMENT PENNSYLVANIA VOLUNTEER CAVALRY

I think it was between 10 and 11 o'clock a.m. when the battery was retired, and the squadron hurried off to the right of the Second Brigade line to reinforce the regiment, a portion of which we found fighting against great odds on the Harrisburg Pike. They fought dismounted, with carbines, and when their ammunition for their deadly weapons was exhausted, and lines at points reached close quarters, they used their Colts' revolvers to the best advantage possible. While compelled to fall back from one position to another, as heavy lines of infantry pressed upon their front and flank, sometimes enfiladed by the enemy's artillery, in a few cases leaving the dead and wounded on the hastily abandoned grounds, yet these troops yielded slowly and doggedly, answering every exulting Rebel yell with a ringing loyal cheer, and only gave up the line in front of the town when their powder blackened and grim-visaged companions of the whole field were completely out-flanked and overpowered by the united troops of Hill's and Ewell's Corps.

PICKETT'S CHARGE

The fighting continued on 2 July. On the Federal right, Ewell's men attacked those of the XII Corps that had recently dug in on Culp's Hill. Fighting was fierce, but by 10.30 a.m. it was finished, with the Federals firmly in control of their right flank.

The attack of Longstreet's Corps under Hood and McLaws had come close to crushing the Union left flank. Federals from II Corps, who had been put into position between the I and XI Corps survivors and the III Corps, dashed forward to support Dan Sickles' battered units. Federals withdrew slowly before regaining their original position. Sickles himself was carried from the field with a wound in a leg that he would soon lose. By nightfall, the Confederate attack had sputtered out. Many Federals had been killed, wounded, and captured on both flanks, but the basic Union line, that fishhook running between Culp's Hill and the Round Tops, was still intact.

The evening of the second night found Lee as determined as ever to crush the Federal army. Now up to full strength, with the added division of George Pickett that arrived that night, he saw a partial success against the Union centre on Thursday. Surely

several divisions could exploit that success the next day, cracking through the Union centre, splitting Meade's numerically superior army. At the same time, a renewed move against Culp's Hill would shatter a Federal army Lee thought already on its last legs. Moreover, as the Confederate's cavalry division, led by Major-General J.E.B. Stuart, arrived that night, they could be used in an assault around the Federal lines, against their rear, to destroy Union units attempting to escape.

At dawn of the third day, Southern troops pressed forward against Culp's Hill. They ran into a Federal force preparing its own attack to regain trenches lost the day before, and in fierce fighting that broke down into small unit actions in rocky, wooded terrain, the attack came to a stand-still. Worse, the Confederates in the centre were not ready to launch their main attack at dawn, so the idea of a two-pronged attack that would crush the Federals was not to be.

Lee himself came to Longstreet's headquarters at dawn, only to find that the main attack was not yet ready. Harking back to his original plan of moving around the Federal right, Longstreet had ordered two of his divisions to move in that direction, while

▲ Brigadier-General Lewis Armistead, black hat stuck on the end of his sword, leads the men of his brigade of Pickett's Division across the wall and into the position of the 69th Pennsylvania. Moments after putting his hand on the cannon muzzle, he received a mortal wound.

LIEUTENANT JOHN H. LEWIS, 9TH VOLUNTEER VIRGINIA INFANTRY REGIMENT

Pickett has carried the line. Garnett and Kemper are both down. Armistead dashes through the line, and, mounting the wall of stone, commanding follow me, advances fifty paces within the Federal lines, and is shot down. The few that followed him and had not been killed fall back over the wall, and the fight goes on. Death lurks in every foot of space. Men fall in heaps, still fighting, bleeding, dying. The remnant of the division, with scarce any officers, look back over the field for the assistance that should have been there; but there are no troops in sight; they had vanished from the field, and Pickett's division, or what is left of it, is fighting the whole Federal center alone.

neglecting to order Pickett's men into position at dawn. It was not until mid-morning that, on learning this, Lee and Longstreet examined the Federal position on Cemetery Ridge and Lee made his plan. He decided that Pickett, reinforced by two divisions from A.P. Hill's Corps, would attack a small clump of trees on the Federal centre. That spot would be softened by a massive artillery barrage, with every single Confederate available turned loose.

Much time had been already lost, and placing artillery and infantry into correct positions would take several more hours. By 1 p.m., however, all was ready, and two quick cannon shots were the signal for the artillery barrage to begin.

Some 150 Confederate cannon opened slow, deliberate fire in what was said to be at that time the greatest man-made noise ever heard on the North American continent. Windows in Baltimore, Maryland, were rattled by its concussion. Around 60 Federal guns returned their fire.

As it turned out, the smaller number of Union guns were more effective. Both sides fired high, the Southern shells bursting well behind Union lines. Meade had to evacuate his headquarters behind the front line, leaving scores of dead horses in the farmyard there. But his infantry, huddled behind a low stone wall on the front, were relatively secure. On the other hand, Federal shells bursting behind the Confederate gun line took a heavy toll on Southern infantry waiting to move past the guns to attack. Hundreds of dead or badly wounded men were carried off before the attack even began.

After an hour, the Federal guns began to fall silent and many were withdrawn over to the back of the crest. The Union chief of

artillery had decided to conserve ammunition for an infantry attack he felt sure was soon due. The Confederate artillery chief, knowing that the ammunition in his limber chests was also running too short to protect the infantry effectively in its attack were the rate of fire to be maintained, sent word for the assault to begin. Wordlessly, Longstreet nodded his assent as Pickett asked if he should go forward.

Within moments the grey troops emerged from the woods and formed their battle lines. As Federal artillery opened up, the Confederates also advanced as if on dress parade. They pressed on, units obliqued towards the centre as Federal infantry units came out on both flanks to fire into the advancing columns. The first two Virginian brigades almost crossed the stone wall when they were finally broken up. A third brigade dashed over the wall, its commander himself reaching a Federal cannon when a bullet brought him down. But they could not hold the position, and hordes of Federals swarmed around the few Confederates who looked back in vain for reinforcements. The Federal centre held.

▲ Men of the 1st Minnesota, a regiment sacrificed on 2 July to stem a Confederate attack, lie as they fell at Gettysburg. Photographed days after the battle, which was fought in very hot temperatures, the bodies have started to decompose badly.

SERGEANT MAJOR GEORGE N. CARPENTER,
8TH VERMONT VOLUNTEER INFANTRY

The service required in the trenches was very exacting, and one half the regiment was on duty while the other rested on their arms, ready in turn to relieve their comrades, or to spring into line at any sudden word of command. The natural result of this arduous, irregular life, the privation and exposure, the strain of constant watching, was that large numbers of the men fell sick and were unfit for duty; so that the service bore more and more heavily on those who could endure it.

THE MISSISSIPPI RIVER FREED

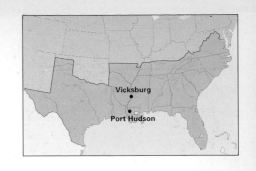

◄ Large Parrott siege guns line the Union lines in the siege of Port Hudson. This would become the longest lasting siege ever seen on the American continent, the Confederates only giving up after Vicksburg's fall made defence pointless.

◄ The pieces of a dismounted bronze Confederate howitzer lies in the foreground in this scene of the defences of Port Hudson. By the end of the siege, the Confederates were down to eating meat of mules and rats. Most had to surrender.

▼ A regiment raised in New Orleans of African-Americans loyal to the central government, the 2nd Louisiana, makes an attempt to take Port Hudson. The African-American units raised in Louisiana were formed into a Corps d'Afrique and eventually became U.S. Colored Troops.

While Vicksburg was the most important point the Confederates held on the Mississippi River, it was not the only one. There was still a sizeable force in Port Hudson, Louisiana, where its guns frowned out over the Mississippi River.

On 21 May, some 30,000 Federals under Banks left the state capital of Baton Rouge to begin a siege of the Confederate works at Port Hudson. The main Federal forces approached from Alexandria towards Bayou Sara on the west side of the river. They ran into minor resistance at Plains Store on the 23rd, but the Confederates there were too few to stop them. News of their move, however, reached the Confederate commander at Port Hudson.

Because Major-General Franklin Gardner, the Confederate commander, knew his 7,000-man garrison was weaker than that of his opponent, he vacillated and by the 25th the Federals had begun to encircle his position. There was no longer any chance of his getting up the river to join forces with Pemberton at Vicksburg.

The area around Port Hudson was heavily wooded and cut by deep ravines through which shallow creeks fed into various bayous and the river itself. This both aided and hurt the defenders: aided in that it was difficult to mass an attack, but hurt in that an assaulting party would often be hidden in the ravines and woods until the moment of attack. On the evening of 26 May, Banks assembled his generals in a conference of war. The group decided to attack the next morning, using heavy naval gunnery from the boats off the post in the Mississippi.

As it turned out the attacks were uncoordinated. A short bombardment was planned to damage the works, after which the entire force would move at once on the Confederate fortifications. The bombardment came off as planned, and Federals on the right dashed forward to the attack. Nothing, however, was heard from the Federals on the left, a group which included some of the first

African-Americans used by the Union army in combat. Attacks continued through the morning on the right and were driven off, but it was not until well past noon that the Union troops on the left attacked. By then the attack to the north had totally fizzled out and the spent troops could not be brought up to attack at the same time as those in the south. Hence Gardner could move troops from point to point to stand off the Federals, including the Louisiana Native Guards, the African-American regiments. The attempt had obviously failed and was called off. The Federals had lost some 2,000 men, while the Confederates suffered casualties of fewer than 300.

Banks had his army dig in and reorganize after their losses. Time was on their side, as ships could easily resupply the Federal forces, while the Confederates were cut off from any supplies. Moreover, it was unlikely that a relief force would be sent to save Port Hudson while Vicksburg was still besieged.

Nonetheless, Banks planned another assault to take the position. On 13 June both land- and water-based artillery opened fire in a major bombardment of the Confederate line. After an hour, Banks sent word under flag of truce to Gardner calling for a surrender. Although Gardner knew in the long run his force had no chance, he replied that his duty would not allow him to surrender the post that been assigned him to defend. Infuriated, Banks resumed the bombardment and ordered another general assault.

This one, on 14 June had a much more focused goal, a large fortification in the centre of the Confederate line known as the Priest Cap. Federal cavalry was ordered to stand by to cut off any Confederates attempting to escape after the fort had been captured.

Before dawn on the 14th, Banks hurled a division at the Priest Cap, but only a small number actually reached the Southern lines. Reinforcements could not cross the fire-swept fields to save them. Further Federal attacks were equally futile, and Banks was convinced by his subordinates to discontinue any further attempts.

The Federals then resorted to traditional siege methods, including rolling saps forward and digging new trenches ever closer to the Confederate lines. They hurled hand grenades into the Confederate positions, while the poorly supplied Confederates had to improvise their own grenades to toss back. Federal engineers attempted a mine under the Confederate line, a difficult enough job in the wet ground of the area. This failed when a Confederate counter-mine was dug and powder was placed in it and exploded, collapsing the Federal mine.

Finally, Gardner learned of Vicksburg's surrender. Knowing that meant his post was no longer defensible, or even vital, he surrendered on 8 July, after a siege of 47 days, the longest of the entire war. A handful of Confederates managed to make their way to safety through Union lines the night after the decision to surrender was made, but most became prisoners. And the Mississippi was in Union hands. 'The father of all waters flows unvexed to the sea,' Lincoln declared.

THE KANSAS WAR

In many ways the Civil War could be said to have started in Kansas. In 1854 Congress passed the Kansas-Nebraska Act that divided the great plains of the Louisiana Purchase into two territories which could become states, the inhabitants choosing if their territory was to be free or slave. In Kansas, bordering the slave state Missouri, the decision broke down into open warfare, as abolitionist societies tried to pack the territory with its settlers, while pro-slavery men from Missouri crossed into the territory to do battle. On 21 May 1856 pro-slavery forces attacked the largely anti-slavery town of Lawrence. This act was later revenged by an unhinged individual, John Brown, and his sons who killed five pro-slavery men in cold blood.

Federal troops were sent in to oversee elections. Pro-slavery men from Missouri, nevertheless, managed to get a pro-slavery state constitution sent to Washington for approval. The U.S. Congress sent it back for a popular election in which, despite widespread fraud, Kansans rejected it. After three more attempts, a free-state constitution was adopted and in 1861 Kansas joined the Union.

These years of guerrilla warfare created a social group who had learned to live by the gun. Among these was a young man named William Quantrill, born in Ohio, who had come West to be a schoolteacher. He soon turned into an outlaw, something that was easy to become in a society where all forms of law and order had broken down. When the war broke out, he found himself in the fellowship of others who had minimum respect for the law, men like 'Bloody Bill' Anderson, Cole Younger, and Jesse and Frank James, many of whom later gained fame as Wild West outlaws.

The first Confederate Congress, aware of the overwhelming numbers that Northern forces could put into the field, thought to use some unconventional methods to fight their war. At sea they commissioned privateers, privately owned warships authorized to capture Northern shipping, even though this practice had by that time long been considered contrary to international law by most of the world's nations. On land they authorized the raising of regiments of 'Partizan Rangers': irregular units organized behind Union lines of civilians who would be armed to fight a guerilla war, striking at night and whenever the chance arose, whilst otherwise living apparently normal civilian lives.

Most conventional commanders, such as Lee, decried these rangers not long after they came into being. They robbed the regular army of recruits while doing very little damage. Indeed, Lee recommended they all be disbanded, save for one battalion in Northern Virginia ably led by Major John S. Mosby. In the far West there were fewer regular battalions, and soon Quantrill organized a company, which elected him captain, in 1862. Quantrill had seen some action in the regular forces at the Battle of Wilson's Creek, but preferred the free-wheeling style of a bandit to regular army discipline.

▼ *Left:* Frank James, a guerrilla during the war and an outlaw before and after it, sits in an unauthorized Confederate officer's coat with an obviously civilian pair of checked trousers. His more famous brother, Jesse James, stands right. The James boys served with William Quantrill in Missouri and Kansas during the war.

▼ The burning of the anti-slavery town of Lawrence, Kansas, by Quantrill's band of guerrillas was one of the worst acts this band of terrorists performed during the war. As a result of the uproar that followed it, Quantrill's men had to leave that state.

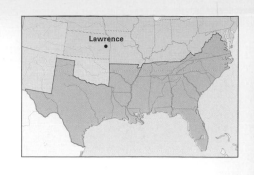

Quantrill received a partizan ranger's commission as a captain and went to work. In November 1862, his band captured a Federal wagon train and later investigation found that all but one of the dozen Union soldiers there had been shot in the head, obviously after being taken prisoner. Word of this and similar raids reached Richmond. When Quantrill first went there he was given a colonel's commission, but, after reconsideration, this unsavoury individual's commission was later revoked.

Nonetheless, he returned to his two-company band bearing the stars of a colonel and set about doing more damage. On 21 August 1863, he and his 400-odd men rode into Lawrence, which was undefended. There his men pillaged and burned the houses and killed men, boys, and even pet dogs. A few men, along with women and small children, either escaped by hiding or were spared, and the cost of damages reached $1.5 million, a staggering sum in the days when a private soldier earned $13 a month.

Quantrill decided that this would make the territory too hot for his men and they decided to head south to the pro-slavery Indian Territory, then defended by Confederate troops. On the way, on 6 October, they captured two Union wagoners who said they were headed to Baxter Springs where there was only a small garrison of largely African-American cavalrymen. Quantrill decided to raid that post and attacked the unprepared fort. Only quick action with a mountain howitzer saved the garrison.

While that attack was going on, Quantrill learned that a Federal wagon train was passing nearby, and he switched his attack to the train. As the outlaws were wearing blue coats captured in earlier raids, the wagon guards took them for an advance party from Baxter Springs. The truth was discovered too late, and the wagon train fell into Quantrill's hands. Union soldiers later found at the site 90 dead bodies shot in the head, many stripped and mutilated.

Quantrill and his men then fled to Texas, only to return later on more raids. Quantrill himself was killed in May 1865 while raiding in Kentucky. Bloody Bill Anderson was shot dead in Missouri in October 1864. The rest of their associates had varied post-war careers; the James brothers and Cole Younger remained with their lives of crime, while others had a radical change of career and became sheriffs and prison guards.

▼ **This pro-Union etching of Quantrill's burning of Lawrence perhaps overdoes the murder of defenceless men, women, and children in that town. Nevertheless, the guerrillas did murder men and boys and even pet dogs in the attack for no military purpose.**

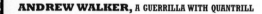

ANDREW WALKER, A GUERRILLA WITH QUANTRILL

The engagement of any importance that I participated in was on August 18, 1863. Quantrill was in command of 273 men and boys. Captain Todd was second in command and there were in the band Frank James, Cole Younger, Bill Anderson, John Kagen, William Jones, William Doagg, Hicks and Hi George, Ab Hallum, Jack Bishop, Dick Berry, Ike Berry, John Jack and W.W. Welch. The battle I refer to was what is called the sacking of Lawrence, Kansas. We got there between daylight and sunup.

We didn't see any pickets, and hence rode up the main street unannounced and unmolested. There was a bunch of tents upon the right of the main street. But I want to say right here, for myself, that I never set fire to a house in my life.

THE CHATTANOOGA CAMPAIGN

After 3 July, both armies rested on the field at Gettysburg. Then, on the 4th, Lee began his withdrawal south. It rained heavily, and movement over muddy roads was slow. Meade, new to his command and still becoming acquainted with his subordinates, made only a token effort to pursue. Northern cavalry clashed with Southern rear-guards at a number of points, capturing some wagons, but essentially doing the Army of Northern Virginia little harm. Meade did have a chance to do a great deal of damage to Lee's army when the Southern troops reached the Potomac, only to find it swollen with all the rain and the ford at Williamsport unusable. Moreover the bridge at Falling Waters had been partially destroyed.

Meade scuffled with Lee as pioneers worked to repair the bridge, but on the 13th it was ready for use. That night Lee crossed into Virginia, undeterred by Meade's troops. By the end of the month the Army of Northern Virginia was back where it had started in June.

In the West activity had resumed. In August, Major-General William Rosecrans led his Army of the Cumberland towards the city of Chattanooga, known as 'the Gateway City'. By September his army, moving in three widely separated wings, was closing in on the Confederate defender, Braxton Bragg. On 4 September the last of Rosecrans' troops crossed the Tennessee River, and the next day reached the mountains of north-western Georgia, south of Chattanooga.

The authorities in Richmond decided then to adopt a plan considered before Lee's invasion of the north to send a part of his army to Tennessee. The movement began on 9 September, but with the paucity of railway carriages, which had largely been made in the north before the war, it was not until the 25th that Longstreet's artillery finally caught up with the infantry. Because of Federal positions that threatened closer railway lines, the trip was a roundabout one, through North and South Carolinas to Augusta, Georgia, and then through Atlanta to Dalton and Ringgold, Georgia. There were constant changes of trains as the pre-war, privately owned Southern railway lines were of different gauges. The men enjoyed the adventure, however, and in North Carolina even received new uniforms of a blue-grey cloth that made them look quite different from the soldiers they would find in the West.

▲ **Major General William Rosecrans, seated, fourth from the left, sits with his staff. There were no staff schools in the U.S. Army at the time, and most of the officers were civilians picked because they had some specialist knowledge or, too often, were relatives of the unit commander.**

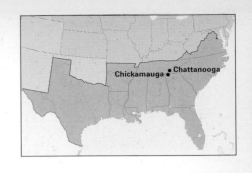

On the very day Longstreet's men started on their trip west, Bragg retreated from Chattanooga south, aware that Rosecrans was moving to his south to cut off his line of communications to Georgia. The same day the first Federals entered the city, while others of Rosecrans' army moved straight after Bragg's men. Bragg himself retreated to La Fayette, Georgia, to await Longstreet's arrival. His scouts reported that Rosencrans' Federal troops were spread out over 40 miles of mountainous terrain, isolated and incapable of supporting each other. Bragg began to plan to strike one or another of these exposed corps.

Bragg did not have good relations with his subordinates. He ordered attacks on exposed Federal forces on both 10 and 11 September, but neither attack was made. However, his advance parties and those of Rosecrans clashed across a wide front, alerting Rosecrans to the potential danger at his front. By 15 September, Rosecrans had ordered his corps concentrated essentially around Lee and Gordon's Mills along the Chickamauga Creek in Georgia, just south of the state border line. By the evening of the 17th he had posted the XXI Corps and the XIV Corps near this spot, with the XX Corps not far off. The army's Reserve Corps was north on Rossville, where the road led to Chattanooga.

Advance parties of Longstreet's Corps arrived the same day. Making their way to a relieved Bragg's headquarters, Longstreet's subordinates learned of the assault which Bragg had ordered to be made the next morning. With Longstreet's 10,000 men and others added to the 33,000-man Army of Tennessee for the attack, Bragg now outnumbered the 54,000 men of the Army of the Cumberland.

Bragg basically planned an attack on the Federal left, turning it, getting by it and up to the road to Chattanooga to cut off the rest of the Federals. He could then get back into Chattanooga, as well as capture any forces trying to retreat to Tennessee after the battle. The ground, however, was against him. It was heavily wooded, cut with creeks that ran north and south as natural lines of defence. Small occasional farmed clearings provided some places to reformed shattered formations, but also offered clear fields of fire for the defenders.

The Federal right was held by the XIV Corps under Virginia-born Major-General George H. Thomas. It had been posted there by Rosecrans on the 18th specifically to block any move such as Bragg planned. It was skirmishers of Thomas' troops who, on the morning of the 19th, ran into dismounted cavalry under Major-General Nathan Bedford Forrest to open the battle. In the dense woods, nobody exactly knew where the enemy lines were. One of the hardest fought battles of the war had begun.

▼ Camouflage was rarely used by either side. The U.S. Sharpshooters wore green to better blend with woods, but that was a rare exception. Here is another exception as a Union sketch artist shows attacking Confederates using pine branches for cover as they attack.

SECOND LIEUTENANT AMBROSE BIERCE,
TOPOGRAPHICAL ENGINEER, U.S. ARMY

Then the guns opened fire with grape and canister and for perhaps five minutes—it seemed an hour—nothing could be heard but the infernal din of their discharge and nothing seen through the smoke but a great ascension of dust from the smitten soil. When all was over, and the dust cloud had lifted, the spectacle was too dreadful to describe. The Confederates were still there—all of them, it seemed—some almost under the muzzles of the guns. But not a man of all these brave fellows was on his feet, and so thickly were all covered with dust that they looked as if they had been reclothed in yellow.

◄ Major General George Thomas, the 'Rock of Chickamauga', tended to frustrate Grant, who always wanted immediate action, with his insistence on careful preparation before any move. Still, he was one of the best Union generals in the war.

THE BATTLE OF CHICKAMAUGA

The Confederate infantry came up and in short time a battle raged over a line almost four miles long through woods and into clearings. Attacks were beaten back and counter-attacks failed. The Confederates could not dislodge the Federals, although they bloodied the Federal left badly. As Longstreet's men arrived by railway, they jumped down, formed up, and were marched towards the sound of firing without a pause. Rosecrans brought up the XX Corps, under one of the 'Fighting McCooks', Major-General Alexander M. McCook, which countered the weight of Longstreet's men.

Much of the fighting was done uphill for the Confederates, a fact, which added to the woods, creeks, and ravines, balanced their superior numbers. By the end of the day the Confederates had not budged the Federals, who continued to hold the road to the city.

The night of 19 September, Longstreet and his staff arrived, making their way to Bragg's headquarters where he learned of the day's progress. That evening, Bragg announced that Lieutenant-General Leonidas Polk would command the right wing of the army, the wing which would continue its push the next morning, while Longstreet would take the left. Both wings were to continue their attacks as soon as possible.

Rosecrans also met with his generals that night. Rosecrans put to his generals the question of what to do next, retreat to Chattanooga or stand. A bone-tired Thomas, who had been dozing through much of the meeting, called out to reinforce the left. Rosecrans decided to sent his wagon train back to Chattanooga, but stand where he was and follow Thomas' advice. That night Federal troops dug in using their tin cups, plates and bayonets, in the absence of issued entrenching tools, to dig earthen fortifications.

Polk was one of those Southern commanders who was no friend to Bragg. Although a West Point graduate, he had gone into

▲ This post-war print of Chickamauga compresses much of the action, as it shows impossibly well-clad Confederates crossing the Chickamauga River in the background and then attacking the Union lines. The actual ground was just about as rough as shown, however.

▲ Major-General Thomas Crittenden, a Kentucky lawyer before the war, had seen limited staff duty in the Mexican War before assuming command of his state's guard and being commissioned a Union brigadier general in 1861. He made the army his career after the war ended.

▲ Union infantry manning the defences of Chattanooga stand off a Confederate cavalry raid along Crawfish Creek. Bragg made no real attempt to storm the Union lines, figuring that he would starve the garrison out there before it could be reinforced.

PRIVATE THEOPHILUS F. BOTSFORD,
47TH ALABAMA VOLUNTEER INFANTRY REGIMENT

In starting this charge just after crossing the LaFayette and Chattanooga dirt road there was a house, as I ran between the house and ash-hopper the old lady was out in the yard with her specks up over her forehead. Some of the men ran against the ash-hopper, knocking it down. I heard her say there goes my ash-hopper. I said look at your garden, they were running through it, making all the pailings rattle. I heard her say: I don't care about the garden, I have lost all my good ashes.

seminary right after graduation and spent his life as an Episcopal priest. He was Bishop of Louisiana when the war broke out. A close friend of Jefferson Davis, his orders were to attack at daybreak. He did not. It was not until around 9.30 a.m. that he finally sent a division forward. Thomas's men held their breastworks against this and the other attacks that followed.

In the Union centre Brigadier General Thomas J. Wood received orders from Rosecrans to redeploy to the left and block a supposed hole in the line. Rosecrans, screened by trees from where he directed Wood, did not realize that this move would cause a huge gap at that point. Earlier Wood had not followed orders and received a tremendous tongue-lashing as a result. These new orders seemed dangerous, and he first replied that there was no gap in the line at that point. Then, determined to obey his orders to the letter, he pulled his brigade out of its place in the line. Quickly Longstreet's veterans found the hole Wood's departure made, and shortly before noon dashed through the gap. They first threw back two Federal divisions, and then as Rosecrans' army began to dissolve rolled up more and more Federals, who fled back towards Rossville and then to Chattanooga. Among them were their generals, Rosecrans, McCook, and Major-General Thomas L. Crittenden, commander of the XXI Corps.

Thomas, however, stayed cool. He drew up his brigades in a semi-circle centred on the crest of Snodgrass Hill in the rear of the

Federal line and there the 'Rock of Chickamauga' withstood Confederate attack after Confederate attack. To this day the U.S. Army's 19th U.S. Infantry Regiment, part of Thomas's Corps there, wears a unique insignia that includes the Union army infantry cap badge and bears the motto, 'Rock of Chickamauga'. The Confederate assaults were ferocious and at times came near to breaking through. But none of these small successes were reinforced sufficiently, and Thomas's men held. At dusk, as ordered, Thomas withdrew his battered command to Rossville where he set up another rear guard. On the 21st, the last of the Army of the Cumberland withdrew to Chattanooga. Casualties had been horrendous. The Federals lost some 16,000, while the Confederates lost some 18,500 men.

Bragg originally ordered his men to pursue Thomas's rear guard into Chattanooga itself, but then reconsidered and, told how broken his formations were, decided not to. The result was a useless victory for him in that he held the field, but Rosecrans' army had escaped and Chattanooga was still in Northern hands. Finally, on the 23rd he moved forward from the south, reaching the heights that loomed above the city. He deployed his men along those heights and began a siege of the city. A day later, however, the Federals loaded two corps from the Army of the Potomac, the disgraced XI Corps and the XII Corps, on to trains to send them to the relief of Rosecrans' army.

THE SIEGE OF CHATTANOOGA

Bragg, sitting on Lookout Mountain that overlooked Rosecrans' position, figured the Federals would evacuate Chattanooga. The Federals did not. True, there were repercussions, with corps commanders McCook and Crittenden relieved and ordered to a court of inquiry. On 24 September, a worried Lincoln hurried the two corps of the Army of the Potomac on to the railway in Washington, with all of them reaching nearby Bridgeport, Alabama, within nine days, a trip of 1,159 miles. Excellent Northern organization and rail facilities made such a transfer possible.

Bragg learned of the transfer by 28 September, but it did not greatly concern him. If Rosecrans would not evacuate the city, the Confederates would starve him out. The Confederates pushed their lines around the city, controlling the roads on the city's south side, and the road north to Bridgeport. The only line open to Rosecrans' men was a narrow, winding mountain trail over Walden's Ridge and through Sequatchie Valley. All rations, ammunition and equipment needed to keep an army in the field had to pass this trail. Bragg sent cavalry under Brigadier Joseph Wheeler on 1 October to cut this path. Over the next nine days Wheeler's men repeatedly destroyed wagon trains on this 60-mile trail but never totally closed it.

Federals inside the city went on reduced rations. Once despised hardtack became greatly prized, and soldiers became too weak from hunger to add greatly to the original earthworks around the city. The Confederates contented themselves with harassing artillery fire, not attempting any attacks or mining, as they were confident of soon receiving the Federal surrender.

In early October Lincoln appointed Grant the Commander of the Military Division of the Mississippi, and told him to go to Chattanooga to replace Rosecrans with George Thomas. Grant arrived there on 23 October.

Grant was not happy with the lethargic, ill-supplied garrison he found. Each soldier had only a handful of cartridges. The day after his arrival he ordered the troops in the garrison to cross the Tennessee River at Brown's Ferry, seize the ground there, and open what they called a 'cracker line'. From here Federal supply depots in Alabama could more easily supply food and equipment to the besieged city.

On the 26th, Joe Hooker led his two Army of the Potomac corps over the Tennessee at Bridgeport towards Chattanooga. The next day the city's garrison threw a pontoon bridge across the river at Brown's Ferry as Hooker sent men to the western foot of Lookout

▼ This Civil War period Currier & Ives print shows Union troops storming Lookout Mountain and driving Bragg's forces away, relieving the city's siege. The Confederate flag shown was not in use by Bragg's troops at this time.

▲ The Union garrison at Chattanooga set up tents on frames and floors made from timbers taken from abandoned houses in the city. Only the lack of sufficient food and the boredom of being besieged made their life hard during the siege.

CAPTAIN EDMUND H. RUSSELL, SIGNAL CORPS, U.S.A.

We found the army at Chattanooga subsisting on one-fourth rations, which were brought on a crazy little steamboat from Bridgeport to the place I mentioned, and thence hauled on wagons to Chattanooga. I saw our soldiers follow these wagons for miles at a time in hope that a cracker box would fall out, or break open upon the heavy rough road, and, when that happened, eagerly gather up the prized fragments of hard-tack out of the dirt and stuff them into their scanty haversacks, thankful to get them.

Mountain, the Wauhatchie Valley. This combination punch broke the siege, and in a few days sufficient supplies began flowing in.

Bragg was caught unprepared by Grant's quick action. He was not going to sit quietly, however, and he sent Longstreet's men on a night attack on October 28 on Hooker's force at Wauhatchie. The attack, planned for ten that night, actually got under way around midnight. The Confederates surprised the Federals, but Union reinforcements soon turned the tide. In the dark, many units were confused as to where they were, and by three in the morning, the Confederates retired to Lookout Mountain.

Then Bragg sent Longstreet and his men towards Knoxville, Tennessee, to destroy Burnside's corps there. This would, he hoped, draw Grant's attention and men to that post, cutting his numbers in Chattanooga. On 4 November, Longstreet's troops left the main army, but Grant was not to be deterred from his main task.

On 14 November, William T. Sherman and his 17,000 men of the Army of the Tennessee, who had come from Memphis, arrived in Bridgeport. The railways were proving invaluable in this war. Sherman's orders were to march into Chattanooga and repair its rail lines. Grant, ever anxious to attack, changed these orders, telling his friend to attack the north end of Missionary Ridge at once.

Thomas, who had been previously ordered to do the same thing but declined, citing paucity of numbers, was directed to divert the enemy's attention by threatening the rifle pits on the bottom of Missionary Ridge at the same time.

The attack was delayed by rains, but on 23 November, Thomas's men cleared Confederate trenches around Orchard Knob, a mile before the main line of defences at the foot of Missionary Ridge. Two days later, Sherman moved against Tunnel Hill on the Confederate right, while Thomas's men were ordered to take and hold the rifle pits at the bottom of Missionary Ridge. Sherman's men ran into a stubborn defence by one of the south's finest generals, Irish-born Major-General Patrick Cleburne. On the right, however, the rifle pits fell easily to troops under Hooker. Once there, however, the men saw that they were in danger from Confederates firing almost vertically along Missionary Ridge above them. With the briefest of pauses, they dashed up the side of the ridge, at times having to pull themselves up from tree to tree. Confederate cannon could not be depressed enough to fire on them. The Confederate infantrymen threw down their arms and ran. The Confederate line was broken at a number of places, and its troops fled towards Chickamauga Creek. The siege was over.

▲ A rather fanciful post-war drawing of the Battle of Lookout Mountain compresses the action, on top of showing impossibly well-clad Confederate soldiers. As well, gaiters, as shown being worn by Union troops, were rarely actually seen.

THE BRISTOE CAMPAIGN

Meade's pursuit of Lee's beaten army after Gettysburg was far too slow for Lincoln, who bombarded the general with demands that he move more aggressively. It took, however, almost three months before Meade began a move against Lee. By that time, Meade's army had drawn up its lines on familiar ground, just north of the Rapidan River. The Army of Northern Virginia took ground east of the Blue Ridge mountains, near Culpeper, Virginia.

Both armies had not only been weakened by losses in the Gettysburg campaign, but they had also been reduced by having units withdrawn. Longstreet's Corps went to Tennessee, soon followed by the Army of the Potomac's XI and XII Corps.

Lee, always looking for an opportunity to exploit, moved shortly after learning of the departure of the two Federal corps. He sent his remaining two corps, led by veteran Lieutenant-Generals A.P. Hill and Richard S. Ewell, their movements covered by J.E.B. Stuart's cavalry, to turn Meade's right flank. He could not only threaten Meade's army this way, but also Washington, a move that in the past had always caused the national government to react by

bringing troops back to the city. On 9 October 1863, the Confederates started their move, skirmishing with Federal pickets and videttes on the way. By the 11th they were in Culpeper, as Meade reacted by withdrawing slowly to place his army between Lee and Washington.

As at Chancellorsville, Lee decided to split his army. He had Ewell follow the withdrawing Federals along the line of the Orange & Alexandria Railroad. At the same time, A.P. Hill's corps swung wide around to the west, in an attempt to cut around the retreating Federals and trap them.

By the morning of the 14th, Hill's troops were some five miles north of Warrenton, near New Baltimore and not far from Ewell's corps. Hill, a professional, U.S. Military Academy trained soldier who had been an excellent division commander of his famed 'Light Division', was not an equally good corps commander. Often laid low by various ailments at important times such as at Gettysburg in which he played little part, he tended to be impulsive and lacking caution. It was Hill who had struck without waiting for Jackson's men

◄◄ *Far left, top:* Henry Heth was honoured by being the only General whom Robert E. Lee addressed by his first name. A West Pointer and professional soldier before the war, he served throughout the war and surrendered at Appomattox.

◄◄ *Far left, bottom:* Brigadier General John R. Cooke, who served in the 8th U.S. Infantry Regiment before the war, followed the South, becoming Colonel of the 27th North Carolina Infantry.

◄ Governor Warren made his name when, reading signals almost alone on the top of Little Round Top, Gettysburg, July 2, he saw Hood's advancing Confederates and, on his own, called up reinforcements to save the vital position. Despite this neither Sheridan or Grant thought much of him.

At noon we were again ordered forward, marching down the pike through the earthworks already mentioned, behind which an occasional dead Rebel was seen, lying as he fell. The haversack of one of these which we investigated, contained nothing except a quart of raw, uncracked corn, and the body was clothed with an amount of clothing inadequate to the season. How can one do otherwise than admire a devotion to a cause, so intense as to endure these two hardships of scanty fare and exposure!

back couriers to his lead elements ordering them to come up and be ready to attack immediately.

A division commanded by Major-General Henry Heth, the same Confederate general whose troops brought on the battle at Gettysburg, were first on the field. Hill ordered them deployed without even waiting for skirmish lines to be sent forward, and sent two brigades straight from column into battle line and then forward.

They were aimed at an obtuse angle that had been formed by the railway line and a stream. As the Confederates charged down the hillside, Hill shouting encouragement and waving his slouch hat, a line of Federal infantry hidden along the railway, rose and delivered a shocking volley. The unexpected Federals were men of Major-General Gouverneur K. Warren's II Corps, some of the best troops in the Army of the Potomac, men who had stood along the stone wall at Gettysburg to repel Pickett's Charge. The two Confederate brigade commanders, Brigadier-Generals John Cooke and William Kirkland, went down badly wounded as the Confederates wheeled to their right and charged the embankment. They couldn't make it, driven off by fire. As they fell back, their supporting artillery was exposed and the Federals leaped over the embankment and seized the Southern guns. An attempt to recover them failed.

Confederate losses were some 1,300, while the Federals lost fewer than 550. Lee, visiting the field the next morning listened as Hill admitted his failure, giving, for him, a major rebuke: 'Well, well, General, bury these poor men and let us say no more about it.'

At this point both the Federal retreat and Confederate advance halted and for the next three days both sides probed to find a possible point of attack. Neither side finding any, on 17 October Lee began to fall back. The Confederate retreat took three days, with Confederate cavalry catching Federal cavalry under Brigadier-General Judson Kilpatrick in an ambush at Buckland Mills on 19 October. The startled Federals fled in what became known by the Southern press as the 'Buckland Races'. By the 20th the Confederate army was back across the Rappahannock and the campaign ended.

◄ Judson Kilpatrick was a graduate of the U.S. Military Academy's Class of 1861. Although young and lacking experience, he nevertheless rose quickly in the war, serving as a brigadier-general by the war's end. Sherman called him a fool, but said he needed a fool to command his cavalry in the march to the sea.

at the opening of the Seven Days, and he would repeat that type of action here.

Learning that the retreating Federals were apparently moving along the tracks, he determined to strike them immediately and split their line of march. He rode ahead of his following corps to a hill that overlooked Bristoe Station where he saw elements of the Federal III Corps crossing Broad Run east of the station. He sent

THE MINE RUN CAMPAIGN

Lee, who apparently had heart problems throughout much of the war, suffered some pain after the Bristoe Campaign, to the point of being unable to ride in late October/early November. Fortunately for the Confederate army, he had recovered sufficiently to take part in a review of the Army of Northern Virginia's Cavalry Corps on 5 November because, two days later, Meade began another attempt to move around Lee's army.

The plan called for the army to be divided into two wings. The right would be under Sedgwick and would be sent across two fords located at Rappahannock Station. Major-General William H. French commanded the left wing, and he was to blast the way across Kelly's Ford, which the Confederates had fortified with two semicircular works.

On 7 November, Federal cavalry and infantry crossed the Rappahannock at Kelly's Ford, after a failed attempt to halt them by quickly overwhelmed Confederate infantry and artillery. Engineers laid a pontoon bridge at the ford site, and Federals poured over the river. At the same time, Sedgwick hurled his men successfully over his target fords, and the Federals had a firm beachhead on the Southern side of the river. Some 2,000 Confederates were captured in the brief action.

French, however, moved too slowly in the fog that descended on the scene to exploit this hole in the Confederate line, and Lee was able to bring up reinforcements to plug the gap. A new defensive line was drawn up and in place by the morning of 9 November. Meade's men, however, did not attack and a day later Lee, in a bad position, began to withdraw. On 10 November, the Army of Northern Virginia was back in position on the south side of the Rapidan River, the very spot from which they had started the Bristoe campaign.

Meade then planned an attempt to turn the Confederate right to coordinate with Grant's attack on the Army of Tennessee in late November. Planned for the 24th, rain over several days held up the attack. Then, on the 26th, French was slow in starting his command, delaying the rest of the army. Rain had also swollen the Rappahannock so that engineers had to repair the pontoon bridges to let artillery join the infantry.

French now compounded the problems by taking his troops down the wrong road, a way that would bring him closer to a Confederate division whose mission was to delay the Federals until reinforcements could arrive. French's error would make this task easier to perform. A day was wasted convincing French, whom some said was 'in the slightest degree under the influence of liquor', of his error and getting him on the right road. On the left, in the meantime, Confederate cavalry captured an ammunition train to further compound confusion.

Finally, in the rain on 28 November, the army was drawn up in position to attack Lee's troops defending the far bank of Mine Run, a tributary of the Rapidan. Lee's troops were well positioned and had spent the time they'd unexpectedly received in strengthening a naturally good position with abatis (a deterrent of slashed tree limbs bound together with branches facing the enemy) and digging earthen fortifications.

The troops on both sides spent a miserable 29 November as temperatures dropped and Meade and his engineers reconnoitred the position. A conference of war that evening produced a decision to attack the next day, led by the II Corps under Warren. At daylight, after a bitterly cold night, Warren saw the strength of the position before him but still gave the orders to attack. The troops, many pinning their names to their coats so their bodies could be identified after the attack, waited. Others turned over valuables to regimental chaplains to be sent home after their deaths. In the meantime Warren sent word to Meade of the enemy's strength and his doubt he could carry the position in front of him. Displaying tremendous moral courage, Meade countermanded the orders for the attack. 'I am conscious that my head is off,' he said as he

▶ The U.S. Army used two types of pontoon bridges. The ones carried at the head of a column to bridge rivers quickly were canvas-covered wood frames that were light enough to be put down and taken up quickly. All wood ones were used for more permanent bridges.

▼ Major-General William French, a U.S. Military Academy graduate from Maryland, lost his reputation during the Mine Run campaign when his corps' slowness caused him to be blamed for the failure to exploit a potential advantage over Lee's army.

▶ Union troopers water their horses in the Rapidan. Horses served both armies in a number of ways, as carriers of important officers, bringing cavalrymen into battle, and hauling cannon and supply wagons.

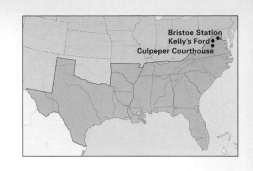

brought his army back to its old camp. 'There will be a great howl.' Meade expected to be relieved as commander of the Army of the Potomac for not attacking, but there were those who knew that his courage had saved the army from another Fredericksburg. He remained in command.

Lee, however, reacted to the Federal retreat slowly. He decided to attack the Federals on 2 December, but his advancing troops found only cold camp fires where they had been. 'I am too old to command this army,' Lee told his staff officers. 'We should never have permitted those people to get away.'

Both armies were exhausted, however, and ready for winter quarters. Indeed, Meade took cold in January, 1864, and this developed into pneumonia. He went to recover in Philadelphia on leave and stayed to recover for three weeks, while his army built log huts and began preparing for the following campaign that would, they hoped, end the war.

PRIVATE JOHN O. CASLER, 33RD VIRGINIA INFANTRY REGIMENT

While we lay in line of battle on Mine Run two men belonging to the Louisiana Brigade were sentenced to be shot, and were taken out in front of the works to be executed, but they broke and ran to the enemy's line and escaped. The guards fired at them, but did not hit them, and did not try, I suppose, for we did not want to see any of the soldiers executed, and would give them every chance to escape that we could so as not to incriminate ourselves.

THE SIEGE OF KNOXVILLE

In a move that brought mutual pleasure to both generals, Bragg detached Longstreet from his army outside Chattanooga. The force would include his two divisions from the Army of Northern Virginia with sufficient artillery and four brigades of cavalry and horse artillery. Another 3,000 men were ordered to join Longstreet as he took command against a force under Ambrose Burnside, then garrisoning the Tennessee city of Knoxville.

The Confederates, believed to outnumber Burnside's troops, left Bragg's army on 4 November, heading towards Knoxville across roads, in wagons and on rickety trains. Confederate cavalry, under Major-General Joseph Wheeler, scouted ahead, reaching the Little Tennessee River near Loudon on 14 November and advancing as far as the banks of the Holston River, west of the city, by the 17th. Burnside, learning of Longstreet's approach, gathered his men, and began to pull back desperately towards Knoxville. At one point Confederate scouts gathered up over a hundred wagons filled with valuable supplies, as the Federals moved north as quickly as possible. Moving parallel to Longstreet's advancing forces over ice-covered dirt roads, Burnside's men narrowly escaped Longstreet at Campbell's Station as it came under Confederate artillery fire. Had Burnside's men reached there a half-hour later than they did, they could well have been cut off south of Knoxville. Instead, they poured into prepared fortifications around the city on 17 November.

Most participants afterwards agreed that had Longstreet aggressively pursued Burnside as closely as possible, he would have taken the city. Indeed, Confederate infantry drove a line of defending Federal cavalry, killing the defenders' commander, Brigadier-General William Sanders, back to the line of fortifications that ringed the town. Instead of employing a wide front attack, however, the Confederates grew cautious, advancing skirmish lines to test the city's defenders.

Federal lines around Knoxville featured full forts with small lines between them. Fort Loudon, renamed Fort Sanders after the dead cavalry commander, was one of the most prominent of these. The Confederate commander in the north-west area, where Fort Sanders was located, Major-General Lafayette McLaws, dug parallels from nearby Confederate lines towards the Federal position. On 22 November, he planned a night attack and reserves were called up to exploit the position's capture. That evening, however, McLaws was talked out of the attack by officers who preferred waiting for the visibility of daylight.

The 23rd brought news of a reinforcing body of two infantry brigades, commanded by Major-General Bushrod Johnson, on the way from Loudon. Longstreet decided to postpone the attack until these troops could arrive.

Confederate Brigadier-General Daniel Leadbetter, chief engineer of the Army of Tennessee, arrived from Bragg on the 25th

▼ *Left*: Looking out from the heights opposite the city of Knoxville. The University of Tennessee appears dimly on the hill at the right. The leafless trees indicate the photograph was taken roughly the time of the city's siege.

▼ Confederates assault the Union lines unsuccessfully. One Union light artilleryman, marked by his short jacket trimmed with red, has leaped to the top of the wall and fires a shot from his personal revolver at a Confederate. Such revolvers were privately purchased.

with orders for an immediate attack. Longstreet was reluctant, wanting to wait for further reinforcements, said to be on the road from Virginia. They were expected in fewer than ten days, which would not be enough time for the Federals to lift the siege. Moreover, the Confederate high command had word that the Federals in Knoxville were on half rations. Surely starving them out, or at best waiting until they were weakened from hunger, would be better than an immediate assault.

Leadbetter insisted, however, on Bragg's orders being carried out and, reluctantly, Longstreet agreed. Plans called for an attack on the 28th, but bad weather delayed the attack until the 29th. That dawn found the trench around the fortification filled with water that had turned to ice, slowing down the assaulting Confederates who became excellent targets. Wire strung around the fort at ankle height further broke up Southern formations. Without axes to get through the staked wires and abatis, Confederates at the front reported back that they could make no progress. 'At first we seemed to be going right ahead, shoving everything aside,' recalled one of Longstreet's staff officers, Moxley Sorrel, 'but some stops were made and the wounded men began coming back.' The attack was defeated.

Longstreet prepared for another try. Before anything could be attempted, however, he received a telegraph from Davis announc-ing Bragg's failure before Chattanooga and ordering Longstreet's men back to support the Army of Tennessee in Northern Georgia.

Longstreet did not obey Davis' orders immediately, remaining at Knoxville where he learned that Federal troops were on the way to relieve the city. Finally, on 4 December, he abandoned the siege and retired to Rogersville, where he resupplied his troops from the local countryside. The Federals, under Major-General John Parke slowly followed. On 13 December Longstreet turned to attack Parke's advanced infantry and cavalry at Bean's Station.

Before dawn on the 13th, Confederates ran into Federal pickets who raised the alarm. The Federals deployed into line in the village, their artillery posted on the hills above them. The Federals fought off frontal attacks, while foiling attempts to flank their position. Finally they were forced out of the town, retreating three miles that night to Blain's Cross Roads. There they set up stronger positions, using railway sleepers for breastworks. Longstreet planned another attack the next morning, but saw the strength of the Federal position and called off his attack. The Federals were allowed to retreat and the Knoxville Campaign was at an end.

▼ *Left*: **The barren field over which actions were fought around Fort Sanders during the siege of Knoxville. Wherever armies camped for any time, trees disappeared into fires and stoves.**

▼ **Orlando Poe, a native of Ohio, served in the Corps of Topographical Engineers before the war, as an infantry colonel until 1863, then returned to engineer duty. He was chief engineer of the Army of the Ohio and the Military Division of Mississippi, becoming a brigadier-general before the war's end.**

CAPTAIN ORLANDO M. POE, STAFF ENGINEER, U.S. ARMY

Early on the 18th eight or ten of the enemy had established themselves in the upper story of the tower of a brick house which stood about 750 yards beyond Sanders's line, and from this advantageous position greatly annoyed his command by their accurate fire. He sent a request to Benjamin, in Fort Sanders, to try the effect upon these sharp-shooters of a few shots from his 20-pounder Parrots. The distance was 2500 yards, but Benjamin's gunner put a short directly through the compartment occupied by the sharp-shooters, badly wrecking it (as was ascertained by examination after the siege), and abating the nuisance.

GOING AFTER CHARLESTON

Most Northerners considered the city of Charleston, South Carolina, and its inhabitants guilty of the crime of starting the war to break up the Union. It was the city in which the convention had been held that had voted for secession, and its inhabitants were considered fire brands. Indeed, Charlestonians had earlier seen Federal troops arrive when they threatened to 'nullify' any Federal laws with which they disagreed.

It would therefore be expected that a major Federal thrust could be aimed at capturing the city. Indeed, many may have thought God also wanted Charleston destroyed, as a major fire on the evening of 11 December 1861, levelled 540 acres of the town including the Charleston Theater, the Carolina Art Association, the Apprentices' Library, and the Circular Church.

The Federals had an excellent launching pad for attempts to take the city, which had fallen to the British after a siege in the War of American Independence. Hilton Head, South Carolina, had come into Federal hands quite early in the war, and by June 1862 troops from there were ready to nibble away at the edges of Charleston's defences. After the fall of Ft. Sumter, Confederates had prepared extensive fortifications around the city. However, they were hampered by the geography of the area, where large islands were separated by narrow streams and vast swampy areas.

On 2 June 1862, Federals landed at the end of one of these islands, James Island, where they faced little immediate opposition. The Confederates had drawn up a defensive line through the middle of the island, centred on Secessionville, a pre-war resort area. There they had a fort, with heavy artillery, and a signal tower that could observe Federal movements. On 16 June, the Federals attacked this position. A large cannon in the centre of the Confederate works forced the attacking line to split in two, heading towards either side of the fort. The open field over which they charged was bordered by dense woods through which they could not pass, but even so the attack was narrowly beaten back. The Federal commander of the attacking force, Brigadier Henry Benham, was relieved of command, and forced out of the army until Lincoln intervened.

In August 1862, Beauregard was named to command in the city, Davis figuring that this backwater post would occupy the general, whom the President disliked. Beauregard went right to work strengthening defences, and encouraging idiosyncratic ideas that might improve his city's chances. For example, he had faith in submarines, even supplying army troops to crew one of the them, the *Hundley*, after she had sunk several times, taking navy crews to their deaths.

Submarines were only part of the naval force assembled in Charleston. Local subscriptions had largely paid for two iron-clad gunboats the *Palmetto State* and the *Chicora*. similar to the *Virginia*. They were supported by a number of conventional boats that had been turned into armed gunboats.

On 30 January 1863, the two iron-clads and the other boats of their flotilla slipped their anchor chains. In the pre-dawn haze they approached several Federal blockading vessels. Two of them, the *Mercedita* and the *Keystone State*, were surprised and quickly surrendered. Other Federal ships, none of which were iron-clad and therefore extremely vulnerable, fled, easily escaping the slower Confederate iron-clads. The Confederate army and navy authorities then brought British, French and Spanish counsels out to sea to show that the blockade had been broken, an act that would have forced the Federals to officially re-establish a legal blockade. During that time the city would have been open to commerce of all sorts.

However, four of the U.S. Naval ships that had initially fled returned that afternoon to their posts off Charleston Harbor, and the British government decided that the blockade had not been officially broken.

The Federal Navy decided to end the threat from Charleston by sea, if the army could not take the city by land. The flagship of a squadron sent to do the job was the *New Ironsides*, an iron-clad that looked much like a regular sailing ship, but mounted fourteen 11-inch guns. She would be accompanied by a squadron of eight Monitor-style boats, each mounting a minimum of two 15-inch guns in their single turrets.

On 7 April, 1863, the Federal flotilla entered Charleston Harbor. Confederate guns at Forts Sumter and Moultrie, as well as at other positions ringing the harbour opened fire on the ships. A mine exploded near one Monitor, but she simply rose up in the water, and then settled down, essentially unhurt. However, the land-based guns took their toll. In all, the defenders fired some 2,209 shots, hitting Federal ships a total of 520 times. The *New*

▼ A U.S. Navy flotilla of Monitor-class ironclads and the more conventionally designed ironclad the *New Ironsides* go into action in Charleston harbour. They essentially learned that ships can't sink forts, and land forces would have to take the city.

Ironsides was especially battered. The Navy decided it could not sink land-based guns, and withdrew. The squadron's commander, Rear Admiral Francis DuPont called for a new joint army/navy venture, admitting, 'These Monitors are miserable failures where forts are concerned; the longest one hour and the others forty-five minutes under fire, and five of the eight were wholly or partially disabled.'

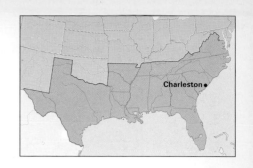

▲ A contemporary Currier & Ives print depicting Battle of Secessionville, an ill-planned attempt at reconnoitering a Confederate position that turned into a bloodbath for the Union. The Union commander lost his command, and almost his commission, over this battle.

CAPTAIN WILLIAM H. PARKER, C.S.N.

We went to quarters an hour before crossing the bar, and the men stood silently at their guns. The port-shutters were closed, not a light could be scene from the outside, and the few battle-lanterns lit cast a pale, weird light on the gun-deck. My friend Phil. Porcher, who commanded the bow-gun, was equipped with a pair of white kid gloves, and had in his mouth an unlighted cigar. As we stood at our stations, not even whispering, the silence became more and more intense. Just at my side I noticed the little powder-boy of the broadside guns sitting on a match-tub, with his powder-pouch slung over his shoulder, fast asleep, and he was in this condition when we rammed the *Mercedita*.

AFRICAN-AMERICANS JOIN THE FIGHT

Although there were a number of free Northern African-Americans who were able and willing to fight for the freedom of their brothers and sisters in the south, only the U.S. Navy was willing to enlist them as full service members at the outbreak of war. African-Americans were allowed to rise in the Navy as high as petty officer, the senior enlisted grade. The Army, even the volunteer forces, however, were 'lily-white' as far as combatant roles went.

That is not to say that no African-Americans were to be seen among the fighting land forces. Both sides made liberal use of them as cooks, servants, teamsters and labourers. Indeed, the Confederate Congress authorized the recruiting of African-Americans into its companies to serve as cooks and musicians, and, with the many personal servants brought to the front, many Northerners were surprised to see so many in the ranks. Indeed, often they were mistaken for actual combatants. During the last months of the war, the Confederate government, pressed to it by generals ranging from Patrick Cleburne to Robert E. Lee, authorized the recruiting of black combat companies. At least two companies were raised in Richmond, where they paraded to the general disapproval of the civilian population, but the war was over before they ever got into combat.

Acceptance of African-American soldiers in the U.S. Army was quicker, although it was not much easier. It started when escaping slaves entered U.S. Army lines seeking freedom. In 1861 and 1862 their masters often followed them and demanded their property back. Most Federal commanders, who were often fighting for the Union than the abolition of slavery, returned these unfortunate individuals. Major-General Benjamin Butler, however, a Massachusetts Democrat before the war, and a clever lawyer, declared that if escaped slaves were property, and this property had been used in building fortifications for the Confederates, they were property with war-like uses and said they were 'contraband of war', not liable to be returned. This definition became widespread.

In various theatres local commanders began to form many of these slaves into military units. Off the South Carolina coast, Major-General David Hunter formed the 1st South Carolina of escaped slaves in May 1862. In New Orleans, where there had long been a tradition of black volunteer militia companies, Butler formed an entire Louisiana Native Guard (Corps d'Afrique), that

included infantry, cavalry, artillery and engineers. The first regiment was mustered in on 27 September 1862, and was the first full African-American regiment in American military history. Officers were mostly white, although there were some African-American officers in the Corps d'Afrique. Lincoln, afraid of disturbing slave-owning interests in pro-Union states such as Delaware, Maryland, Kentucky and Missouri, refused to authorize their actions.

However the move was not to be denied. Massachusetts Governor John Andrews authorized two black infantry regiments, the 54th and 55th, and, when the U.S. War Department would not pay them the equal of what white infantrymen made, had the state make up the difference. African-Americans in Kansas formed the 1st Kansas, and saw the first action of black troops at Island Mounds, Missouri, on 28 October 1862. Finally, with the issue of the Emancipation Proclamation, Lincoln called for four regiments of U.S. Colored Troops (U.S.C.T.) to be raised, a number that soon mushroomed. Existing black regiments were taken on as U.S.C.T. regiments; the 1st Kansas became the 79th U.S.C.T. By the war's end, some 145 infantry regiments, 7 cavalry regiments, 12 heavy artillery regiments, one field artillery regiment and one engineer regiment made up of African-Americans took part in the war, with a total of some 178,895 African-Americans serving.

There was prejudice at first against them actually fighting, with theatre commanders tending to use them as labourers rather than as soldiers. Nonetheless, they did manage to see combat. U.S.C.T. units took part in the assault on Port Hudson on 27 May 1863 and defended their position at Millikens Bend, Louisiana. The 8th

▲ This corporal of U.S. Colored Troops holds a privately purchased 1849 Colt pocket revolver. African-Americans fought long and hard for the right to join the white soldiers in fighting for an end to slavery.

► This illustration taken from a U.S.C.T. recruiting poster shows a typical company, complete with its white officers. Officers were virtually all white, but were screened by tests and came from combat units so man-for-man were likely better than those in all-white units.

▲ Angry Confederates killed both blacks and native southern whites serving in the Union garrison at Fort Pillow, Tennessee, long after the fort had been overrun. If the killings were intended to awe African-Americans and keep them from fighting, it backfired.

SERGEANT ACHILLES V. CLARK, 20TH TENNESSEE CAVALRY, CSA

The bugle sounded the charge and in less than ten minutes we were in the fort hurling the cowardly villians [sic] howling down the bluff. Our men were so exasperated by the Yankees' threats of no quarter that they gave but little. The Slaughter was awful. Words cannot describe the scene. The poor deluded negros [sic] would run up to our men fall upon their knees and with uplifted hands scream for mercy but they were ordered to their feet and then shot down. The whitte [sic] men fared but little better. Their fort turned out to be a great slaugter[sic] pen – blood – human blood stood about in pools and brains could have been gathered up in any quantity.

U.S.C.T. took heavy losses in the battle at Olustee, Florida, in February 1864. But their most infamous engagement was the Battle of Fort Pillow, Tennessee.

This post overlooked the Mississippi River north of Memphis and was garrisoned by Battery F, 4th U.S. Colored Light Artillery; the 11th U.S.C.T., and loyal whites in the 13th Tennessee Cavalry. Nathan Bedford Forrest's cavalry overran the position on 12 April 1864. Eyewitnesses agree that Forrest's men killed a number of Federals there, both black and white – indeed, they were as angry at the whites joining Lincoln's army as they were at the blacks – as they tried to escape. While the Confederates suffered only 14 killed and 86 wounded, some 231 Federals, mostly black, were killed, and another 100 wounded. From the 262 who were part of the garrison, only 58 African-Americans were taken prisoner.

If the plan was to deter slaves from fighting against their masters, it failed to work. Indeed, the massacre led to fiercer fighting from both blacks and their white officers, who were under sentence of death from the Confederates if captured in action.

DEFENDING TO THE END

DuPont was relieved of command of the Federal ships off Charleston in June 1863, after the failure of his attack. The next approach would be by the army, which landed troops on James Island on 9 July and on Morris Island on 10 July, under cover of naval gunfire. The Confederates there had erected several large forts that overlooked entrances to Charleston Harbor, the leading one of which was named Battery Wagner.

The Federals, having established a firm beachhead, decided to assault Battery Wagner on 11 July. The daybreak attack, however, was driven back causing tremendous losses. In one regiment, only 88 of the 196 men who made the attack answered the roll call the next day.

The Federals decided to try again with a larger force and heavier artillery fire for ten hours prior to the infantry assault. As the artillery fire was going into sand, it did less damage than it would have done on more solid ground. Indeed, the Confederates actually covered some of their smaller guns with sand to protect them during the bombardment, digging them out afterwards and using them to deadly effect during the attack.

The Federals then sent 6,000 men against the 1,300 Confederate defenders. In the first wave was one of the first African-American regiments, the 54th Massachusetts which, prior to that, had mostly been used in rear echelon jobs. Many men who made the night-time assault actually crossed the moat and got into the fort, but the defenders had so weakened their forces, that few survived even to surrender. The attack was valiant but useless. The Federals brought up heavy artillery and began a siege of Battery Wagner.

The siege dragged on, the men roasted by the hot South Carolina summer sun. The Federals dug trenches towards the fortification, while Confederate sharpshooters made it impossible to be exposed for more than a minute. The Federals used large calcium lights to expose the fort at night, blinding the defenders and making them easy targets. Finally, in September, Beauregard ordered the fort's garrison to withdraw. By 7 September, after 58 days, it was in Federal hands.

Elsewhere, Federal engineers designed works for guns that could reach Fort Sumter and by early July their guns opened fire on the battered brick fort. On 17 August 1863, these guns were joined

▲ While a U.S. Navy flotilla of Monitor-class vessels and the USS *New Ironsides* head towards Charleston harbor, Union ground troops batter Battery Wagner on one of the peninsulas that protected the way into the city's harbour.

► This photo was taken of the insides of Fort Sumter after the 1861 Confederate bombardment. By 1863 virtually no brick walls stood, only piles of brick dust underneath sand bags. But the garrison held on.

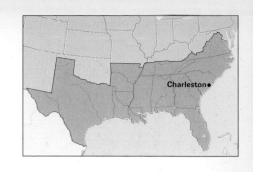

by naval guns in two Monitor-type boats. By 24 August, the fort was described as 'a mass of broken masonry'. Still, the fort's guns replied, and the bombardment continued. Finally, on the night of 8 September, a group of 500 sailors and marines landed on the island, but they were met by a heavier fire from the piles of bricks making up the fort than they expected. Fire from the *Chicora* added to their problems, and they withdrew with a loss of 127 men.

The U.S. Navy withdrew to lick its wounds, but returned to open a second bombardment of Fort Sumter on 26 October. This bombardment lasted 41 days and nights. By the time they were done, the only answering fire from the fort came from four sharp-shooters' rifles aimed at Union cannons across the bay. On 30 November, the Federals tried again to take the fort with a landing force. The barges were spotted before they could land, and fire from all quarters forced them again to retire.

Finally, the Federals decided to order the Confederates to abandon Morris Island and Fort Sumter or face a bombardment of the city as a whole. Large Federals guns were specifically placed to accomplish this. The Confederates rejected the ultimatum and on 29 August 1863 the first shells landed on the city's streets. The bombardment would carry on for 18 months. Many of the city's citizens moved inland, often to the estates of relatives or friends, while some simply moved uptown out of artillery range. The city would not, however, surrender. Indeed, remaining citizens kept up as much of their pre-war social activities as possible. The city's Jockey Club held its annual three-day meet to the end. But towards the end of 1864 an end was in sight. An outbreak of yellow fever in October weakened morale, while the fall of Savannah, Georgia, in December 1864 made eventual capture a very real prospect.

CAPTAIN LUIS F. EMILIO, 54TH MASSACHUSETTS VOLUNTEER INFANTRY

Wagner's wall, momentarily lit up by cannon-flashes, was still the goal toward which the survivors rushed in sadly diminished numbers. It was now dark, the gloom made more intense by the blinding explosions in the front. This terrible fire which the regiment had just faced, probably caused the greatest numbers of casualties sustained by the Fifty-fourth in the assault; for nearer the work the men were somewhat sheltered by the high parapet. Every flash showed the men dotted with men of the regiment, killed or wounded.

Many of the city's garrison had been sent to reinforce the Army of Tennessee prior to the fall of Atlanta and it was obvious that the city could not be defended against attack from the sea and Sherman's men if they chose to come. On 2 July 1864, a large Federal force again took part of James Island but the Confederates held on and the Federals withdrew on 11 July. A third bombardment of Fort Sumter opened on 7 July, by now so reduced that it was a captain's command. This bombardment lasted 60 days and nights, but again ended in failure.

By now, Sherman was on the move, apparently towards Charleston. By early February it was clear that he would bypass the city and on 14 February, Beauregard ordered it abandoned. Early in the morning of 18 February, Federal soldiers entered the city and raised the flag over Fort Sumter.

▼ The African-American 54th Massachusetts storms Battery Wagner in this post-war. The regiment's white colonel, seen being shot on top of the wall besides the colour, was thrown into a single burial trench with his black troops. His family left him there, a mark of honour.

FIGHTING IN MISSISSIPPI

The garrison in Vicksburg, commanded by Major-General William T. Sherman, now took the war into the rest of Mississippi. On 3 February, Sherman marched his 26,000 men out of the city on what would amount essentially to a raid to destroy enemy rail lines and stores in Meridian. Another 7,600 cavalry from Memphis, under Major-General William Sooy Smith, were sent to cooperate with Sherman's troops. Smith's orders were to sweep 'down near the Mobile & Ohio Railroad, disable that road as much as possible, consume or destroy the resources of the enemy along that road, break up the connection with Columbus, Mississippi, and finally reach me at or near Meridian as near the date I have mentioned as possible [10 February].' Defending the state were some 20,000 men under Polk.

Polk's men fought a delaying action on the battlefields of the Vicksburg Campaign, at Champion's Hill and Liverpool Heights, Edwards' Ferry, and Bolton Depot, but fell back as, on 5 February Sherman's men entered Jackson. Their main opponents on the march were cavalry who were easily brushed aside by the more heavily armed infantrymen.

By 7 February Sherman's men skirmished with Polk's troops near Brandon, Morton and Satartia, but opposition was relatively light and their raid was not halted. The Confederate high command was in a panic. Davis telegraphed the overall theatre commander, Joseph Johnston, that the Federals had to be stopped before they reached their obvious goal, Mobile, Alabama. The great fear was that once there, Davis said, he could establish a base 'to which supplies and reinforcements may be sent by sea'. Sherman, however, had no intention of driving all the way to Mobile, although Grant would have liked to have taken that city after the fall of Vicksburg. Indeed, on 31 January, Sherman telegraphed Banks, then attempting to establish a Federal foothold along the Texas coast, that: 'I want to keep up the delusion of an attack on Mobile and the Alabama River, and therefore would be obliged if you would keep up an irritating foraging or other expedition in that direction.'

In the meantime, Smith's troops made progress, too, although Sherman was unaware of it. He decided to wait for a brigade of cavalry, without which he thought his forces would be too weak to advance. The brigade did not join his troops until 10 February. The next day his troops were beyond Collierville, Tennessee. In all, he would have to march some 250 miles to reach Meridian, but his troops had only penetrated some 150 miles into the state before they were stopped. One of the things that considerably slowed up Smith's column was that hundreds of African-Americans, having heard of Lincoln's Emancipation Proclamation that proclaimed freedom from slavery in rebellious territories as of 1 January 1864, joined his column to escape to freedom.

Smith's troops ran into stiffer than usual opposition from 2,500 Confederate cavalrymen led by superb cavalry commander Major-General Nathan Bedford Forrest at Okolona, where Smith reported that, 'we had the worst of it for a little while, but finally checked the enemy handsomely, and continued our return march, fighting at the rear and on both flanks.' In fact, a loyal Tennessee regiment gave way under attack, and the Federals were forced to retreat five miles under fire before finally halting the Confederates. Smith's column pulled back towards Memphis. They reached there on 26 February. Sherman never forgave Smith for his failure to play his part in the campaign.

In the meantime, on 13 February, Sherman's part of the force reached the outskirts of his true objective, Meridian. The following day, Valentine's Day, his troops marched into Meridian, as Polk's Confederates continued to fall back in front of them, towards Demopolis, Alabama.

The Federals spent five days in Meridian, destroying an arsenal, immense storehouses and the railways in every direction. Sherman's infantrymen spent the time breaking up the Mobile & Ohio Railroad, south and north, and the Jackson & Selma Railroad, east and west, so that they could not be used again for the rest of the war. In all, Sherman's troops destroyed some 115 miles of priceless railway lines, 61 bridges and 20 locomotives.

▲ **General Leonidas Polk, a classmate of Jefferson Davis at the U.S. Military Academy, spent very little time in the army after school, instead becoming an Episcopal priest. The Bishop of Louisiana when the war broke out, he was quickly commissioned a Confederate general.**

◄ **Major-General Nathan Bedford Forrest, an almost illiterate slave-trader before the war began, proved to have a hidden talent as a brilliant cavalry leader. It was said his trick of winning battles was to 'get there firstest with the mostest'.**

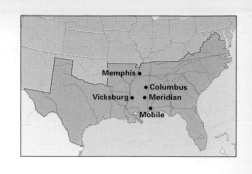

▲ Wherever Union soldiers went, African-Americans who had been slaves in nearby towns and plantations joined them, seeking freedom. This group, as had many, managed to take a wagon and mules from their former owners, who have also probably fled south as refugees when Union troops approached.

MAJOR-GENERAL WILLIAM T. SHERMAN, U.S. ARMY

Intending to spend the night in Decatur, I went to a double log-house, and arranged with the lady for some supper. We unsaddled our horses, tied them to the fence inside the yard, and, being tired, I lay down on a bed and fell asleep. Presently I heard shouts and hallooing, and then heard pistol shots close to the house. My aide, Major Audenried, called me and said that we were attacked by rebel cavalry, who were all around us. . . I went out into the back-yard, saw wagons passing at a run down the road, and horsemen dashing about in a cloud of dust, firing their pistols, their shots reaching the house in which we were. Gathering the few orderlies and clerks that were about, I was preparing to get into a corn-crib at the back side of the lot, wherein to defend ourselves, when I saw Audenried coming back with the regiment, on a run, deploying forward as they came.

Finally abandoning hope of being joined by Smith's column, Sherman began his return to Vicksburg on 21 February. By the 26th they were near Canton, Mississippi, and by 4 March they were safely back in Vicksburg. Although the campaign by itself had accomplished very little, save for a great deal of destruction of Confederate war material, it taught Sherman that he could safely guide a large body of Federal troops a great distance through Confederate territory, living off the land rather than depending on transportation from the rear. Moreover such a body could do considerable damage to the enemy that could not be largely repaired until after the war was over. Civilians would see that their attempt at independence was futile; their own forces could not protect them if Federal forces decided to invade their territory. This lesson would serve him well on a larger scale during his famed 'march to the sea'.

INTO THE WILDERNESS

▼ Grant sent Meade's Army of the Potomac, plus Burnside's IX Corps, south, first meeting Lee's Army of Northern Virginia, then constantly heading south, moving around Lee's right flank until he could be pinned down around Richmond.

On 9 March 1864 U.S. Grant, who had been summoned to Washington, was handed a commission as lieutenant-general, the first since George Washington, and given overall command of all Federal armies in the field. He immediately began a plan for an offensive at all points, with Sherman heading after Johnston's Army of Tennessee in Georgia and Meade aiming at Lee's Army of Northern Virginia. Lesser forces would advance into the Valley of Virginia, along the Louisiana front on the Red River, and a new Army of the James, under Benjamin Butler, would land below Richmond and take it.

Grant briefed Lincoln, explaining, as he later said, 'that it was necessary to have a great number of troops to guard and hold the territory we had captured, and to prevent incursions into the Northern States. These troops could perform this service just as well by advancing as by remaining still; and by advancing they would compel the enemy to keep detachments to hold them back, or else lay his own territory open to invasion.'

Grant himself decided to make his headquarters with the Army of the Potomac, rather than in Washington. A highly efficient telegraph service made sure he was as closely in contact with all his far-flung forces in the field as he would have been in an office building, and with Meade he could directly supervise operations against Lee's army.

On 3 May 1864, Grant directed Meade to move across the Rapidan, turn Lee's right flank, and head towards Richmond, i.e. almost a repeat of the Chancellorsville campaign. The idea was to get through the wooded terrain called the Wilderness before Lee could react and reach the more open fields where superior Union numbers would tell. By midnight the advance elements of Meade's 122,000 men were on the road. Lee could put only 66,000 men against him.

The Federals sent their army along two roads, the Germanna Plank Road and the Ely's Ford Road, and then through the Wilderness so that as many as possible could get through as quickly as possible. The Southern cavalry soon discovered the Federal march, and Lee sent his forces to intercept Meade's army in the Wilderness. Again, the Federal army failed to use its cavalry well, letting its infantry march blindly into the Wilderness while the cavalry was tied down watching the Federal supply train. Only one division, the weakest one of the Cavalry Corps, was deployed as scouts.

On 5 May, Lieutenant General Richard Ewell's Second Corps, coming up the Orange Turnpike at around dawn, hit the V Corps of the Army of the Potomac strung out on its line of march. The Federals advanced, but were driven back by the Confederates, who followed the retreat. Lines became broken up in such dense underbrush that entire regiments would leave the roads, heading into the brush and within minutes entirely disappear from sight. Heavy clouds of grey gun smoke made keeping contact even more impossible. Lines could not be maintained. Soldiers fired at what they thought were sounds of enemy action. Few regimental officers knew where their lines ended on either side. At one point Generals Lee, Hill, Stuart and their staff officers found themselves in a clearing. Suddenly a Federal skirmish line emerged from the woods within pistol shot range of the Confederate high command. Both sides were shocked by the encounter, unable to move. Then the Federal company officer ordered his troops to right about and they disappeared back into the woods. So dense and impenetrable was the terrain, such was the confused and chaotic nature of the fighting everywhere in the Wilderness.

N

Harpers Ferry

Winchester

Leesburg

Potomac River

0 5 10 15 20
Miles

SIGEL
8,000

Washington

Shenandoah River

BURNSIDE
20,000

Manassas

New Market

GRANT
120,000

MEADE
100,000

Mine Run

Fredericksburg

LEE
60,000

The 'Wilderness'

Gordonsville

Spotsylvania

Charlottesville

Hanover Junction

Cold Harbor

Richmond

Appomattox Court House

BEAUREGARD

Petersburg

BUTLER
33,000

▼ Major General Winfield Scott Hancock, a Pennsylvania graduate of the U.S. Military Academy, was nicknamed 'Hancock the Surperb' for his abilities. After the war, he was a Democratic candidate for president.

▼ Soldiers with one of the two volunteer Engineer regiments in the Army of the Potomac, the 15th and 50th New York Volunteer Engineers, work on a road in the Wilderness in May 1864. A third New York Engineer regiment, the

1st, served in the deep south and with the Army of the James.

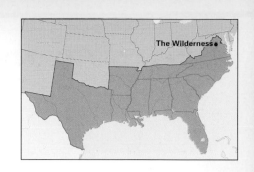

The Wilderness

Grant, never one to avoid a fight, was notified of the battle and sent word to Meade that, 'If any opportunity presents itself for pitching into a part of Lee's army, do so . . .'. The V Corps hit Ewell's line with force, nearly breaking it, but the attack had been so delayed by its commander, Gouverneur K. Warren, that Ewell had been able to bring up reinforcements to plug the gaps. Grant ordered Burnside to bring up his IX Corps, which was not under Meade's command, as quickly as possible and to go into action alongside Major-General John Sedgwick's VI Corps, then to try moving to the aid of the V Corps.

Still more troops were added by both sides to the fighting. Now A.P. Hill's III Corps struck Major-General Winfield Scott Hancock's II Corps who had arrived on the Orange Plank Road. To add to the horror, sparks from wadding in muskets set the brush on fire in many places. Many of the wounded, unable to drag themselves to safety, burned to death, the cartridges in their leather cartridge boxes exploding, adding to the overall din.

Fighting generally died out at around eight that evening. Lee ordered his men to stay where they were for the night, expecting Longstreet's First Corps to arrive that morning. Grant, anxious that the Confederates should not repeat anything as they had at

Chancellorsville, determined to maintain the initiative. He ordered a further attack at 4.30 the next morning to keep the Confederates reeling. 'Today we have fought because the enemy chose that we should,' wrote a *New York Tribune* correspondent that night. 'Tomorrow, because we choose that he shall.' The face of war in the east had changed forever.

 CAPTAIN GEORGE D. BOWEN, 12TH NEW JERSEY VOLUNTEER INFANTRY

When we fell back, Emanuel Cober, a member of my company, halted a dozen yards in our front got on one knee and one foot under a small peach tree, using the tree as a rest, here he fired several shots of the enemy as he would see a party to shoot at. He was just on the point of shooting again when he was struck by a minnie ball in left breast just above the heart. He dropped his gun and came back to me cursing, calling the man who shot him all kinds of a S-n of a B—-h. The swearing was partly in English and partly German.

OUT OF THE WILDERNESS

At early dawn of 6 May, however, it was Confederate scouts who found that the Sedgwick's right flank was unprotected, while the Confederate line extended beyond that point. Before they could make much use of the fact, however, Hancock's Federals hit the whole front on the Orange Plank Road at about 5.00 a.m. The Confederates were overwhelmed and many fled back through the woods and along the roads. As A.P. Hill's men ran for the rear, Lee ordered the Confederate wagon trains to be sent further back and asked that Longstreet make all haste with his corps to reach the battle scene.

By 6.30 a.m. the leading elements of Longstreet's corps were on the field, deploying for action on the Orange Plank Road. Lee himself met many of them, finding some of the first troops on the field were from his famous Texas Brigade. 'Hurrah for Texas,' he shouted, waving his grey felt hat in the air. The Texans halted Hancock's advance. Hancock shoved more units into the fray to restart his attack, but more of Longstreet's men were on hand, and progress had halted.

At 10.00 a.m. Longstreet received word from the Army of Northern Virginia's chief engineer that an unfinished railway track led around the Federal forces left flank, south of the Plank Road. Longstreet told his chief of staff, who had never before commanded troops in combat, to gather some scattered brigades, take them around on the railway track and attack the Federals. The staff officer, G. Moxley Sorrel, found elements of Georgians, Mississippians and Virginians and had them into position at about 11.30 p.m. when they hit the unsuspecting Federals. The Federal line was rolled up as Longstreet ordered his other units up to reinforce the assault. The 20th Massachusetts made a gallant but desperate attempt to stop the attack in the centre of the road, and were torn to shreds, while the Federal division commander, Major-General James Wadsworth, was shot dead at the same time.

At the height of the Confederate success, however, Longstreet, one of his generals, and his staff were fired on by South Carolina troops, the generals being removed from the field badly wounded.

▲ A period Currier & Ives shows Union troops advancing into the Wilderness in a much more military formation than the actual woods and undergrowth allowed. In fact, one could hardly see 10 feet away from one in any direction there.

Longstreet would survive, but it would take months to recover. It must have felt like Chancellorsville all over again. Longstreet's attack ground to a halt.

While all this was going on, the Confederates on the far Union right, under Brigadier-General John B. Gordon, prepared to hit the Federals on that flank. However, General Ewell delayed allowing Gordon to make the assault. Time passed. By 2.00 p.m. Burnside's corps was on the field. They launched an attack against the centre of the Confederate line, but the defenders threw them back with ease. Two hours later Lee himself sent as many as 13 brigades against Hancock's and Burnside's men, but the Federals had gained enough time to build field fortifications and bring up their supporting artillery. The Confederate attack failed.

Hancock received orders to counterattack at 6.00 p.m., but pleaded ammunition shortages and the attack was called off. At the same time, however, Gordon was finally authorized to turn the Federal right. As earlier, they found the Federals unprepared for such an attack, but darkness and the wilderness tore up the Confederate line more than Federal gunfire did, and the attack failed. The Battle of the Wilderness was over. It had been as hard fought a battle as any previous ones; the Army of the Potomac had losses of 17,500, while the Army of Northern Virginia lost some 12 per cent of its men, around 7,500 in all.

Now the question for soldiers on both sides was how quickly the Army of the Potomac would return to its quarters across the Rapidan. After all this is what every previous Federal commander, from McDowell to Meade, had done after a campaign had been blocked by Lee's troops. Indeed, Lee reported to Richmond on 8 May that, 'The enemy has abandoned his position and is moving towards Fredericksburg.'

PRIVATE JOHN O. CASLER, 33RD VIRGINIA VOLUNTEER INFANTRY REGIMENT

Sergeant Bradly, nicknamed 'Doggie' because he could bark like a fice, of Company F, was on the skirmish line on the fifth. He always held to the theory that if a man was born to be killed he would be killed anyway and there was no use in trying to protect himself from the bullets.

As the firing was heavy, and each man behind a tree on the skirmish line, some one hallooed to 'Doggie' to get behind a tree or he would be killed. He replied that if he was 'to be killed the tree wouldn't save him,' and remained where he was. In a few moments he was shot dead.

This time, however, would be different. As Grant later recalled, 'I had, on the 5th, ordered all the bridges over the Rapidan to be taken up except one at Germania Ford. . .'. On the morning of 7 May he ordered Meade to prepare for a march that night south, not north, to Spotsylvania Court House with one corps and to Todd's Tavern with another, while a third should go to the intersection of the Piney Branch and Spotsylvania Road.

Federal skirmishers found on the morning of the 7th that Lee had pulled his men back to form a new defensive line. The front line soldiers on both sides rested as best they could as quartermasters brought up food and ammunition. Then, that evening, the Federals began their march, cheering and tossing their hats when they realized they were heading south, and not back to north. Their new commander-in-chief was made of sterner stuff than his predecessors – this was to be a fight to the finish.

◄ Sergeant R.K. Williams, left, is the acting company commander of all that is left standing of a company of the 57th Massachusetts after the meat-grinder known as the Wilderness. The men, however, are recovered with bright weapons and dress brass shoulder scales.

▲ Brigadier-General John B. Gordon, a lawyer from Georgia before the war with a native talent for battle, could not convince his superiors to allow him to attack quickly enough to win. He would go on after the war to become his state's governor.

SPOTSYLVANIA COURT HOUSE

At around 9.00 p.m. on 7 May the first troops, those of Warren's V Corps, began to move silently out of the breastworks they'd built in the Wilderness, heading towards Spotsylvania Court House. Major-General Richard Anderson, who had been picked by Lee to command the First Corps of the Army of Northern Virginia in Longstreet's absence, began moving his troops in much the same direction, not because he knew of the Federal advance, but because Lee had told him to retreat to rest his troops.

At about 1.00 a.m., the advance party of V Corps suddenly found themselves out of the Wilderness and on their way south. The rest of the army followed. As dawn rose that day Confederate skirmishers approached the Federal breastworks back in the Wilderness, only to find them deserted.

By 8.00 a.m. the first Federal troops approached Spotsylvania Court House, where they could cut off Lee from Richmond. Grant was already thinking ahead, planning to move south and link up with Butler's Army of the James which was landing below Richmond. At the Court House road section, however, the Federals ran into Confederate cavalry holding the heights of Laurel Hill. While the horse soldiers delayed the infantry, hard-pressed officers sent word back to Anderson, imploring him to bring the First Corps up. By marching hard the weary Confederates reached the ground, saw the advancing Federals, and raced to deploy behind the breastworks the cavalry had built. The Confederates had won their race.

The Federals assaulted, but they were exhausted from their overnight march. The Confederate line held as both sides sent more units in piecemeal. Hancock's II Corps concentrated around a crossroads next to Todd's Tavern between the Wilderness and Spotsylvania Court House. From there he could react to attack or defend. But in fact they were not attacked there, as Early's corps simply bypassed the position on their way south.

Lee arrived near Spotsylvania in the early afternoon and saw his position on Laurel Hill was holding well against repeated attacks. By evening further attacks were called off. That night Grant ordered the Federal cavalry, under western Major-General Philip Sheridan, to head south, move around Lee, destroy rail lines and supply depots, and eventually link up with Butler.

The next day Confederate engineers found that reinforcements arriving that night had made their defences as a salient that jutted far out from the rest of the Confederate line. Agrarian Southerners called the position the 'Mule Shoe'. As they continued to dig in, Federals also improved their lines.

Fighting continued on 10 May with another failed attack on Laurel Hill. That evening, however, a young brigade commander, Colonel Emory Upton, decided to attack the Mule Shoe using different tactics from a sweeping charge by a line of infantry two deep. He would assault with only four battle lines, three regiments in each. Only the first line would have weapons ready to fire, while

► A post-war Kurz & Allison print, as inaccurate as all their prints were, of the Battle of Spotsylvania does emphasize the importance of the pontoon bridges to the Union army in getting its troops across Virginia's many rivers and streams quickly.

▼ Major-General John Sedgewick, to inspire his men in face of Confederate sniper fire, declared that, 'They couldn't hit an elephant at this range', while standing in the open. Seconds later he was mortally wounded.

◄ Attacking in a solid column without pausing to fight, Union troops smashed into the Mule Shoe and quickly drove out the defending Confederates. The attack was poorly supported and Confederates were able to rebuild their line and retake the position.

the rest would be loaded but not primed, so no one would be tempted to stop to fire before reaching his objective. The attack was like a freight train and the Federals simply shoved their way over the works and into a broken Confederate line. But reinforcements were too little and too late, advancing over ground swept by Confederate fire, and Upton, who received a general's star on the spot for his work, was forced to withdraw.

Grant figured that if such an assault would work for a brigade, a full corps would be certain to make it a total success. At the same time, Lee grew concerned for the security of the Mule Shoe, and ordered the withdrawal of artillery.

Before dawn on 12 May, the Federal II Corps, using Upton's tactics, smashed into the Mule Shoe at a point referred to as 'the Bloody Angle'. Although the Confederates fought bravely, they quickly lost 4,000 as prisoners, including two generals, and a number of regimental colours. Simultaneous attacks by Burnside and Warren, however, were easily beaten off. Confederate reinforcements arrived around the inside edges of the Mule Shoe, where victorious Federals milled around, many of the Union officers down. Fighting carried on until some time after midnight, ending with the Confederates able to set up a new line across the salient base that held. Fighting had cost the Federals some 6,800, while the Confederates lost about 5,000 men, which they could ill afford.

SERGEANT J.W. REID, 1ST REGIMENT OF ENGINEER TROOPS, C.S.A.

Our engineer regiment was sent on ahead of the main army to repair bridges, work on roads and all such work as might be needed. Some of our companies were sent one way and some another on all the roads leading in the direction of Richmond. My company, after repairing some small bridges and corduroying the road in some places, finally got to Mechanicsville, and fixed up the bridge I had stood on when we were halted the night previous to going into the seven days fight commencing at Mechanicsville, and there we remained several days.

Now both sides dug in for siege warfare. Grant made headlines by sending word back to Washington: 'I propose to fight it out on this line if it takes all summer.' However, he actually continued his slide to the south by sending two corps to the left on 13 May. Rain began to pour on exhausted men on both sides. Meade attacked Lee's lines, again unsuccessfully, on the 18th. Then on 19 May Ewell led the 6,000 men of his depleted corps against the Federal right flank in an effort to determine if Grant's army was moving. The green troops opposing him held, marking the end of the battles around Spotsylvania Court House. In all, the Federals lost some 17,500 during the campaign, while the Confederates lost 9–10,000.

SHERIDAN'S RAID

From Spotsylvania Court House Sheridan got his three divisions of cavalry moving early in the morning on 9 May, aimed at the south side of the North Anna River where they could find forage before being forced to give battle. By the evening of the 10th they had fought some rear-guard skirmishes with Confederate cavalry along the North Anna and near Beaver Dam Station, and were situated south of the South Anna. There they were less than 20 miles from Richmond, causing alarm in the city.

Sheridan wasn't interested in raiding Richmond, however. His orders were specific: 'to break up General Lee's railroad communications, destroy such depots of supplies as could be found in his rear, and to defeat General Stuart's cavalry.' In the meantime, Stuart set off to defend the city and to foil Sheridan's plans.

Sheridan sent a brigade of Michigan cavalry under Brigadier-General George A. Custer to break up railway lines. He cut the Virginia Central railway at Beaver Dam Station, where he recap-

tured some 400 prisoners taken at Spotsylvania, as well as destroying the station, two locomotives, three trains, 90 wagons with a large amount of the Army of Northern Virginia's medical and food supplies, and laying waste some nine miles of rail and telegraph lines. While this destruction was going on, Stuart marched to a defensive position near Yellow Tavern, some six miles north of Richmond, arriving at 10.00 a.m. on 11 May.

At about 2.00 a.m. that same morning, one of Sheridan's brigades set off for Ashland to destroy the Fredericksburg railway that passed through there. The brigade destroyed a complete train and tore up some miles of tracks before rejoining Sheridan's main force.

Sheridan's main force reached Yellow Tavern and charged into the Confederate cavalry. The result was one of those rare cavalry fights where the troopers on both sides were mounted and fought with sabres and revolvers rather than carbines. The Federals generally pushed the Confederates back and at about 4.00 p.m. a Federal

▲ Union cavalry, by now superior in numbers, horses, and weapons, are met by Stuart's battle-worn troops at the Battle of Yellow Tavern. Most Union cavalry regiments trained one battalion in the use of the sabre in particular, while the other used carbines more.

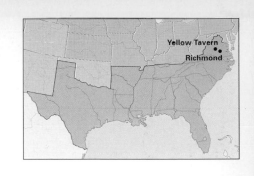

sent a reconnoitring party up the Brook Turnpike directly towards Richmond to test the city's defences. They actually breached the first of the two rows of forts around the city. Sheridan himself joined the party, deciding to cross the Mechanicsville Pike on the south side of the Chickahominy where there had been such hard fighting two years earlier, and camp the next night at Fair Oaks. He had heard that Major-General Benjamin Butler's Army of the James was on the south side of the James river, some four miles south of Richmond, and decided to join him.

During the Peninsula Campaign, some Confederates short of manpower experimented with land mines, then called 'torpedoes', that would detonate either on the pressure of a man's or horse's step or when a wire had been tripped. Now Sheridan's troopers encountered such land mines, resulting in the loss of several horses and men. Enraged, Sheridan forced some of his prisoners to lead the column, probing for wires which they would follow to the mines, which they would then unearth.

On the 12th Sheridan's column reached the outer works of the city, which were now fully manned so that the cavalrymen found they could not pass as planned. Forced to take another route, Sheridan's men fought off a cavalry attack that day, then crossed the Chickahominy. By the 14th they reached the James, released their prisoners to the guards of the Army of the James, and drew provisions. Three days later, Sheridan's cavalry started back to the Army of the Potomac, crossing the Pamunkey on a bridge that the troopers built on the 22 May. That night they learned that Lee had withdrawn from Spotsylvania Court House and made for Chesterfield Station, where Sheridan finally reported to Meade on 24 May.

Summing up, Sheridan recalled that, 'our success was commended highly by Generals Grant and Meade, both realizing that our operations in the rear of Lee had disconcerted and alarmed that general so much as to aid materially in forcing his retrograde march, and both acknowledged that, by drawing off the enemy's cavalry during the past fortnight, we had enabled them to move the Army of the Potomac and its enormous trains without molestation in the manoeuvres that had carried it to the North Anna.'

▲ **Major General of Volunteers George Armstrong Custer,** a member of the U.S. Military Academy class of 1862, rose with astonishing speed to this, his final rank, by the war's end. The same impulsiveness he showed in the Civil War would eventually cost his life and many 7th U.S. Cavalry lives.

▲ *Right:* **Major General J.E.B. Stuart was a natural born cavalryman, but too often more concerned with what was said about him in the newspapers and halls of government than what his command, the cavalry corps of the Army of Northern Virginia, could do for the rest of the army.**

brigade struck the Confederate left. The blue-coated troopers overran an artillery battery and Stuart himself, marked by a plume in his broad-brimmed hat and bright yellow facings on his jacket, rode into their midst to rally his men. A Federal trooper who had been dismounted in the fight, saw Stuart and fired his revolver at him.

Stuart, obviously wounded, rode off, to be taken by ambulance back to hospital in Richmond. There, on 12 May, shortly after being visited by Davis, he died before his wife could reach his side. The Confederacy was not only losing its lower ranks, but its best generals as well.

As the Confederate cavalry, shattered by their leader's loss, withdrew towards the ring of forts around Richmond, Sheridan

COLONEL J.H. KIDD, 6TH MICHIGAN CAVALRY

As soon as our line appeared in the open – indeed before it left the woods the Confederate artillery opened with shell and shrapnel; the carbineers and sharpshooters joined with zest in the fray

and the man who thinks they did not succeed in making that part of the neighborhood around Yellow Tavern an uncomfortably hot place, was not there at the time. It was necessary to take

advantage of every chance for shelter. Every Wolverine [Michigan soldier] who exposed himself was made a target of. Many men were hit by bullets.

THE BATTLES OF NORTH ANNA AND COLD HARBOR

The Army of the Potomac continued its slide to the east and south around Guiney's Station in a race with its opponents to reach the North Anna River. In the early hours of 22 May, Ewell's and Anderson's corps of Lee's men beat the Federals to Hanover Junction, and found themselves sandwiched between them and Richmond. Every one of these races, however, ended with the Confederate army closer to the ring of forts around their capital city. Once there, Lee spread out his army with Ewell's Second Corps on the right, Richard Anderson's First Corps in the centre, and A.P. Hill's Third Corps on the left.

During the afternoon of the next day, the Federals began to cross the river. Hancock's II Corps attacked the Confederates at Chesterfield Ford, Burnside's IX Corps struck at Jericho Mills, and Warren's V Corps and Wright's VI Corps attacked west of Jericho Mills. Federal engineers laid a pontoon bridge at Jericho Mills over which their infantry poured, only to be beaten back by A.P. Hill's troops.

Federals elsewhere were only able to take advance works on the north side of the river at Chesterfield Ford before being stopped. The IX Corps probed Lee's works at Ox Ford, but found these, too, formidable. Grant decided to slip further south instead of trying any further frontal assaults. Lee was ill for much of this action, unable to find the strength to defeat the Federals, split as they were in their attacks, something a healthy Lee was likely to have done. Indeed, on the 24th the Army of the Potomac was in a

critical situation, with the VI and V Corps on the right, while the II Corps crossed, along with some of the IX Corps, at Chesterfield Bridge, so that the army was essentially in three parts, because of the bend in the river and Lee's salients.

On 26 May, however, the Army of the Potomac started to move to cross the Pamunkey River and head towards Hanovertown, well beyond Lee's right. Federal cavalry reached the town, riding all night through driving rain, by 27 May, while Lee began to move his troops in reaction to Grant. The next day Lee was again moving to block Grant in new lines around Cold Harbor. A 'cold harbor' in 17th century Virginia was an inn that sold no food or alcohol, and the town took its name from such an ancient inn. Grant ordered his cavalry to take the town, and on the evening of 31 May, blue troopers found it defended by Confederate cavalry, who they drove off, and infantry, who stopped them. Sheridan had to withdraw. Grant ordered him back, and the Federals re-took the town, dug in, and lay that night on their arms.

Lee also wanted that vital crossroads, and ordered Anderson to take it with his First Corps. At dawn on 1 June, Southern infantry advanced, but were beaten back by repeating carbine fire. By noon Federal infantry, in the form of the VI Corps, replaced the weary cavalrymen. They were shortly joined by the XVIII Corps, and the Federals hurled six divisions against the Confederates. Despite a momentary breakthrough, a Confederate counterattack held the line and drove back the attackers.

Grant wanted a breakthrough, and ordered up the II Corps to attack the next day. It was a miserable hot day, with dust flying thick on the dirt roads. The fatigued Federal infantrymen took all day to get into position, not being ready until about 6.30 p.m. on 2 June. Grant decided to call off the attack until the next morning.

This was all that Lee needed to prepare his lines. As the II Corps came up and through that night, Confederate engineers laid out what was probably an even better defensive line than that which they held at Fredericksburg. They planned their works during the day, then, under cover of darkness, sent out engineer officers holding a long cord, marked with pieces of cotton cloth for visibility. Each officer advanced a set distance and then secured his piece of the cloth. The officers retired, and men with spades and picks advanced, digging a line of trenches that followed the cord.

Federals, who heard the sounds of digging, knew they would face an almost impossible task. Many pinned their names on pieces of paper to their coats so that their bodies could be returned home.

Before dawn on 3 June the attack was launched, in two lines, along a two mile front. Caught in prepared fields of fire, the Federals had no chance. In several places the attack carried some lines, but the Federals there were quickly driven back. In all the Federals lost some 7,000, compared to Confederate losses of fewer than 1,500. Grant surveyed his corps commanders and all agreed not to attack there again. 'I have always regretted that the last assault at Cold Harbor was ever made,' Grant later wrote.

▼ Confederates destroyed the bridges that crossed Virginia's many rivers ahead of the advancing Union army. This one crossed the North Anna River. They would be rebuilt as needed by men of the U.S. Military Railroad.

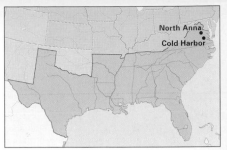

North Anna
Cold Harbor

▼▼ *Bottom:* Major-General William F. Smith, standing centre and looking left, commanded the XVIII Corps which had been part of the Army of the James until attached to the Army of the Potomac in time to take part in the assault at Cold Harbor, for which he bitterly criticized Meade.

▼ Men of the XVIII Corps drive the first line of Longstreet's Corps in the opening phases of the Battle of Cold Harbor. They would later meet well entrenched Confederates in one of the worst blood-baths of the war. It was a battle Grant was always to later regret.

PRIVATE JOHN D. BILLINGS, 10TH MASSACHUSETTS ARTILLERY

The Fourth Detachment piece is struck twice... Its No. 7 man, John Bradley, has a 'close call' made for him by a shot which, just scaling the works, strikes the edge of the pit in which he crouches when not carrying ammunition, covers him with the loose earth, whirls his overcoat away, and sends his canteen flying into the ranks of a neighboring regiment. 'Why don't you get up, John?' some one asks; and he convulses us by responding from the depths of his safety pit, 'I'm waiting for that thing to bust,' not being aware that it had ricochetted.

THE BATTLE OF NEW MARKET

▼ A German native and revolutionary in the 1848 rebellions, Franz Sigel came to America in 1852. A leader of his people in America, he was commissioned brigadier-general in 1861 and a major-general in 1862. He proved, however, to be a poor soldier.

In May 1864, the Valley of Virginia was again threatened and this time there would be no Stonewall Jackson to save it. Grant had picked the Valley as one of the doors into the Confederacy that would be knocked on. The knocker there was Major-General Franz Sigel, a German officer in the 1848 rebellions and an American resident since 1852. Sigel had some 23,000 men under his command; many of his top officers were fellow Germans and communicated with their men only with difficulty. Facing him was a Confederate army under Major-General John C. Breckinridge, a veteran of the Mexican War and one-time U.S. Vice-President. Breckinridge had fewer than 5,000 men, many of them cavalry who were dismounted for lack of forage for their horses.

Sigel, with orders to march on Staunton, started his campaign into the Valley on 29 April. Breckinridge, reinforced but still considerably fewer in numbers than his opponent, headed up to meet him on 6 May, the day Sigel's men reached Winchester. Confederate cavalry, meanwhile, raided behind Sigel's advance, destroying a vital Baltimore & Ohio Railroad bridge across the Potomac and causing considerable consternation in Washington. Sigel, forced to detach some his cavalry to go after the raiders, stopped his advance. Breckinridge reached Staunton on 8 May, while the Federals were still bivouacked in Winchester.

Breckinridge now planned to move against the Federals. He called on the nearby Virginia Military Institute, known as the 'West Point of the South' because of all the officers it supplied the Confederacy, to send its 264-strong Corps of Cadets to supplement his command. He now had 3,500 infantry, 1,500 cavalry, and 12 cannon. A further reinforcement would bring his total to 5,300 men and 18 cannon, still considerably fewer than Sigel's force.

On 9 May, Sigel's men took the road south again and on 13 May Breckinridge put his men on the road north. Confederate cavalry, in the advance, ran into Federals near Moorefield and drove them back, giving the German general yet more worries. He had his men dug in and ordered weapons constantly loaded.

On 12 May, Breckinridge's cavalry reached New Market, the point he wanted to defend. There they ran into Federal skirmishers. Behind these cavalrymen, on both sides, the infantry were making for the same town through heavy rains which did nothing to cool the increasing temperatures. Confederate infantrymen reached the town on 15 May and went into position on defensive lines held by the cavalry on Shirley's Hill, south of New Market. There Breckinridge planned to allow Sigel to attack him. The Federal lines, made up of only lead elements of Sigel's army, were centred on Manor's Hill on the northern side of the New Market Valley.

The Confederates sent out a skirmish line that then retreated, but the Federals would not be drawn out of their lines to attack. Breckinridge decided to attack them instead. On the morning of 15 May the Confederate line, with V.M.I. cadets marching in reserve, advanced. Sigel himself reached the field just in time to see the three lines of advancing Confederates and ordered an advance to meet them. However, when he reached the front, he decided that his men would have the worst of it, and ordered a retreat before the two lines could close.

The advancing Confederates halted from time to time to dress their lines and regroup in the rain. Sigel called for the rest of his army to join his pressed force at New Market, unfortunately barking out orders in German which his subordinates did not understand. However, the Federal line finally halted the advancing Confederates, and even counter-attacked. Breckinridge was forced to commit his reserve, the young V.M.I. cadets. The cadets

Winchester
New Market

▼ Major-General John Breckinridge had served as vice president of the United States before the war. After Richmond's fall, he would accompany Jefferson Davis and the remainder of the Confederate government in its escape from the city.

were ordered to attack in the front, drove the enemy and captured a Federal cannon. They had lost 10 killed and 47 wounded in gaining a victory that is commemorated at VMI every year with the calling of the 'roll of honor'. In all, Breckinridge lost some 550 men, while Sigel lost 96 killed, 540 wounded, and another 225 men missing, mostly prisoners of war.

By 3.00 p.m. Sigel's troops were in full retreat, a retreat that quickly turned into a rout. The Confederates followed with the cadets capturing as many as a hundred prisoners. Only a fresh Federal regular artillery battery managed to stop the Confederates where they were. Sigel ordered his battered army to retreat to

Cedar Creek, near Strasburg, where they would reform. They reached there on the morning of 17 May. On 19 May, the German general was replaced with Major-General David Hunter, who found his new command to be 'utterly demoralized and stampeded'. He would later start a campaign of destruction in the Valley from early June, eventually to be met by an enlarged Confederate army under Jubal Early, detached from Lee's main force battling Grant.

After the battle, on the Confederate side, the Corps of Cadets returned to its classrooms, which were eventually burned as the school moved to Richmond in the last days of the war.

◄ Brigadier-General John D. Imboden of Virginia was a lawyer and politician before the war began. He quickly rose from captain of the battery he organized to brigadier-general by January 1863 and ended the war on prison duty in South Carolina.

BRIGADIER-GENERAL JOHN D. IMBODEN, C.S. ARMY

It so happened that when they came to within about three hundred yards of the battery they had to cross a deep rocky gulch, grown up with scrub cedars, thorns and briers, and filled here and there with logs and old stumps. Many men had fallen

before Smith and Ship had reached this gulch, but whilst in it they were sheltered by its banks. As it was difficult to get through, Smith and his veterans took their time, gaining thereby a slight breathing-spell before making the deadly run

necessary to reach the hostile battery. The boys from the Military Institute were more agile and ardent than Smith's veterans, and got out on the bank first.

▲ While Virginia Military Institute cadets began the war in formal grey uniforms similar to U.S. Military Academy uniform, they soon adopted a plain grey outfit of Confederate soldiers.

THE BERMUDA HUNDRED CAMPAIGN

While Sigel was to advance in the Valley, and Meade to advance against Lee, a new army, christened the Army of the James, was created from elements that had been stationed along the Southern Atlantic coast. Assigned to Major-General Benjamin Butler, it was to be aimed at Richmond from the south, landing not far from where McClellan's Peninsula Campaign came to an end.

Mistrusting Butler, the politician, Grant assigned a trusted professional officer to be one of Butler's subordinates, Major-General William F. Smith, who, he believed, could correct any of Butler's mistakes. Butler produced a rather professional plan by himself, however, calling for a landing at Bermuda Hundred, a piece of land that jutted into the James on the east and north and bounded by the Appomattox River on the south. From there, he would be only 14 miles from Richmond. His troops would then move against Richmond, across the large naval guns at Drewry's Bluff. Their movements coordinated with that of the Army of the Potomac, he could besiege the city until Meade's men linked up with his and the two armies could easily take it.

For his army, Butler received the X Corps and the XVIII Corps, which included 35 units of the US Army's U.S. Colored Troops. Butler himself was a strong supporter of U.S.C.Ts, who was noted for treating them fairly and making sure they received the best officers possible. He gathered his army at posts at Yorktown, Gloucester Point and Fort Monroe, preparing them for the advance which began on 5 May 1864.

The short river voyage took just a morning and the first of Butler's troops ran ashore, totally unexpected. A spy from Richmond brought news that Richmond was almost unprotected, with only a few infantry and artillery units at Drewry's Bluff. The rest of the city's defenders had been sent to Lee. In fact, the Confederate defenders south of Richmond included 75 infantry and cavalry regiments and 36 artillery units under Beauregard. The fortifications they manned included three rings carefully designed by military engineers.

Butler moved seven miles towards the city and then dug in for the night. The next day he sent two brigades towards Port Walthall Junction, three miles west, to destroy the railroad there. Not all the designated troops actually moved, and those who did found Confederate infantry under George Pickett dug in on the same side of the tracks as themselves. After a brief skirmish, the Federals retired. The next day Butler sent a larger force, which again failed, as did another attempt on 9 May. By now Butler learned of the Wilderness battle and, fearful that Meade would be turned back and Lee could then attack the Army of the James, the Federal commander ordered his troops to fortify their lines.

Still, Butler was aware of his orders to take Richmond and, learning that the Army of the Potomac was still on its way south, on 11 May he sent his troops out of their trenches towards the Confederate works at Drewry's Bluff. This was a well defended post, with not only Confederate soldiers, but also sailors and marines

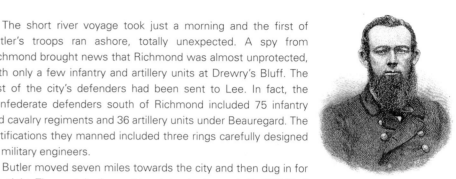

▲ **Major-General William Smith, a professional soldier before the war, was named to command one of Butler's Army's corps so that he could correct any mistakes Butler made. He turned out to have the wrong personality for the job.**

► **Union soldiers faced these Confederate fortifications at Fort Darling during the second battle at Drewry's Bluff in 1864. On the extreme left lie the paddle wheels of a sunken vessel, possibly the victim of a mine, or 'torpedo'.**

►► *Far right*: **Major-General Benjamin Butler, a Democratic politician from Massachusetts, was commissioned to bring all parties into the war for the Union. He became the most hated soldier in the Union army among southerners during his command of New Orleans.**

Bermuda Hundred •

manning the large guns that protected the city from an attack up the river. At the same time Butler sent his poorly-led cavalry to raid the Richmond & Danville Railroad, a raid which did little good.

Butler's troops attacked the Bluff on 13 May and were thrown back. They dug in and probed for weaknesses. Smith suggested a place to attack on the 15th, which Butler approved, but Smith then declined to accept responsibility for the attack, and Butler cancelled it. While in this position, Sheridan's Army of the Potomac cavalry arrived and the cavalry general told the army commander that Meade's army was headed in their direction. Hearing this, Butler decided to retreat and await the Army of the Potomac.

Beauregard had no intention of letting this happen. In an early morning fog on 16 May, the Confederates struck with some 16,000 men, forcing the Federals back to their original lines in a heavy downpour. By 10.00 p.m. Butler's men were back in position, the XVIII Corps on the lower flank and centre and the X Corps on the northern flank. They immediately began work to improve considerably the quality of their defences.

The Confederates followed, attacking what Beauregard thought to be a weak spot on the XVIII Corps front. At first the Confederate attack went well, with the Federal line penetrated, but Federal reinforcements counter-attacked and retook their trenches. Beauregard decided then the Northern position was too strong to assault, and dug in himself. Now neither side could successfully attack the other, nor would either side make the attempt. An engineer officer reporting on Butler's position to Grant showed the general a map of the positions of the Army of the James, saying, 'It's like a bottle, General, but the enemy has corked it.' Grant added the phrase to his official report, much to the chagrin of Butler. Indeed, the lines penning Butler's army remained a part of the Confederate defences until the fall of Richmond, being finally abandoned in April 1865.

▲ Mountains of supplies unloaded at the docks on the James River and due to be distributed to Union forces show the vast economic potential which the north was able to unleash in its war to maintain the country.

8 JUNE	**1864** Lincoln nominated for a second term.
10 JUNE	Battle of Brice's Crossroads – N.B. Forrest beats an 8,000-man force.
11 JUNE	Trevilian Station, Virginia – Confederate cavalry blocks a move to the Valley.
15-18 JUNE	Attacks on Petersburg – Beauregard stands off attempts to take Petersburg to begin a siege.
19 JUNE	USS *Kearsage* sinks the CSS *Alabama*
27 JUNE	Battle of Kennesaw Mountain – Johnston stands off Federal attacks.
11 JULY	Confederates approach Washington – Early's drive from the Valley nears the Federal capital.
17 JULY	Hood replaces Johnston – For constant retreats to Atlanta, Davis replaces the popular Johnston with the fiery Hood.
20 JULY	Battle of Peachtree Creek – Hood begins to destroy his army by attacking at Atlanta.
22 JULY	Battle of Atlanta – Another of Hood's attacks fails.
30 JULY	Battle of the Crater – Federals explode a huge mine under Confederate lines at Petersburg but fail to exploit their initial success.
5 AUG	Battle of Mobile Bay – 'Damn the torpedoes,' says David Farragut as he leads a successful U.S. Navy squadron against the Confederate Navy.
18-19 AUG	Battle of the Weldon Railroad – Grant continues to extend his lines west at Petersburg, bringing Lee's army to the breaking point.
25 AUG	Battle of Reams' Station – A.P. Hill surprises the II Corps.
1 SEPT	Fall of Atlanta
13 SEPT	Third Battle of Winchester – Sheridan begins the final clearing of the Valley.
22 SEPT	Battle of Fisher's Hill – Federals drive past Strasburg in the Valley.
19 OCT	Battle of Cedar Creek – Despite early successes, a Confederate attack in the Valley fails, virtually destroying its army there.

The Army of the Potomac continued its southern slide until it linked up with the bottled-up Army of the James. The two would then begin a trench warfare outside Petersburg that would look very much like the Western Front of World War 1. Lee's attempt to repeat past successes in terrifying the Federal government by sending troops north through the Valley of Virginia would fail. In the west, however, the Union forces were not to be stopped. Sherman would manoeuvre his way to Atlanta, finally capturing it and, in the process, assuring Lincoln would be re-elected in the 1864 Presidential election.

HEADING TOWARDS PETERSBURG

Both sides spent the day after the Federal assault at Cold Harbor dug in, often in trenches that were only yards apart. As men and units sorted themselves out, Grant and Lee argued in writing, Grant proposing that, 'Hereafter, when no battle is raging, either party be authorized to send to any point between the pickets or skirmish lines, unarmed men bearing litters to pick up their dead or wounded, without being fired upon by the other party.' Lee suggested that a flag of truce should be required, Grant responding that he would send out men on 6 June between noon and three to pick up the many dead and wounded between the lines. Lee continued to resist and it was not until the next day that the Federals were able to clear the field. By that time, according to Grant, all the wounded but two had died.

As the two armies lay there, Grant detached Sheridan's cavalry to head west and join Hunter in the Valley of Virginia. Confederate cavalry under Major-Generals Wade Hampton, Stuart's replacement, and Fitzhugh Lee met the Federals at Trevilian Station on 11-12 June. There one Federal cavalry brigade, commanded by Custer, drove his troops into Hampton's rear, but Hampton was able to stabilize his lines. Lee was forced back, leading to an apparent Federal victory. However, after considering his situation, Sheridan decided his force was not strong enough to cross Virginia to unite with Hunter. He therefore retired back to the Army of the Potomac, finally joining it on the James River in late June.

Hunter was having very much his own way in the largely undefended Valley. His troops entered Lexington and burned the Virginia Military Institute, along with many farms in the lush agricultural area. Despite pressure from Grant, Lee decided to detach a division under Major-General Jubal Early to march to the Valley to defend it. On 13 June, he sent word to Early to take his Second Corps of 8,000 men, with two of its artillery battalions, to the Valley. He was ordered, he later wrote, 'to strike Hunter's force in the rear, and, if possible, destroy it'. Thereafter he was to move north to 'threaten Washington City'.

Grant resolved not to attempt another frontal assault, but to continue slipping around to Lee's right. In this case it would mean crossing the James. On 12 June, he and Meade began what is still considered one of history's most brilliant military manoeuvres. Without Lee having any idea what the Federal forces were doing, four corps started off for the James. One corps went by water down the Pamunkey and York and then by boat up the James to meet the other corps which would go by land, with volunteer and regular army engineers laying down pontoon bridges as they advanced, taking them up after they had passed.

A day later Lee learned that Federal lines at Cold Harbor were empty and his opponents were headed south. He figured that the Federals were aiming at Richmond from the Long Bridge area of

▶ Brigadier-General Fitzhugh Lee, a nephew of Robert E. Lee and a professional soldier before the war, was a special favourite of General J.E.B. Stuart. He particularly distinguished himself at Spotsylvania Court House where his division held the crossroads.

▼ A guard, left, checks that all those who cross this pontoon bridge across the James River at Deep Bottom, Virginia, are authorized. As desertion rates ran high, soldiers going to the rear had their papers checked at many spots along the way.

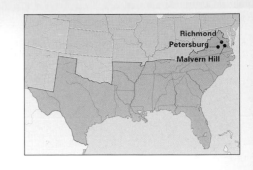

the Chickahominy. Planning to block this drive on the city, Lee then moved his army, drawing up defensive lines from Malvern Hill to White Oak Swamp. According to Longstreet, by then, 'My men had become experts in fortifying, so that parapets and dams along the front grew apace.' But these lines were to be left alone; Grant had no intention of going that way.

By the late afternoon of 13 June, the II Corps was at Wilcox's Landing on the James where engineers were working on one of the longest pontoon bridges of the war. In all, the engineers used 104 pontoons to build a bridge 2,200 ft long. Regular army engineers started building on the east end, while New York volunteer engineers began at the west to meet them. Gathering Federal infantrymen watched as the engineers scrambled around with their boats and timbers until the bridge was ready. They could start crossing this bridge to Windmill Point on the southern side the next morning; in all it would take three full days for the entire army to finish crossing.

Lee, in the meantime, was entirely in the dark about Grant's Southern crossing. A young Confederate artillery battalion commander complained that his troops were not sent to block Grant's move quickly enough. 'The root of the matter was in Gen. Lee's disbelief that Grant had crossed the James,' he later wrote.

But from the south, Beauregard sent hurried word of a massive attack on his lines at Petersburg. Such an attack, which was successfully defended, struck on 16 June, but still Lee felt it his duty to remain where he was to defend Richmond which was Grant's primary target. He did, however, detach Pickett's division to clear out lines occupied by the Army of the James on the Bermuda Hundred that day, but the bulk of his army was to stay where it was. It was not until attacks continued on the 17th that Lee relented and finally sent two corps under A.P. Hill and Richard Anderson south to fill in the Petersburg lines. It was almost too late.

▲ In many places a wide swampy belt lay between solid land and a river so engineers had to build bridges out to a point where they could use pontoons. Pontoon bridges were also used as temporary piers where boats could dock.

CAPTAIN JULIAN W. HINKLEY, 3RD WISCONSIN VOLUNTEER INFANTRY

When we had first come within range of the grape-shot, my scabbard had been struck and cut in two at a point just below where I grasped it with my left hand. Later, when my men had sheltered themselves and had commenced firing, I was again struck. I was at the time resting on one knee in a position where I could watch the battery, and direct our fire upon it, for I was determined that the enemy should not have an opportunity to take it away so long as we had a chance to capture it. My attention had just been called to something on the left, when a bullet struck the front of my cap, cutting the figure '3' out of the bugle, and glancing from the bone, cut a gash across my forehead.

THE CAMPAIGN TO ATLANTA

In Tennessee, Grant had left his trusted colleague William T. Sherman to command part of his multi-pronged assault on the Confederacy. He was to capture the vital rail and manufacturing centre of Atlanta, Georgia. Sherman had almost 100,000 men in three forces. The Army of the Cumberland under Thomas was near Ringgold, Georgia. The Army of the Ohio under Major-General John Schofield was north of Dalton, Georgia. The Army of the Tennessee, recently having lifted the siege of Chattanooga, under Major-General John McPherson was on the old battlefield of Chickamauga.

Facing him was a Confederate Army of Tennessee under General Joseph Johnston. Johnston's 60,000 men would find defending the entire path to Atlanta easy, since the area was broken up by heavily wooded ridges made for resistance, while the poor road system would make marching and bringing up supplies difficult for the Federals. Johnston's force was firmly entrenched at Dalton on a ridge line with only a few gaps.

Sherman recognized that his men had no chance of driving Johnston's troops from their positions and therefore ordered probing attacks in an attempt to find a weak spot. In the meantime, he sent McPherson to capture and hold the railway line to the Confederate rear. This should force Johnston to retreat. On 9 May the head of McPherson's column passed through a gap at Snake Creek defended only by Confederate cavalry. These were easily driven off by his infantry and artillery. Although he headed towards Resaca, in Johnston's rear, McPherson halted because he felt Southern defences were too strong, and pulled back to the lower mouth of Snake Creek Gap.

Retreating Confederate cavalry brought word of McPherson's flank march, and Johnston immediately ordered Hood to take three divisions to Resaca to block it. Furthermore, he learned that a 10,000-man corps under Polk was on its way from Mississippi as reinforcements.

Seeing McPherson's success, Sherman now decided to send his entire force through Snake Creek Gap, to take Resaca and trap Johnston north of the Oostenaula River. On 12 May, as the Federals advanced, Johnston, fearing he would be cut off, retreated to Resaca. By 13 May the Confederates, now aided by Polk's arrival, dug in around Resaca. The next day Sherman launched an attack on Johnston's centre, which was driven off. Johnston then sent Hood against the Federal left. After initial success, he was stopped.

After some unsuccessful fighting the next day, Sherman sent troops across the Oostenaula to threaten Johnston's rail supply line. Johnston counter-attacked this successful move, but it was in vain. To avoid capture, Johnston evacuated Resaca during the night, heading towards Calhoun and Adairsville, Georgia. On the 17th, the Confederates dug in around Adairsville, while Sherman sent two of his armies around the Southern flanks. That night, in fear of being trapped again, Johnston ordered yet another retreat.

► **Union troops break through the Confederate defences at the Battle of Allatoona Pass, the Confederates fleeing. One Confederate officer attempts to rally his unit by waving his regimental colour. Although a post-war print, the uniforms shown here are reasonably accurate.**

► **Johnston, master of the defensive battle, pulled back into strong positions, but Sherman was constantly able to manoeuvre his army around the Confederate flank until finally at the gates of Atlanta.**

▼ **General John Bell Hood leads his troops against Union troops under Hooker and Schofield at Culp's House, near Marietta, Georgia, June 22, 1864. Hood was never to learn that the direct assault was a dinosaur, tactically speaking, by this point in the war.**

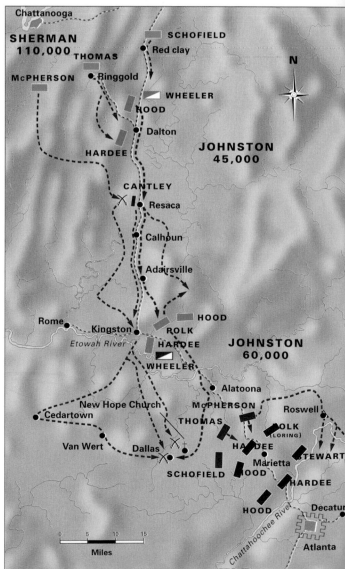

On the 18th, Johnston was in the Cassville-Kingston area, where he skirmished with advancing Federals. There Johston saw an opportunity and on the 19th ordered Hood and Polk to attack one of the separated Federal armies. While getting into position, Hood received faulty intelligence that the Federals were approaching his flank and rear, and he set up defensive lines instead of attacking. Johnston then set up defensive lines in Cassville, but was persuaded by Hood and Polk that the ground could not be held, and ordered a retreat. His next defensive line would be at Allatoona Pass.

On 22 May Sherman, who allowed his men a couple days of rest in Cassville, sent his troops towards Dallas, Georgia, bypassing Johnston's left flank. It was not until the 24th that Johnston realized what Sherman was up to, so he ordered his army to Dallas. On the 25th his men were in line around New Hope Church, Georgia, 25 miles north-east of Atlanta. Sherman immediately attacked in a heavy thunderstorm, but the Confederates held. Most of the rest of Sherman's army arrived in the New Hope Church area the next day, and both sides dug in and skirmished. Both sides initiated major attacks, the Union XI Corps on the 27th and Hardee's Confederate corps on the 28th, which failed. On 1 June Federal cavalry captured the important Allatoona Pass, with its railway connection to Chattanooga, which allowed easy Federal resupply. This done, Sherman shifted to his left, forcing Johnston to give up his Dallas lines on 3 June.

COLONEL ADIN B. UNDERWOOD, 33RD MASSACHUSETTS VOLUNTEER INFANTRY REGIMENT

Resaca was a myth, for all the men of the Thirty-third saw of it, but on the other side of the Coonasauga, a river which was crossed by a temporary bridge, they found what they cared more for than all the towns of Georgia – a pile of tobacco hidden in a secesh house. Every man of the brigade got his half pound, and such a cheering went up. In the luxury of the moment, yesterday's battle, with all its horrors, was forgotten. The death wounds, and the partings of comrades, and the song of the hour was – the weed – the Army's solace.

On 4 June Johnston was well dug in along Lost, Pine, and Brush mountains north-west of Marietta. Sherman advanced to attack and Polk was killed by a stray cannon shot on 14 June. Federal attacks forced Johnston to adjust his left flank on June 16, and after failing to hold the Federals on 17 June, retreated to Marietta on June 18. The Army of the Ohio struck these new lines on Kennesaw Mountain 27 June, losing almost 2,000 either killed or wounded in a disaster. This success was but temporary, and Johnston retreated to another line at the Chattahoochee on 2 July. Federals followed, finding a weak spot on the Confederate right. This forced Johnston across the river to the very defences of Atlanta. There he prepared to defend the city against an inevitable siege.

THE FIRST ASSAULTS ON PETERSBURG

◀ **Butler's attack from Bermuda Hundred failed, his Army of the James 'bottled up like a corked bottle'. Grant sent his Army of the Potomac around to take the vital rail lines from Richmond west through Petersburg, but moved too slowly. A siege was the last option.**

Butler saw his chance of military glory fade – his Bermuda Campaign had resulted with him being the butt of jokes. To try to win success, he turned his attention to Petersburg, as yet still thinly defended. On 5 June 1864, he sent 200 of his cavalry to reconnoitre the approaches to the city and was told that only one regiment, along with some unreliable militia, guarded it.

Before he could plan an attack, however, he received word that the Army of the Potomac was going to cross over to the south side of the James with the goal of taking Petersburg. He determined not to wait for them, but to strike quickly to win fame for its capture. On the 7th he ordered an attack with his infantry and cavalry. The morn-

ing attack, which was poorly led and totally mismanaged by Butler's inferior subordinates, failed.

Grant was shortly on the scene and called for a new attack on Petersburg. This time the main effort would be made by Major-General W.F. Smith, augmented by cavalry, U.S.C.Ts from City Point, and lead elements of the Army of the Potomac, the II Corps. In all, this would be a force of some 16,000 Federals against a defending force under Beauregard of no more than 3,000 troops. Luck was on Beauregard's side that day: Federal orders were mixed up by signal officers, maps were incorrect, rations never got through to hungry troops, water supplies ran short, and commanders delayed too long. Hancock's II Corps, delayed as rations were brought up to augment the two days' worth they had with them, did not arrive at the front until after dark and Smith decided not to attack, despite the bright moonlight. Even Grant, usually so clear in his orders, did not let Smith know exactly what he expected the roles of the two armies to be. This is not to take anything away from the Confederate defenders who fought bravely when they had to.

Grant himself did not come to the attack, instead supervising the crossing by the Army of the Potomac over the James. Smith and his men approached the Confederate defences warily, well aware of the power of entrenched Confederate infantry. By the late afternoon they took Lunettes 5 - 11, over a mile of the city's outer lines. But the Confederates had created a series of deep defences, and simply fell back to their next line. Petersburg was still safely in Confederate hands, a fact that probably caused the war to last at least six months longer.

However, the attacks had seriously worried Beauregard, who stripped the lines facing Butler's men, and managed to put 14,000 men into the city's defences. This still wouldn't be enough for a serious assault. The Army of the Potomac's IX Corps arrived in front of

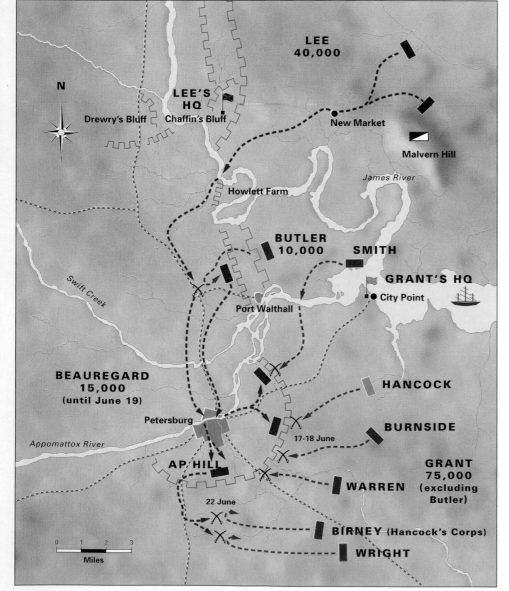

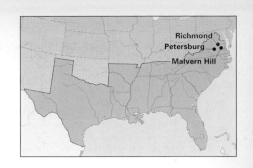

A Pennsylvania light artillery battery of 12-pounder bronze Napoleon cannon prepares to fire against Confederate lines outside Petersburg. Famed photographer Mathew Brady, whose eyesight was by then too poor to take his own photographs, stands in the straw hat front and center.

PRIVATE JOHN D. BILLINGS, 10TH MASSACHUSETTS LIGHT ARTILLERY

At the conclusion of the assault we unharnessed and spent a peaceful night, and the next morning, the Sabbath, opened quietly enough. But before soon we were sent for from further front, and Lieut. Granger rode forward in company with a staff officer to find a place for us in the new line. He returned with a bullet-hole through the sleeve of his blouse, and gave the order to 'limber up.' 'What kind of place are we going into, Lieutenant?' inquired one of the men. 'That's the kind,' as his rejoinder, holding up to view his riddled sleeve. 'Look at this!'

◄ Petersburg, one of Virginia's major cities and an important rail gateway into Richmond, was a sleepy southern town before mid-1864. Nevertheless, as it was obviously an important target, the Confederates garrisoned it throughout the war.

the city in the mid-morning of 16 June, followed by the V Corps at midnight. During the day, the Federals continued to attack, capturing four redans and some trenchline. Confederate counterattacks failed, while Army of the James troops attacked the weakened defences they faced. Only quick movements by Pickett's Virginia Division stabilized the situation.

The IX Corps attacked a point called the Shand House on the Petersburg lines in the morning of 17 June. Initially successful, a Confederate counter-attack late in the day recovered that position. Still, the Confederates were forced to retire to a shorter line of defences. But help was on the way. Lee, still around Malvern Hill, finally accepted the fact that Beauregard's men were facing the bulk of the Army of the Potomac and began sending troops to his aid.

Orders for the V Corps in conjunction with the IX Corps on the morning of the 18th were to strike at 4.00 a.m. with maximum effort and as quickly as possible. The troops moved off well enough, but soon the right wing surged ahead of the rest of the

line and had to wait for them to come up. Burnside reported that his men had been stopped short of their goal, partly because they were 'much wearied' from their long marches to get into position. V Corps men, whose experience from the Wilderness to Petersburg taught them to dig in every time they stopped, dug in while the artillery came up and scouts went out to reconnoitre their front. Beauregard had slowly pulled back, trading a mile of lines for time to allow Lee's lead element to arrive.

By 8.00 a.m. a brigade of the Confederate First Corps was on the scene and the door to Petersburg was being barred. Meade ordered the attack to continue, with a new push to begin at noon. Warren, however, reported at 1 p.m. that he hadn't heard any firing, so he had not bothered to attack, figuring that Burnside wasn't attacking. By darkness it was obvious that Petersburg was not going to fall to the Federal forces that day, and Meade ordered his army to form the best lines they could and dig in. What could have been a quick assault would now be a full siege.

THE BATTLE OF THE CRATER

On the morning of 18 June 1864, there was scattered fighting towards the Confederate lines around Petersburg. Grant decided the moment had passed for Petersburg to be taken easily by assault, and he ordered Meade's troops to dig in for a siege.

The Federal army was in a good position. Grant assigned Butler's army the job of defending the lines north of the Appomattox, while the Army of the Potomac and the IX Corps, independent since its commander, Burnside, outranked Meade took the south. This latter force had captured two railways and a number of roads that led into the city and had a point on the river from where they could be easily resupplied. Engineers on both sides now went to work to set up or improve their works as the armies sniped at each other across lines often as close as a hundred yards apart.

A traditional job assigned to military engineers is to dig mines under enemy works which are then blown up while infantry pour through the gap in the lines. In this particular situation, however, Colonel Henry Pleasants, a mining engineer in civilian life, commander of the 48th Pennsylvania Volunteer Infantry Regiment, made up largely of coal miners, came up with the idea of digging a mine under a Confederate position some hundred yards away. He told his superior that such a job could be done with some picks, shovels, and some surveying instruments. With such tools, his men could dig up to 50 ft daily, bringing them under the Confederate line in little over a fortnight.

Major James Duane, the chief engineer of the Army of the Potomac, a professional who actually wrote the army's engineering manual, said that the idea would not work as nobody had ever dug a mine so far. Yet Pleasants and Burnside received permission to begin the work, which began on 25 June. Duane was of so little use that he even refused to give the miners surveying equipment he had on hand, the diggers had to obtain what they needed in Washington privately. Indeed, the diggers even had to improvise wheelbarrows by making them out of biscuit boxes and hickory poles.

The ground was clay with few rocks, and the miners made good time. By 17 July they had gone 510 ft from their lines. Although the Federals concealed their activity, the Confederates suspected that a mine was being dug. They began sinking countermines. Some of their listening shafts ended up rather near Pleasant's mine, but they had so few personnel to man them, they did not discover the actual mine.

The miners actually reached their destination on 23 July. Then they built an area in which to deposit the six tons of powder that were to be exploded in it. This done, they laid a fuse to the mine entrance and on 28 July were ready.

In the meantime, Burnside selected the troops to make the assault and began training them. The first wave was to consist of U.S.C.T. division, who were relatively new to the service, but were not as exhausted as Burnside's other divisions. Late into the planning process, however, Grant and Meade decided not to use African-Americans as the first elements in the assault, as, were they to be unsuccessful, the uproar would be tremendous. Burnside was told to substitute a white division, although the U.S.C.T. division could be in a later element.

▶ Moments after the mine the 48th Pennsylvania lay was exploded, Union infantry rushes forward. A last-minute change switched trained black troops for untrained white troops, who milled around in the crater and allowed the Confederates to reinforce their position.

▶ Windslow Homer, a young artist before the war, served as a combat artist for *Harper's Weekly* in several eastern campaigns and produced paintings of what he saw thereafter. This painting shows a Confederate who has dangerously climbed on top of his works to dare a Union soldier to shoot him.

MAJOR WILLIAM M. OWEN, WASHINGTON ARTILLERY, ARMY OF NORTHERN VIRGINIA

Mounting the parapet to get a better look, and while standing there, a sharp-shooter of the enemy fired from his rifle-pit twice; his second shot wounded me in the right cheek. He raised his head to see the effect of his aim, and, being indisposed to gratify him with the knowledge of his accuracy, I stood for a moment, and then jumped down into the trench. My wound bled profusely; but it was a mere flesh wound, and the men running up with canteens of water, I saturated my handkerchief and tied it around my face, and went back to my tent, which was pitched in Mr. Cameron's yard.

▲ Coal miners serving in the 48th Pennsylvania dig a shaft under the Confederate defences of Petersburg. The project was not approved of by the Army of the Potomac's engineers, and the coal miners had to do all the mining work, even obtaining their own equipment, themselves.

Throughout 29 June the troops who were to make the attack gathered in position. Then in the early morning of 30 June the miners lit their fuse and waited. At around 4.45 a.m. the powder in the mine exploded in a huge pillar of smoke directly under the line held by the 22rd South Carolina Infantry, some 300 men. Most were thrown into the air, then buried alive or badly wounded by the earth that fell back into the crater caused by the explosion. In all, some 278 men from the 22rd and two other South Carolina regiments, as well as a Virginia artillery battery, were lost in the explosion. The crater that resulted was some 170 ft long, 60 – 80 ft wide, and 30 ft deep.

Approximately 110 Federal cannon and 54 mortars opened up on the general area, as Federal infantry pulled themselves out of the trenches and prepared to advance. Dust from the explosions mixed with gunpowder smoke to make vision impossible, delaying these formations. In the meantime, Confederates in the rear and on the sides of the crater scrambled to gather troops to hold their line.

The Federals advanced, jumping down into the crater which they used as a fort. Nobody pushed them on. By 8.30 a.m. some 15,000 troops, including U.S.C.Ts, were in the crater and the surrounding Confederates poured heavy fire into them. They also covered the field behind the crater to the Federal trenches with fire so no reinforcements could join them. By early afternoon the attack's failure was obvious, and such men as could escape were ordered back to Union lines.

THE SIEGE OF PETERSBURG

With the failure of the crater, the Federals returned to a normal siege. The men dug their trenches deeper, adding bombproof shelters to the rear. The skies were filled with fire from cannon, mortars, and rifles. 'The scenes along the trenches at night were grand beyond description,' wrote Confederate engineer officer W.W. Blackford. 'For miles the bright little flashes of the musketry in two parallel lines were the brilliants surrounding the brighter gems of the cannon flashes. Darting across with the rapidity of a meteor from side to side, in opposite directions, flew the lighted shells in almost horizontal lines, while high above all in the heavens in graceful, arching flight flew in flocks of six or eight at a time, the mortar shells, looking as if they were chasing and passing and re-passing one another in their eagerness to perform their deadly mission. The flocks of mortar shells from the opposite sides sometimes crossed each other's path and seemed for an instant tangled together, but then they would glade away and separate with the utmost grace.'

The Federals had brought up naval mortars, huge things, one called the 'Dictator', which they mounted on railway carriages. Other railway lines, built by the expert U.S. Military Railroads, passed behind the lines to the main supply depot at Point Comfort. Engineers had built huge piers there where supply ships could unload and hospital ships could pick up the wounded and ill to be brought back to hospitals in Washington, Philadelphia, and New York. Civilians built restaurants in this area where off-duty Federal soldiers could gather for a rest from the tensions of being in the front line trenches.

Indeed, life in the trenches was both tremendously boring, from the lack of any activity, and nerve-racking from the constant threat of death. Sharpshooters grew so good that one Confederate officer noted two of his men crossing an exposed point in different directions were killed by the same bullet. In the trenches, many Confederates dug bore-holes into the ground in an attempt to uncover any new Federal mines. Water was poured into the bore-holes, draining out instantly if a mine were detected. Despite these efforts no new Federal mines were detected.

Confederates in their trenches could return to Petersburg where life essentially went on, despite the constant shells that exploded in

▲ The Union army brought up a Naval mortar, which they called the 'Dictator', to use in bombarding Petersburg and its defences. The mortar was mounted on a railroad line so it could be moved from spot to spot as needed.

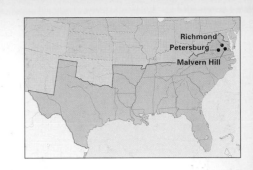

▼ Sharpshooters, well protected within their trenches, made life miserable for both sides during the Siege of Petersburg. It was almost certain death to expose a part of one's body any where near the front lines.

the city's streets and buildings. Indeed, many Confederate officers kept dress uniforms safe in Petersburg rooms. When back in the town they could change from their dirty day-time uniforms into these to take part in the many 'starvation balls', as Southern women called their socials of the period. While food was often in short supply, clothing was not. Indeed, imports of British-made cloth and even entire uniforms, as well as a production system that had become highly efficient, assured the average Confederate soldier of a new pair of trousers every month and a new jacket every three months.

Grant was not the type of person who could take simply sitting in trenches and waiting for his enemy to surrender easily. To fill in time, he brought his family to the small cabin that had been built for him behind the lines, while constantly ordering probes and demonstrations at points along the Confederate lines in order to find weak points and possibly exploit them. On 18 August, he sent Warren's V Corps west in heavy rain to capture the vital Weldon Railroad. Lee sent troops under Heth to halt them south of Petersburg. The next day troops from A.P. Hill's Corps added their strength, hitting the V Corps and forcing Warren to pull back to the Globe Tavern, although he still held the railway line. The Confederates, unable to retake the line despite renewed attacks, dug new lines.

The Federals began destroying their section of the Weldon Railroad. To stop them, on 25 August A.P. Hill's Corps struck at the troops there, now including the II Corps. The surprise attack, however, did not halt the line's destruction.

On 29 September the Federals launched a two-pronged attack against Lee's Army. One came from north of the James against

Richmond itself, while the other continued Grant's usual turning of Lee's right, this time to the west. These attacks aimed to extend Lee's already stretched line and stop him sending reinforcements to Early in the Shenandoah valley. They would also allow the capture of the vital the South Side Railroad. On the right, the Federals captured a vital spot in the Confederate line, Fort Harrison, which they converted into one of their own defences. On the west, they slogged towards the railroad, fighting successfully at Peebles Farm at first, but then being driven back by A.P. Hill counter-attacks. Nonetheless, the Federals had succeeded in stretching the Confederate lines almost to the breaking point. By 2 October, the Federals had extended their line west by some three miles. Grant knew that Lee's Army of Northern Virginia could not defend such lines for long.

▲ Union soldiers pose in captured Confederate fortifications at Warren Station after they had captured the position. In the heat of a Virginia spring, many have removed their jackets and blouses and wear shirt sleeves.

CAPTAIN GEORGE W. BOWEN, 12TH NEW JERSEY VOLUNTEER INFANTRY

Had notice that the wagon train was up with Officers baggage. Went back, got my Valise got a complete suit from cap to shoes, layed them down beside a stagnant pool of water; walked off; took from my pockets what was in them; and went off

and left them, no doubt leaving a half a pint of body lice in them, skimmed the scum off the pool and washed myself. This is the first change of clothing I have had since the 3rd of May.

THE RED RIVER CAMPAIGN

The final assault on the Confederate heartland was to come in the west, to take Shreveport, Louisiana. This town had become the home of the Confederate government of that state, as well as the headquarters of the Confederate Trans-Mississippi Department and an important supply depot. It was, moreover, the gateway to Texas.

The plan called for a joint Army-Navy attack along the Red River, and was under the joint command of Banks for the Army and Rear Admiral David D. Porter for the Navy. Porter was personally leery about the plan, concerned that the Red River could fall and trap his fleet which included a dozen ironclad gunboats, two large wooden steamers, and four smaller steamers. Grant shared his concern and was, besides that, not at all confident in Banks' abilities.

However, in March 1864 Banks got his army under way from Vicksburg, while Porter brought his gunboats. Opposing them was Fort De Russy, which defended the Red River, and a force of several divisions under General Richard Taylor, son of the famed Mexican War commander. On March 14, the Federals, having landed nearby the day before, marched on and surrounded the unfinished Confederate fort. The Confederates quickly surrendered 185 men, eight heavy guns, and two field pieces. A day later the boats reached Alexandria, from which the Confederates had hastily removed all their stores.

Banks' main body of troops, marching overland on a road that ran roughly parallel to the Red River to Shreveport, were delayed, but this mattered little since it took until April 3 for Porter to get the troops he was transporting over the rapids past Alexandria to where they were to meet Banks' force. The hospital ship in Porter's fleet was a casualty of this part of the expedition. Finally, however, these troops reached Grand Ecore where most started to join Banks' troops at Natchitoches. From there they would attack Shreveport. This was, however, not to be.

On April 7 Taylor, having been reinforced, and now commanding a force of some 9,000 men, heard of Banks' advance. He knew that the troops directly under Banks were separated from the troops on Porter's boats, and decided to fight before the two groups could unite and present overwhelming numbers. He chose to draw up lines to defend near Mansfield on the edge of a wood that fronted an open field 800 yards wide by 1,200 yards long. The road to Pleasant Hill, on which Banks' troops were marching, passed through the middle of this field.

On the next day Banks' 12,000 troops ran into Taylor's mounted skirmishers, driving them back on the main line. Then Banks' infantry came into the clearing and having deployed into line, halted there. Seeing that they did not advance, Taylor ordered a general

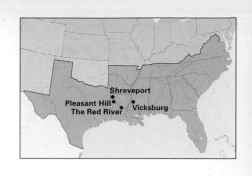

assault late that afternoon. The Federals were quickly routed in this desperate charge, abandoning some 20 cannon, 250 supply wagons, and 2,500 prisoners. They did not stop until a fresh Union division halted the pursuing Confederates. Then the Federals continued their retreat to Pleasant Hill throughout the night.

The Confederates followed Banks to Pleasant Hill where the next day they attacked the Federal left. The Federals this time stood, actually capturing three Confederate cannon and 426 prisoners in the fight. Nonetheless, Banks having had enough, decided to abandon the campaign. The troops who had planned to join Banks now rejoined Porter's fleet and retreated.

Porter's initial fears were coming true, however, as the waters of the Red River continued to fall and Confederate sharpshooters, including artillery, fired on them as they made their way back down stream. Harassing Confederates actually managed to capture one boat, while forcing Porter to destroy another. Worse news was found at Alexandria, where Porter's commanders discovered that the rapids had fallen too low for his boats to pass over.

An Army officer, a former logging industry man, however, suggested building a dam to raise the water level. When the water was high enough, a gap would be knocked in the dam, and the boats would escape in line. Sailors and soldiers began work together and in eight days had a completed dam in place. Work crews knocked a gap in the dam and four of the boats escaped before the water level fell too low again. The dam was rebuilt, a new hole knocked in it, and the rest of Porter's boats were away.

Finally all the Federals were back to safety. But the campaign had been a failure, and blame was placed on Federal officers who spent much time during it acquiring cotton, which had become valuable in hungry northern cotton mills. Indeed, Porter reported that 3,000 bales of the white stuff had been captured on the Washita and another 2,000 bales on the Red River, all of which was sent to storehouses in Cairo, Illinois. Banks reported that his troops acquired 10,000 cotton bales. The result was that some individuals made a great deal of money, but the cause of the Union had not been advanced at all.

LIEUTENANT FRANK CHURCH, U.S. MARINE CORPS

We had a twenty-four pound howitzer on the hurricane deck which was being fired very rapidly. It was very warm and one of the men was ramming a cartridge in it when it exploded sending the poor fellow off the top of the boat down into the 'forecastle'. They picked him up and carried him to the Doctor. He had his whole right arm completely mashed to a jelly and filled with powder. He will probably get over it by the loss of his arm.

THE DEFENCE OF ATLANTA

By 3 July 1864 Sherman's army was at the gates of Marietta, only 18 miles from Atlanta. As the wounded arrived there by the trainload, many citizens made preparations to flee, while others were pressed into the ranks of the home guard. Sherman probed the Confederate left, forcing Johnston's troops to fall back again slightly. The main hope in Atlanta, though, was that the rain-swollen Chattahoochee River would stop Sherman where Johnston's army had not.

By 8 July the Confederates were forced out of not only Marietta, but also Roswell, although they still held their positions on the Chattahoochee. Federal attempts to cross the river on the 10th were defeated. However, two days later all except one corps of the Army of Tennessee were in lines on the southern side of the river, as rain fell, slowing both sides. Finally, on the 14th, Sherman's men crossed the river and held their hard-won position. The Confederates burned the railway and turnpike bridges across the

river, along with three pontoon bridges built by their own engineers. After this, the final corps of the Army of Tennessee on the northern side of the river crossed over to join its compatriots.

In Richmond, Davis was livid. Atlanta was a vital rail centre, as well as a major production centre, and without it the Confederacy would be hard pressed to produce and ship uniforms, accoutrements, munitions, and foodstuffs to its armies in the field. On 16 July he telegraphed Johnston that he wanted to hear about 'the present situation and your plan as specifically as will enable me to anticipate events'. Johnston's evasive reply was: 'As the enemy has double our number, we must be on the defensive. My plan of operations must therefore, depend upon that of the enemy. It is mainly to watch for an opportunity to fight to advantage. We are trying to put Atlanta in condition to be held for a day or two by the Georgia militia, that army movements may be freer and wider.'

It sounded as if Johnston had already written off Atlanta, and that was simlpy not acceptable. The next day Davis ordered Johnston removed from command and replaced by aggressive John Bell Hood of Texas. Hood, who had lost one leg and the use of one arm in battle, had never been tried in high command positions before, although he had been a top notch brigade and division commander. Some Confederates welcomed him, although Johnston had been a highly popular commander who was seen as not wasting his soldiers' lives.

Changing generals was not stopping Sherman, however. By 17 July his armies were five miles from Atlanta, while McPherson's Army of the Tennessee occupied Decatur. By the 19th, Thomas's Army of the Cumberland troops reached Peachtree Creek, north of Atlanta, while Schofield's Army of the Ohio was headed towards the city further east from Thomas. In these separated movements Hood saw an advantage, although possibly the plan had been Johnston's. He planned to strike the Army of the Cumberland while the three forces were widely separated.

In the late afternoon of 20 July, after some delay which Hood blamed on his subordinates, the Confederates struck Thomas's 20,000 men. At first the Confederates were successful, the Federals appearing to them to be demoralized and panic-stricken. But Thomas would prevail here as he had at Chickamauga, refusing to be beaten, and stiffening his troops' resistance. For some two hours, until dusk, the Federals beat off wave after wave of Confederates, until Hood finally called the fight off.

His first attempt as an army commander a failure, Hood changed his focus to McPherson's force. On the 21st he sent Lieutenant-General William Hardee's Corps to march directly south 15 miles, then to turn east and attack McPherson's flank and rear. At the same time as Hardee's Corps was on the road, a division of McPherson's army took Leggett's Hill, after a strong defence by one of the Confederacy's best generals, Irishman Patrick Cleburne. From here the Federals had a full view of the city that was their goal. The other troops under Hood's command fell back into prepared fortifications which ringed the northern edge of the city.

▼ Major-General William T. Sherman watches, front centre, as his artillery pounds the defences of Atlanta. A staff officer next to him holds binoculars, most of which actually provided very little magnification but did offer 20/20 vision which was otherwise not all that common.

1ST LIEUTENANT WILLIAM M. SHERFY, US SIGNAL CORPS

I discovered the enemy advancing through the interval between the 16th and 17th Corps. This fact I reported to yourself, and immediately afterward, seeing Gen. McPherson about to start through the woods towards the 17th Corps, I rode up and warned him of the danger. He disregarded it, though, and went on, and as he was accompanied by but one orderly I went with him, being followed by several other members of the Signal Corps. We had gone but a short distance when the enemy appeared upon our left, within a few yards of the road, and ordering us to halt fired a volley at us. We all wheeled off the road to retreat, but at that instant the general was struck . . .

The next day Hardee's weary troops smashed into McPherson's flank. Fortunately for the Federals, McPherson had extended his left flank during the night with two divisions, so the attack that should have fallen on an open position, actually ran into prepared Federals. Despite fierce charges, dug in Federals repelled every Confederate attack and held their lines. On a reconnaissance during a lull in fighting, McPherson came too close to some Confederates hidden in the bushes and the 36-year-old general was shot in the heart.

But the Confederate attack was another failure and by now almost a quarter of Hood's 40,000-man army were casualties. The Federals had only lost approximately 3,700. Sherman decided not to attack the city's fortifications directly, but instead to lay a partial siege of the city to force Hood out with minimal casualties.

◄ Lieutenant-General John Bell Hood actively sought to replace General Joseph Johnston with himself. Once in that position, however, he proved he was totally inadequate for the job. Where Johnston was too cautious, he was too reckless.

▲ A post-war somewhat romantic lithograph of the death of Major-General John McPherson, one of the best of the army's commanders. In fact, McPherson was killed during a lull in the fighting, rather than in its midst as shown here.

CAVALRY RAIDING AROUND PETERSBURG

While the infantry and artillery were tied down in the trenches outside Petersburg, the cavalry was still free to do as much damage as possible on lines of communication and supply.

Grant was the first to strike, at 2.00 a.m. on 22 June, sending out all the cavalry still with the Army of the Potomac, as well as the cavalry of the Army of the James, against Burkeville, where two Southern railways, the Southside and the Richmond & Danville, intersected. Once there he destroyed as much of these lines as possible. Meade was against the raid, concerned that the Confederate cavalry would be able to prevent it succeeding. At first things went well, with the blue-coated troopers reaching Reams' Station, on the Weldon Railroad, by mid-morning. They stopped there to burn the station buildings down and tear up track on either side for a short distance. Then they headed off towards Dinwiddie Court House.

They were almost there when Confederate cavalry charged into their rear guard. This attack, not pushed heavily, was easily beaten off. They then reached Ford's Station, a Southside Railroad stop, where two trains loaded with supplies for the Army of Northern Virginia, were waiting. These trains were quickly torched, as were the station buildings, and a nearby saw mill. They built bonfires and piled the tracks on them, twisting them out of shape when they were red hot. Army of the James cavalry at Keysville

burned depots, bridges and trestles, sawmills, and water tanks.

Again, Confederate cavalry attacked the Federal rear guard while those ahead of them were on this destructive rampage. The attack did little to slow up the cavalry which by the afternoon had reached the Roanoke River. The bridge there was guarded by forts which prevented attempts by the Federals to reach the bridge and burn it. Deterred, the weary Federal troopers decided they had fulfilled their mission, and started back on a more southerly route than that by which they came. By the 27th they were near Stony Creek Depot, which they believed was defended by a small force. Heading there, the force they actually ran into was a full brigade of Confederate cavalry supported by two nearby divisions. The Federal attack there failed, and they decided to move around and pass east at Reams' Station. The two sides clashed at Stony Creek Depot while Federals reconnoitred the way to Reams' Station, which they reported clear. On the 29th, Federal cavalry disengaged, and headed towards Reams' Station.

Hearing the Federals' movements, the Confederates attacked and captured the better part of a full brigade. And things did not improve, as Reams' Station was actually garrisoned by two infantry brigades. The Federals decided to burn their supply wagons, left their wounded in the care of their enemies, and headed west, then south, then east, narrowly escaping to Federal lines. By 1 July they were back safely, having lost a quarter of their men as casualties.

Confederate cavalry would have more luck when they learned that the Federals had pastured almost 3,000 cattle, desperately needed by hungry troops in Petersburg, on Coggins' Point on the south bank of the James, some six miles below Union headquarters. Cavalry commander Major-General Wade Hampton took some 4,000 of his troopers on 14 September towards Dinwiddie Court House, where they turned south-east, riding for just over ten miles, and then north-east. They were on the Rowanty Creek, at Wilkinson's Bridge by that evening. The next day they rode 18 miles, still undetected, to Blackwater Creek where they built a bridge and then crossed to a point where they could attack the Federals four miles from Coggins' Point.

Just before dawn the Confederates struck the Federal cavalry pickets, who were easily brushed aside, and the prize was taken. While some cavalrymen rounded up the cattle and got them ready to head out, others destroyed telegraph lines and loaded supplies into wagons to head south. Then they started back.

The Federal high command was taken entirely unawares and reacted slowly. Finally the Navy was notified and sent gunboats to shell the area. By the time they'd reached Coggins' Point the Confederates were long gone. The Confederate line of march, with almost 2,500 captured cattle, stretched seven miles and moved, naturally, at a cow's pace. However, the Federals were unable to move swiftly enough to stop them. While some Southern troopers screened the main line of march against Federal

◄ **Major-General Wade Hampton, wealthy enough to pay for all of his first unit's equipment himself, proved to be an excellent cavalry leader. When Sherman's men approached South Carolina, his home state, he was detached from Virginia to cover General Johnston's retreat.**

cavalry, who ran into them at Ebenezer Church in the late afternoon, the rest moved on throughout the night. They reached Confederate lines by 9.00 a.m. on 17 September, having lost only 61 men. Lee's infantrymen, who had been reduced to eating bacon only one day out of every four, were delighted to see them and more particularly the captured cattle; one of the rare times Civil War infantrymen appreciated the cavalry.

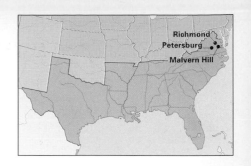

▲ This period engraving of the Battle of Ream's Station shows how it was that by late in the war formal battle lines were largely abandoned as men sought every piece of cover they could, forming a loose, ragged firing line.

CHAPLAIN HENRY R. PYNE, 1ST NEW JERSEY CAVALRY REGIMENT

As the colonel and some of his staff were walking around the house, observing the position of affairs, one of the men informed the adjutant that there was a curious spectacle inside. On entering one of the rooms, he found the walls lined with all the featherbeds and mattresses in the house, and prone upon the floor were fifteen females, from the old woman of eighty to the girl of thirteen, all with bare feet and scanty skirts, all terribly frightened, and all drumming with their heels upon the floor in a paroxysm of fear, whenever a shot struck the house.

THE BATTLE OF TUPELO, MISSISSIPPI

While Sherman's men closed in on Atlanta, the red-headed general himself kept an eye cocked towards where Confederate cavalry leader Nathan Bedford Forrest was creating havoc. Picking two subordinates, he wrote the Secretary of War, 'I shall order them to make up a force and go out and follow Forrest to the death, if it cost 10,000 lives and breaks the Treasury. There never will be peace in Tennessee till Forrest is dead.'

One of the generals Sherman named was Major General A.J. Smith who was given a combined infantry/cavalry command and on 5 July, 1864, started from LaGrange south-east towards Ripley over hot, dusty roads. Forrest's scouts learned about Smith's march immediately and sent a brigade to hold a post south of Pontotoc. The brigade deployed on a ridge behind a swampy piece of ground cut by two creeks. Smith attacked this brigade with cavalry

and infantry on the centre and a cavalry attack on the Confederate right which drove them out of their position. The Federals occupied Pontotoc, from which they sent infantry and cavalry to reconnoitre Forrest's main position.

Smith decided not to attack Forrest on ground of the Confederate's choosing, instead bypassing Forrest's excellently chosen position by marching out on the 13th towards Tupelo, 18 miles in the east, through which the Mobile & Ohio Railroad passed. Forrest, under direct command of Major-General Stephen D. Lee, commanding officer of the Department of Alabama, Mississippi, and East Louisiana, moved along a parallel road and sent out scouts to find a place where his troopers could attack the Federal flanks easily.

The result was that the march to Harrisonburg, a small town a mile from Tupelo, was almost a running fight, involving both

► A dramatic incident from Nathan Forrest's life, as shown in this later illustration, when his horse was killed from under him. Although pressed by advancing Union troops, he calmly stepped away, received another horse, and rode to safety.

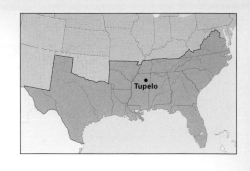

Tupelo

▲ Stephen Dill Lee of South Carolina became the youngest lieutenant-general in the Confederate army. An artilleryman before the war, he commanded Confederate artillery at Vicksburg and eventually ended up a corps commander in the Army of Tennessee.

▲ *Right:* Major-General Andrew Jackson Smith, a professional soldier from Pennsylvania, had been in California when the war began. He was named chief of cavalry under Halleck in 1862 and then moved to an infantry division command and then a corps command by the war's end.

Federal infantry and cavalry. When they reached Harrisonburg the troops were so exhausted that they rolled up in their blankets and went right to sleep, not even bothering to light cook fires. The next morning Smith sent a detachment of his cavalry, the 7th Kansas, through Tupelo north to Saltillo, some ten miles away. On the way there they destroyed all the water tanks and bridges they came across on the Mobile & Ohio line.

After the blue troopers rode out of town, Forrest sent his men just after daybreak at Smith's position. The land was largely clear, except for a wood rail fence and a wide gully on part of the line. This formed the place where the Federals rallied, and repulsed the Confederates. The Confederates reformed and attacked again, being again repelled, two out of four such attacks they would make during the day. While they were reforming, Forrest's artillery did excellent service until it faced counter-battery fire from two Federal batteries. The Confederates attempted to take these guns, but were thrown back, the southern commanding officer dead on the field.

These attacks failing, the Confederates then moved to the left, crossing north of the Pontotoc Road, to hit the other Union flank. The Federals stood for two and a half hours until the Federal commander ordered an advance, which drove off the Confederates. Forrest had been defeated, with a loss of some 1,000 killed, wounded, and missing, while the Federals lost some 650.

Once the cavalry returned from their raid towards Saltillo, Smith decided that he could do no more in the area, especially as ammunition and rations were running low, and headed back towards Memphis. Indeed, the day after the battle Smith's quartermaster announced that he could supply only one day's worth of hard crackers, while artillery ammunition was especially low after the previous day's fight.

Forrest, never one to give up, struck at Smith's camp that evening, before the Federals could get under way. This attack was easily broken up. The next morning Forrest returned to the attack, but his force was, once again, broken up by a Union counterattack and he finally gave up. Smith then moved off, reaching Memphis on 23 July.

While Smith believed he'd done much damage to Forrest's command at Tupelo, Sherman did not, and he ordered another campaign against the amateur soldier. On 29 July Smith took 17,000 men south again. This time the weather was rainy and hot, and the column moved slowly. While the Federals ambled from point to point without any seeming plan, Forrest assembled 2,000 of his best mounted men, starting off on 18 August, he reached Memphis on 21 August. He'd covered a hundred miles in two and a half days.

Panic-stricken Federal commanders ordered Smith's return to Memphis which he did so quickly that he left railroad bridges unburned and even a 97-mile-long telegraph line his own telegraph troops built untouched for the Confederates to use. In fact his only achievement had been the burning of the public buildings in Oxford as an act of revenge for the Confederate burning of Chambersburg, Pennsylvania. By the time he got to Memphis, however, Forrest's men were gone. Forrest had been beaten at Tupelo, but not put out of the game. On the plus side for the Union, however, Smith had occupied Forrest, keeping him from striking at Sherman's lines of communication and supply during the fighting around Atlanta.

FIRST LIEUTENANT JAMES DINKINS, AIDE-DE-CAMP, CS ARMY

We lost about fifteen hundred true and brave men. When General Buford withdrew his command and all the firing had ceased, he rode away from the scene and stood alone under the shade of a large tree. General Forrest passing by asked where his command was. General Buford covered his face with his arm, and said: 'I have no command. They were all killed.' He was deeply grieved, and in no condition to discuss the events of the battle at Harrisonburg.

WAR ON THE HIGH SEAS

Confederate Secretary of the Navy Mallory had more on his mind than just defending his new country's coast. He believed that striking a blow against the huge U.S. merchant fleet would prove a significant contribution to forcing Northern public opinion to veto waging war against the South. He sent an agent, Commander James D. Bulloch, in May 1861 to England with instructions to buy or build six steamers to be used as fast cruisers armed with two large guns and enough room for stores for extended periods at sea. These ships were to become commerce raiders.

As a neutral power, Great Britain could not sanction building ships for either side in the war, but Bulloch secretly managed to get a contract for his first ship to which he gave the cover name *Oreto*. A contract also went to another Liverpool builder for a ship code-named No. 290. Back in the South, Mallory instructed a professional U.S. Navy officer, a newly commissioned Confederate commander, Raphael Semmes to find a ship among the many locked in blockaded Southern ports. Semmes picked a screw-driven ship in New Orleans capable of carrying a battery of four or five guns, the *Havana*, which he had converted to a warship and christened the *Sumter*. Semmes took command of the new warship in April 1861 and began fitting her out. By 12 June she was ready to go, and under cover of darkness at the end of June the Confederacy's newest cruiser slipped past Federal blockades and out to sea.

Shortly after she captured her first prize, the Northern merchant ship *Golden Rocket*, and by early January 1862 she was off the coast of Spain. On the way she had captured 16 Northern merchant ships, burning some and bonding others. However, by this point the small ship was leaking badly and her engines needed overhauling. She put into Gibraltar where Semmes learned he would be unable to get her back to sea. Paying off the crew, Semmes then headed to England.

The *Sumter* had not been the first ship to fly a Confederate flag in a European harbour. That honour went to the *Nashville*, a converted passenger ship, which sailed to Southampton, England, capturing one merchant vessel on the way, arriving there on 21 November 1861. Returning with a full load of munitions, she burned a second merchant ship on the way to Bermuda. She then headed into Beaufort, North Carolina, where she was blockaded for the rest of the war.

In Liverpool, Bulloch got the *Oreto* launched in March 1862, when she was renamed the CSS *Florida* and given to Lieutenant John Maffitt to command. She reached Nassau in May and was converted to a warship. Yellow fever broke out there, and Maffitt took her to Cuba, where he came down with the disease. Recovering, though still weak and with a small crew, Maffitt then aimed his ship at Mobile Bay, slipping through the blockade there under a British flag on 4 September. Refitted and painted grey, the *Florida* slipped past the blockade again during a storm in February 1863. By 7 May 1863, she had destroyed a dozen Northern merchant ships. But by August, she, too, was in need of repairs, and put into Brest, France. She finally left 10 February 1864, under a new command. On 4 October, she arrived at Bahia, Brazil, having destroyed 11 merchantmen and bonded two more. Here, she was illegally captured by the USS *Wachusett* who took her in tow while most of her hands were ashore.

▲ Rear Admiral Raphael Semmes had been a career U.S. Navy officer before resigning to follow his state south. After the *Alabama* fight, he returned to command the James River Squadron near Richmond, receiving an army commission to command his naval brigade in the war's last days.

▶ Famed French painter Edouard Manet was one of many who travelled from Paris to Cherbourg to see the *Kearsage* take on the *Alabama*. In his painting of the scene, the *Alabama* begins to sink, stern first, while small boats circle to pick up survivors.

▶▶ *Far right*: Many of the officers and men of the *Alabama* were captured by the *Kearsage* and brought back as prisoners, held in the ship's hold as shown here. Most of the ratings were in fact foreign, not southern, born, while the officers were native southerners.

Bulloch's other raider was launched on 29 July 1862 and taken to the Azores to be fitted with her guns and crew. Semmes received command of this ship, christened the *Alabama*. After capturing several Northern ships, the *Alabama* arrived off Texas in January 1863 where she was hailed by the USS *Hatteras*. Both sides hoist their battle flags, and in the short fight, the Southern cruiser sunk the Federal warship, taking her men on board as prisoners. It would be the only successful fight between a Confederate cruiser and a U.S. Navy warship.

Both the *Florida* and the *Alabama* put prize crews on captured ships which they then armed to cruise on their own. The net effect was to greatly terrify Northern ship owners.

The *Alabama* was to cruise the world, visiting Cape Town, South Africa in August 1863, then appearing in the Indian Ocean that September. In all, she would burn or bond 68 Northern vessels. But the long voyage told on her and she put in to Cherbourg, France, on 11 June 1864. Hastily summoned, the USS *Kearsage* stood off Cherbourg and sent her a challenge. On 17 June the *Alabama*, her bottom still fouled, put out to meet her. A defective Southern shell, powder perhaps damp, struck the *Kearsage*'s

rudder but failed to explode. Anchors on the sides of the *Kearsage* protected her from other hits, while the Northern shells tore a hole in the Alabama's side. She soon sank, Semmes being rescued by a British yacht.

Other cruisers like the CSS *Georgia* were later launched, but the *Florida* and *Alabama* were the two great Confederate cruisers and between the two of them they virtually swept the Northern merchant fleet from the seas.

SECOND ASSISTANT ENGINEER MATTHEW O'BRIEN, C.S. NAVY

A shell entered, and brought up a few yards from them. It must have been a five-second fuse, from the distance of the *Kearsage* from us at this stage of the action, for it exploded almost immediately. I protected myself as well as I could from the fragments. So soon as the smoke and dust cleared away, I looked, intending to go to their assistance, expecting to find them wounded, or perhaps dead; when, to my amazement, there they stood hauling on the tackle as though attending an exercise drill.

▲ U.S. Navy gunners cheer as the *Alabama* sinks in the distance. Superior northern gunpowder and fuses, fresher than those found on the *Alabama* which had been stored a long time, helped settle the fight in the north's favour.

THE BLOCKADE

One of the purposes of the cruisers, besides inflicting pain on the Northern economy by destroying its merchant fleet, was to draw away U.S. Navy ships which would otherwise be occupied in blockading Southern ports. With ports open, ships bearing arms, food, clothing, munitions, and even mundane things of life that Southern manufacturers were unable to supply such as pins and needles, could arrive from overseas.

When the blockade was declared, the U.S. Navy owned only one screw frigate, then returning from Japan; five screw-sloops, of which only one was in the Home Squadron; three side-wheel steamers; eight screw-sloops; five screw steamers, and two side-wheel steamers. These ships were spread all over from the coast of Africa to the Pacific and the Mediterranean. They were immediately ordered to return to the scene of the conflict. In the meantime, the Navy bought as many ships and boats, ranging from yachts to ferry boats, as they could and began fitting them for the blockade. Thousands of sailors and officers had to be recruited into a Navy that, before the war, had been legally limited to 7,600 officers and men. By the war's end, the Navy had 51,500 men in its service.

The Union officially announced the blockade of the 3,000 miles of Southern coast on 19 April 1861, and almost immediately U.S. Naval ships began to take their places off Southern ports. At first, neutrals approaching the blockade had to be stopped and a warning noted in their logs, after which they were free to leave. Later, however, they could be seized if attempting to run the blockade.

The majority of ships loaded with merchandise for Southern merchants and the government came from Great Britain. At first the blockade was so easy to pass, because of a lack of blockading ships, that these ships were typical merchant ships sailing directly from a British port to a Southern one. Later, however, blockading squadrons were beefed up as more ships came on duty. It proved more viable to use typical merchant ships to bring the merchandise to one of four points, from where it would be unloaded and warehoused until a special blockade-running ship could reload it and take it to a Southern port.

These ships were built low in the water, using hard coal to limit tell-tale smoke, and made with screws or low paddle-wheels. Painted black or dark grey, they would wait until darkness then dash towards their port, usually flying foreign flags to confuse Federal

▶ **An 1861 cartoon showing the original strategy suggested by Major-General Winfield Scott, the U.S. Army commanding general when the war began. Called the 'anaconda policy' after the snake, he basically proposed strangling the south while also invading her. This was the eventual strategy used.**

▶ **Improvisation was the order of the day as a Union military force far outgrew its pre-war rules and regulation. In Port Royal, South Carolina, the U.S. Navy built a machine shop over the hulls of two old ships and in them could produce all the metal equipment its blockaders needed.**

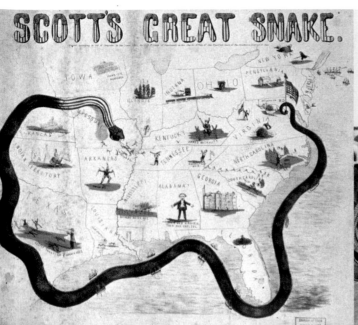

blockaders. Each would have a Confederate Army signal corps officer on board who would display the right signals for the forts that guarded the inlets to the ports. They were crammed with merchandise, often bought the by ships' officers who stood to make a fortune on each trip. Indeed, owners could pay for the cost of an entire blockade runner with one successful trip. Return trips would bring cotton out. While most blockade runners were privately owned, North Carolina bought its own early on, while the Confederate Navy eventually commissioned 43 of its own blockade runners.

The four points from which blockade running was operated were Bermuda, Nassau, Havana, and Matamoras the least important of these locations. Located on the Texas/Mexican border across from Brownsville, Matamoras was potentially valuable because as a neutral port could not be blocked. But routes from Brownsville to points where the merchandise was needed were limited. After the fall of Vicksburg isolated the West, Matamoras could only bring in material to the Trans-Mississippi Department.

As Mobile and New Orleans were the ports that could be reached from Cuba, and New Orleans fell early in the war, while Mobile was usually effectively blockaded, Havana was of less significance. But Nassau and Bermuda became boom towns, with warehouses rented out at high rates to the merchants who brought in goods. The towns were crowded with sailors waiting for a job, merchants' agents, and people waiting for transportation into or out of the South.

Nassau was an easy run from Savannah, Charleston, and Wilmington, North Carolina. Moreover the shallow waters around the island meant that the blockading U.S. Navy vessels, with their

MIDSHIPMAN ALFRED T. MAHAN, U.S. NAVY

I shall not attempt to furbish up any intellectual entertainment for readers from the excessively dry bones of my subsequent blockading, especially off the mouth of the Sabine. Only a French cook could produce a passable dish out of such woeful material; and even he would require concomitant ingredients, in remembered incidents, wherein, if there were any, my memory fails me. Day after day, day after day, we lay inactive - roll, roll; not wholly ineffective, I suppose for our presence stopped blockade-running; but even in this respect the Texas coast had largely lost importance since the capture of Vicksburg and Port Hudson, the previous summer, had cut off the trans-Mississippi region from the body of the Confederacy.

deeper draught who were always on the lookout for blockade runners, had to keep further off-shore. Bermuda was a short run from Wilmington, which, as the war continued, eventually became the South's last free port and therefore Bermuda's importance was even greater in the last years of the war.

By the end of the war the blockade was virtually unbreakable. Indeed, throughout the blockade the U.S. Navy blockaders captured 1,149 vessels, of which 210 were steamers, for which the officers and men shared prize money. Another 355 vessels were burned, sunk, or driven against the shore, a common trick among blockade runners who would dash towards shore when discovered and ground their vessels. Then, protected by land-based guns, the cargoes could often be recovered.

▲ The U.S. Navy could call on many beached civilian sailors to fill its ranks, as Confederate commerce raiders reduced the northern merchant fleet. However, as these sailors on the USS *Unadilla* knew, bounties were greater for army service than for navy service.

THE BATTLE OF MOBILE BAY

▼ *Right:* A post-war cigarette card of Rear Admiral David Glasgow Farragut who was first commissioned into the Navy in 1810 and became the Navy's first rear admiral in 1862. He was named vice admiral for his victory at Mobile Bay, and died a full admiral in 1870.

▼ The two commanders of the CSS *Virginia* meet years after the war. Rear Admiral Francis Buchanan, left, was the ship's first commander, while Captain Josiah Tattnall commanded her after he was wounded and eventually ordered her destroyed to prevent her capture.

Mobile Bay is a large harbour which, before the war, had been the second largest cotton-exporting port in the south. As a result, it became far and away the most important Southern port for blockade runners in the Gulf of Mexico, most of which were smaller craft from Havana, Cuba. The capture of the city of Mobile and its harbour was therefore given high priority by U.S. Navy officials. Indeed, Grant wanted to take them after Vicksburg's fall, but Chattanooga's problems diverted him from that goal.

The harbour has a long, somewhat oval shape, of about 20 miles long, with the city of Mobile at the Northern end. The relatively narrow entrance was guarded on the east by Fort Morgan, with 45 guns, which sat on Mobile Point. In the centre of the entrance was Dauphin Island, and the 26-gun Fort Gaines on its eastern side, forming the other barrier to the main way into the harbour. The Confederate Navy also laid a minefield across this entrance, with a channel only 500 yds wide under the guns of Fort Morgan through which blockade runners could pass. On the western side of Dauphin Island, the Confederates also laid mines, as well as building Fort Powell on a small island that sat in the middle of this channel. It was felt to be entirely secure from Federal approach, and was not used by blockade runners.

Besides static defences, the Confederate Navy's constructors at Selma built a number of ships for the defence of Mobile Bay in case the U.S. Navy passed the initial barriers. These included the CSS *Tennessee*, one of the most powerful iron-clads in the Confederate service. Some 209 ft long, she was armed with four 6-inch rifled cannon and two 7 1/8-inch pivot guns. Command of the vessel was given to Rear Admiral Franklin Buchanan who was wounded taking the CSS *Virginia* against the ships blockading Richmond in the first use of iron-clads in America. The rest of Buchanan's squadron was considerably weaker, consisting of three wooden gunboats that had been converted from river steamers. However, construction was proceeding on three more iron-clads, the Federals learned. Once completed, the squadron would be in a good position to steam outside and dispatch the U.S. Navy's blockading ships.

Opposing Buchanan was Rear Admiral David Farragut, one of the Navy's greatest officers. Farragut was given a fleet that consisted of 17 ships, including four big sloops of war, and was told that iron-clad ships of the *Monitor* class were on their way. Although of dubious stability on the high seas, these would be more effective once inside the harbour in the fight against the *Tennessee*. Farragut planned to charge past Fort Morgan, with ships in tandem facing the fort protected by anchor chains and sand bags. The Monitors were to go in a separate column.

On 5 August 1864, Farragut launched his attack. An early morning flood-tide was washing into the harbour, which would carry any damaged ships along with it, while the winds would drive smoke into the eyes of the gunners at Fort Morgan. The USS *Brooklyn*, a wooden sloop of war equipped with a minesweeping device, would lead as Farragut's flagship. At 5.30 a.m. the squadron got under the way, Farragut climbing into the port main rigging to see what was going on, while the ship's captain sent up a quartermaster to secure the admiral to the rigging with a line.

The *Tennessee*, ready for just such a move, advanced out to meet the incoming ships, and a Monitor, the *Tecumseh*, made for the Southern ship. This move unfortunately took the iron ship into the path of a Southern mine which exploded. The captain gallantly stepped aside to allow one of the crew to escape, but by then the iron craft was sinking so quickly that the captain went down with his boat, taking another 92 crew with her, while only 21 got away safely.

Seeing more obstacles, the *Brooklyn*'s captain also backed his engine to avoid them. But Farragut ordered the squadron forward at flank speed, probably not uttering the famous quote attributed to him there, 'Damn the torpedoes, full speed ahead', which was not written until many years later. Whatever he said, the squadron carried on and soon passed the fort.

The *Tennessee* tried to ram several ships, but the speedier Northern engines allowed them to escape. Once in the harbour, the gunboats lashed to the protected ships were cut loose and headed after the Southern gunboats, the *Morgan*, the *Gaines* and the *Selma*. One soon surrendered, another beached, and the third

EUREKA.

▼ Farragut's ships surround the battered CSS *Tennessee* in Mobile Bay in this period Currier & Ives lithograph. The overall Confederate commander, Rear Admiral Francis Buchanan, was wounded in the first iron-clad battle and again at Mobile Bay.

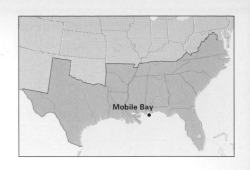

ran for the protection of Fort Morgan's guns, leaving only the *Tennessee*. Buchanan now took this ship right into the Federal squadron. She was rammed in turn by the *Monongahela*, the *Lackawanna* and the *Hartford* but suffered no significant damage, while her armour-plated sides protected her from the Federal cannon fire. However, because of defective fuses, she ceased firing at around 9.40 a.m. Finally, one Monitor battered her stern from 50 yds away, finally jamming her gun shutters and weakening her sides. Buchanan, his leg broken, was taken below.

Further artillery fire cut the tiller chains to her rudder head, so that the *Tennessee* could not be steered. At around 10.00 a.m., unable to fight further and battered by the Federal Monitors, the *Tennessee* surrendered. Mobile Bay was in Union hands.

COMMANDER JAMES D. JOHNSTON, C.S.N.

Realizing the impossibility of directing the firing of the guns without the use of the rudder, and that the ship had been rendered utterly helpless, I went to the lower deck and informed the admiral of her condition, and that I had not been able to bring a gun to bear upon any of our antagonists for nearly half an hour, to which he replied: 'Well, Johnston, if you cannot do them any further damage you had better surrender.'

With this sanction of my own views I returned to the gun-deck, and after another glance about the bay to see if there was any chance of getting another shot, and seeing none of the enemy's ships within range of our broadside guns, I went to the top of the shield and took down the boat-hook to which the flag had been lashed after having been shot away several times during the fight.

THE FALL OF ATLANTA

By 23 July it was obvious that Hood was unable to stop Sherman with desperate attacks, and the Federal general planned to move the Army of Tennessee rapidly to his right and block the only railway still running for the Confederates, the line between Atlanta and Macon. In the meantime, Federal works paralleled those of the Confederates around the city, and Northern guns opened up on the city itself. Civilians watched as shells turned their homes into piles of rubble. Civilian aid organizations gathered food and issued it to newly homeless citizens. On 26 July, as an indication of official pessimism, the Confederate Quartermaster General announced that he would order the vast amount of stores and manufacturing equipment that made the city a centre of production evacuated to Macon and eventually on to Milledgeville, the capital city of Georgia.

Hood had not entirely given up, though. On 27 July, he sent his cavalry to turn the Federal right, from whom he learned that Sherman was marching that way. He followed up his cavalry with parts of two infantry corps the next day. The Confederates planned to march out to Ezra Church to block the Federal advance. However, when they reached there they ran into the XV Corps who were already behind breastworks. Despite this, the Confederates charged

to take the position. Their attacks were in vain, and they lost another 5,000 men, while the Federals, protected behind their temporary breastworks, lost only 562 men. Hood no longer had enough men to continue his planned offensive manoeuvres. From now on, he would be forced to remain behind the city's fortifications. Both sides settled down for a formal siege.

Hood attempted to deceive Sherman into thinking that thousands of reinforcements were pouring into the city. He had all trains enter the city blowing whistles, hoping that the Federals would believe each train to be filled with troops. The result, however, was to make the city's train depot a target for Union cannoneers. Citizens threw up sandbag walls around pavements to protect both buildings and pedestrians.

Sherman meanwhile brought up bigger guns, 30-pounder Parrotts, rifled cannon, with the idea of knocking down buildings in town. While some citizens died in their beds as cannon shells roared through their houses, others dug bombproof shelters in their gardens in which to spend their nights. Some shells caused fires, which had to be fought by the 500 men who remained out of the service and in the city's volunteer fire companies.

▲ A contemporary Currier & Ives lithograph of the capture of Atlanta. The explosion center, which actually took place further out of town, was the destruction of the Confederate munitions which the Army of Tennessee was unable to take with it.

▼ U.S. Military Railroad engines used the old Atlanta railroad roundhouse even though the building around it was destroyed. The Union army made great use of its railroads, setting up its lines to support its troops, over which ran its own equipment.

While the infantry remained in the trenches, Sherman's cavalry was on the loose, tearing up tracks and destroying cars of the Macon Railroad and capturing and destroying a much needed Confederate supply wagon train. However, Sherman realized from their efforts that cavalry alone could not hold the railway and infantry would be needed. On 4 August Sherman ordered an attack on the railway at East Point by two infantry corps. The attack took the main breastworks that defended the railway line at East Point, but Sherman felt that he had gone far enough with the troops he had. He now concentrated on his army's siege works, digging parallel lines ever closer to the Confederate works. On 11 August the *New York Times* reported that, 'General Sherman is making gradual approaches and is very near the enemy's works, with works nearly as strong as theirs.'

On 28 August Federal troops drove back the Confederates and reached the West Point Railroad that ran from East Point to Red-Oak Station where they destroyed irreplaceable tracks and ties. The next few days saw more Federal units inching the Confederates further and further away from where they could defend their lifeline outside the city. In desperation, Hood sent two corps early on the 31st towards Jonesboro, where they were to attack the Federals threatening this line. If the attack were to fail, he told Hardee, the lead corps commander, the city must be evacuated. The Federals at Jonesboro were, however, well entrenched, and they easily repelled the Confederate attacks. By the next day Hood found his forces in a wholly untenable situation. Hardee's Corps had been cut off at Jonesboro, while the following corps, commanded by Stephen D. Lee, was pinned down between Hardee's troops and the city fortifications. A third corps had been almost shattered and

its survivors were making their way to Lovejoy as quickly as possible. All that Hood had in Atlanta was a small corps and the almost worthless Georgia militia.

Hood ordered Lee to disengage and prepare to protect the withdrawal of his evacuating forces. Meanwhile he loaded all the stores he could on the hundred railway carriages available and started them out of the city. What food that could not be packed away was given away to civilians, while any remaining rail stock was set on fire. The latter was a mistake because the carriages contained ammunition which exploded, lighting the night-time sky dramatically, but depriving Hood's surviving soldiers of much needed ammunition.

The Federals also saw the explosions and sent scouts to see what was happening. They found the Confederate works empty and on 2 September Sherman's advanced forces entered the city.

▲ A Union light artillery crew demonstrates the loading procedure for a 10-pounder Parrott rifle in a captured Confederate fort near Atlanta. The men wear their dress uniform short jackets, showing this image to have been taken away from any point of danger.

CAPTAIN JULIAN W. HINKLEY, 3RD WISCONSIN INFANTRY REGIMENT

We found more Union sentiment in Atlanta than anywhere else in the South. As our Brigade entered the city, at about nine o'clock at night, many of the women brought out buckets of water for us to drink. They were very bitter against Hood's army, which they said had robbed them of everything that could be carried off, with the excuse that the Yankees would steal it anyway. They were agreeably disappointed to find that the Yankees did not rob them of a thing.

CAMPAIGNING TO NO PURPOSE

▼ After Atlanta fell, Hood took his army west to try to draw Sherman to where he would destroy his army attacking the Confederates. Sherman followed Hood for a while, then returned to Atlanta to head to the sea. In the meantime, Hood went to his destruction outside Nashville.

After withdrawing from Atlanta, Hood gathered his battered Army of Tennessee at Lovejoy's Station and began to plan ways to regain the offensive. In the meantime, Sherman regrouped his army in Atlanta for some much needed rest and refitting. There he decided that rather than feed the entire civilian population, residents who would not swear allegiance to the Federal government should be forced to leave the city. In all, some 446 families, a total of around 1,600 people, became refugees, leaving behind not only their homes but also most of their possessions. Many of these people made their way to country relatives, but still others had no such places to go, and filled already crowded hotels and boarding houses such as their limited incomes would allow. Confederate officials protested, but Sherman replied that 'war is war and not popularity-seeking'.

While the Confederate infantry rested and resupplied, the brilliant cavalry officer N.B. Forrest set off on 16 September 1864, with 4,500 men on a raid against Sherman's lines of communications. Eight days later his troops captured Athens, Alabama, and by the 27th was in combat around Pulaski, Tennessee. By the end of the month his troops reached Lynchburg, Tennessee. On 1 October his men captured a blockhouse (a fortified wooden building often armed with a cannon or two) which overlooked vital rail lines and bridges, at Carter's Creek Station, Tennessee. The next day they fought at Columbia, Tennessee. By the end of October they were as far north as Fort Henry, site of Grant's early victory, where they captured the gunboat *Undine* and the boat *Mazeppa*, containing 9,000 pairs of shoes. However, they had been expected to join Hood in his move north to lure Sherman out of Atlanta. Instead, Forrest took his men and ships south up the Tennessee River towards Johnsonville, Tennessee. At Johnsonville, Forrest was forced to abandon the *Undine*, but did a great deal of damage to the supply lines around Nashville, as well as drawing out its forces. His raid, however, had peaked.

Greatly concerned, Davis visited Hood's army in late September. Hood requested that Hardee be removed from command. Davis then assigned Hardee to command the Department of South Carolina, Georgia, and Florida.

Following this, Hood set his army in motion in an attempt to draw Sherman out of Atlanta and force him into a fight that the Confederates could win. On 2 October the Army of Tennessee reached Sherman's supply line at Big Shanty and Kennesaw Water Tank, Georgia, where they cut the Western & Atlantic Railroad. Sherman reacted a couple of days later, sending Thomas to Nashville to command the defences there in case Hood would be rash enough to drive on that city. From his lines, he also sent troops north to help protect his supply lines. By 4 October he left only one corps in Atlanta, the rest heading after Hood.

At Allatoona, overlooking a railroad pass, the Confederates ran into a tough defending officer in Major-General John Corse. The Confederates attempted to bombard the dug-in Federals into surrender, but this failed. So Confederate infantry went in, taking some positions around the main line, but not the whole. As Sherman's men advanced to relieve the position, signal flags proclaimed that, although hidden by dense black powder smoke, it was still in Federal hands. As Sherman approached, the beaten Confederates withdrew, having lost almost 800 men out of the attacking force of 2,000; the Federals lost 700.

As a much larger Federal force approached, Hood withdrew to Gadsden, Alabama. Sherman followed, the two armies clashing at Resaca, La Fayette, and Rome, Georgia, on 12 October, and again four days later at Ship's Gap. Hood continued to move, heading out of Gadsden to Guntersville, Alabama, planning to move into Tennessee and further separate Sherman from Atlanta. The Tennessee River at Guntersville was too full to cross and, lacking

▶ Sherman ordered all civilians out of Atlanta prior to leaving on his famous march to the sea so that the city could be destroyed and thereafter be of no military use to the Confederate forces. Here civilians pack up to follow Sherman's orders.

trained pontoon troops, Hood was forced to continue west across Northern Alabama. When they reached Decatur on 26 October they found the Federals too strong and continued westward. By the end of the month they were in Tuscumbia, Alabama, with troops crossing the Tennessee at Florence.

Sherman's troops gathered in Tennessee to meet the Confederate threat. Sherman himself had other ideas. He pleaded with Grant for permission to give up what he felt was a wasted effort in chasing the faster moving Army of Tennessee throughout the wilds, and instead regroup his army in Atlanta. After gathering supplies, he would cut his supply line off entirely. Leaving Thomas to defend in Tennessee, his huge army would drive straight through Georgia, making for the Atlantic Ocean. During this march, his men would destroy much vital Southern industry, burn crops, and demoralize civilians. Neither Grant nor Lincoln thought much of the idea, preferring that he destroy Hood's army first. Sherman, however, wore them down, and they eventually agreed to the scheme. By 9 November, Lincoln having been safely re-elected, Sherman reorganized his army into three wings, cut his wagon train to a minimum, and prepared for the great adventure of the war. Hood would be on his own.

PRIVATE SAM R. WATKINS, 1ST TENNESSEE INFANTRY REGIMENT

For weeks and months the roads were filled with loaded wagons of old and decrepit people, who had been hunted and hounded from their homes with a relentless cruelty worse, yea, much worse, than ever blackened the pages of barbaric or savage history. I remember assisting in unloading our wagons that General Hood, poor fellow, had kindly sent in to bring out the citizens of Atlanta to a little place called Rough-and-Ready about half way between Palmetto and Atlanta. Every day I would look on the suffering of delicate ladies, old men, and mothers with little children clinging to them, crying 'O, mamma, mamma', and old women, and tottering old men, whose gray hairs should have protected them from the savage acts of Yankee hate and Puritan barbarity . . .

WINNING BACK THE VALLEY

By the second week of June 1864, Hunter's men coming south through the Shenandoah Valley were threatening the vital town of Lynchburg, Virginia. Lynchburg, a town of 8,000, boasted an arsenal, several army hospitals, and was a major hub of boat and rail transport. The loss of such a place was not acceptable and, although hard pressed, Lee detached Jubal Early with three infantry divisions and two artillery battalions – almost a quarter of the Army of Northern Virginia – to drive Hunter from the Valley. In fact, Early's instructions were more ambitious than just that. His aim was to repeat Stonewall Jackson's lightening campaign of 1862 and by terrifying the authorities in Washington, force Grant to send men back to defend the capital.

By 16 June, Hunter had besieged Lynchburg, but Early was on the way. The following day Hunter's men heard train after train blowing their whistles as they entered the town. Early's troops had linked up with John Breckinridge's outnumbered Confederates defending Lynchburg. Knowing that he would be unable to capture the rail centre, Hunter, who believed an entire corps had been sent as a reinforcement, sent out skirmishers to mask his withdrawal

the following day. He headed north. Early hesitated, missing an opportunity to destroy Hunter in his position around Lynchburg, but then on the next day followed the retreating Federals. Hunter abandoned the Valley, withdrawing into friendly territory in the new state of West Virginia. On 28 June he telegraphed army headquarters from Gauley, West Virginia, that his army was in good shape and his campaign had been 'extremely successful'.

Considering the Valley now safe, Early slowed his pace, the Stonewall Division, Jackson's old command, passing their old general's grave at Lexington in his last review. By 2 July, they had reached Winchester, where more than a hundred actions had been fought, where they were greeted by enthusiastic residents of this much fought-over place. Sigel, still in command in the Harper's Ferry area, sent out skirmishers against Early as he headed north towards him. On 3 July the sides clashed at Leetown, Darkesville, Martinsburg, North Mountain and North River Mills, West Virginia, and Buckton, Virginia. But Early's men were too many for the Federal defenders, who fled north, across the Potomac into Maryland. Word went out ahead of them that the Confederates were again heading

▼ Sheridan's army in the Valley of Virginia formed a huge camp, as shown by this contemporary sketch. Part of his wagon train of supplies is seen in the foreground, while his troops' tents stretch as far as can be seen beyond.

MAJOR HENRY KYD DOUGLAS, CONFEDERATE STAFF OFFICER

Harry Gilmor of the cavalry and I were riding together and went through the village together. At the end of it we saw some young ladies run out of a house and come to the fence, one of them calling me by name. We rode up to the fence to speak to them, forgetting there was nothing in our front. The girls were full of excitement and semi-hysterical laughter. 'Look there, the Yankees!' cried one, and before they could run away we saw the white jet of several rifles, and a ball buried itself in the gate-post, tumbling from it a glass from which Gilmor had just quaffed the water.

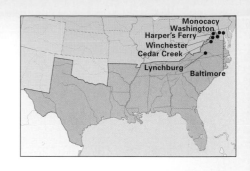

◄ Major General David Hunter had an especially undistinguished career as a Union general. Given the chance to be part of Grant's grand strategy in 1864, his failure in the Valley of Virginia gave Grant a chance to relieve him and he never held important command again.

north from the Valley. Again militias – as many as 24,000 – were called out as authorities in Washington watched the threat with grave concern. In Baltimore Major-General Lew Wallace, disgraced in Grant's eyes by his slow movements at Shiloh, gathered men from his command, including Ohio National Guard regiments who had been enlisted for only three months, and prepared to head west to defend the nation's capital. In the lines around Petersburg, men of the VI Corps were loaded onto boats at City Point to travel north to Washington to defend the city.

On 4 July Early's men were around Harper's Ferry, ready to cross the Potomac. This time the Harper's Ferry defences, armed with 100-pounder cannon, were too strong for Early to waste time on, so he took his men east to Shepherdstown where they crossed the Potomac. Once the Confederates began moving around Harper's Ferry, the Federals began pulling out, and the Confederates dashed in. There the hungry Southern troops found such delicacies as sardines, oysters, meat, wines, fruit, preserves, and alcohol. Many had the finest Independence Day, 4th of July, feast they'd had in years.

By the 6th they were in Hagerstown, with advance parties as far east as Antietam. There Early, obviously not as focused on his mission as Stonewall Jackson had been, spent a day sightseeing at the old battlefield, as well as visiting the father of one of his aides.

At Hagerstown, the Confederates found a non-slave-holding, prosperous population. They decided to demand $200,000 from the city government and population or they would burn the city in retaliation for the damage Hunter's men did in the Valley. This was to be delivered as a complete change of clothing for each man in the town and $20,000 in cash. Given four hours to get all this, the local banks put up the money, but the clothes were unavailable. Finally, the Confederates accepted the cash with several hundred suits, all the locals could manage to find, and the Southern troops moved on.

On the morning of 7 July, Confederate troops were positioned outside Frederick, one of the most important towns in Maryland.

Federal troops were already there, however, and the senior Confederate officer cancelled an attack on the town, fearing heavy losses in street fighting. At the approach of more Confederate infantry, the Federals withdrew from the city on the evening of 8 July.

They headed to Monocacy Junction where most of the Federal troops in the area had been gathering under Wallace and where a creek drew up a natural line of defence. There, reinforced by the first elements of the VI Corps to arrive on the scene, Wallace prepared to drive back this last Confederate invasion of the North.

▲ Jubal Early was not up to the brilliance of Stonewall Jackson, but still received the important job of repeating Jackson's campaign in the Valley of Virginia to relieve pressure from Lee at Petersburg. He was simply one of the best left ready for action by 1864.

THE ATTACK ON WASHINGTON

Several hours after daybreak on 9 July 1864, Wallace placed his troops along ridges on either side of the Washington Pike on the eastern side of the Monocacy River. The Frederick Branch Railroad and the Baltimore & Ohio Railroad both used a bridge that crossed the river in the centre of the Union line, and Wallace expected this bridge and the Pike bridge to be the Confederate goals. He therefore also ordered specifically chosen men to the western side of the river.

At about 9.30 a.m. the Confederate advance began, slowly at first, probing at the Federal defences. Their main attack was at the Federal centre, towards the bridges. Their cannon began pounding the Federal lines and by noon the wooden covered bridge over the river was on fire. Three times the Confederates attacked and three times they were pushed back. More troops came up on the Southern side, while Wallace, after the troops of the VI Corps arrived the previous night, received no more reinforcements. Finally, towards the late afternoon, the Confederates came forward in overwhelming numbers.

Obviously outnumbered, men of the 10th Vermont who had been defending the western side of the river, escaped single file under fire across the railway bridge to safety. Surprisingly few were knocked into the water approximately 45 ft below.

In the meantime, Southern troops under John B. Gordon had crossed the Monocacy south of the Federal position and headed towards the Federal left flank. Wallace withdrew his left back to the fences on the edge of the Washington Pike. Cheering, the Confederates charged twice and were thrown back twice. Then Gordon tried a third time, and the Federal line, badly battered, was broken as the sun began to set.

Wallace retreated towards Baltimore. The fighting had cost him some 1,880 men, but he had delayed Early's army for a vital day. During that day additional troops of the VI Corps filed into Washington's defences. These included 87 forts and redoubts built in a ring around the city north of the Potomac. In all, they were armed with 484 heavy and 33 field guns. Many of the heavy artillery men who had manned these forts earlier had been sent as infantry

▲ In the distance, Early sends out a Confederate skirmish line to probe the defences of Washington in his 1864 raid on the capital. The initial defence included militia, some garrison artillery, and Veteran Reserve Corps members, men who were incapable of active duty.

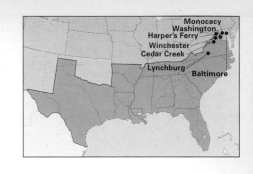

to the Army of the Potomac. There were still many troops available, including three regiments of Veteran Reserve Corps infantry, men incapable of field service who did guard and hospital duty.

In the meantime Early sent much of his cavalry towards Baltimore to threaten it and Point Lookout, a major prisoner of war camp. If the Confederates were able to free these prisoners, they could greatly enlarge their ranks. The cavalry, under Maryland native Colonel Harry Gilmor, was north-west of Baltimore by 10 July. The next morning his cavalry struck the Magnolia Station, capturing the morning train from Baltimore to Philadelphia and New York. The Confederates burned it and then waited to capture the next train coming along. This train Gilmor also set on fire, after running it onto a bridge to destroy both. Then he retired towards Towsontown.

It took two days for Early's weary troops to reach the outskirts of Washington. There, at dawn, the first of the Confederate infantry looked across the lines at Fort Stevens, held by 1,250 men and 126 cannon. Still others destroyed the estate of Francis Blair, a member of the Lincoln cabinet, in Silver Spring. Early himself reconnoitred the Federal defences, ordering a skirmish line to probe Fort Stevens.

Early was not happy with the strength of the city's works. His orders did not demand an attempt on the city. That evening he held a council of war in Silver Spring. His generals there agreed that the city would be hard to take, impossible to hold on to, and delaying there would prove dangerous. Nonetheless, they decided to probe the defences again the next day, at least to so threaten the Federals that they would not follow the retreating Confederates. They drew up their battle lines, partially to cover their retreat, and opened up with muskets on the fort.

One of those standing behind the fort's walls was Abraham Lincoln. Drawn by curiosity, the President was standing near a surgeon who suddenly keeled over, wounded. People nearby shouted at the President to take cover and, according to one eyewitness, reluctantly he did so.

That night Early began his withdrawal, back the way he came towards the Valley. Gilmor, unaware of Early's retreat, headed into Howard County as far as Brookeville on 13 July. But he soon learned of the failure before Washington, and was forced to retire as well.

Grant, aware that he had originally underestimated Early's raid, himself left his headquarters outside Petersburg to come to the Washington area for a conference of war. Finding that Hunter was unaware of even the positions of the Confederates, he accepted that luckless general's resignation, and summoned one of his most trusted lieutenants, Philip Sheridan, to take command of the troops around Washington and in the Valley to once and for all destroy Early's army.

▼ The home of Lincoln's Postmaster General Montgomery Blair in Silver Springs, Maryland, was visited by Early's raiding Confederates in the suburban Washington district. As seen in this photograph, they did some damage to the house in their visit.

MAJOR-GENERAL JOHN B. GORDON, C.S.A.

In the vortex of fire my favorite battle-horse, presented to me by my generous comrades, which had never hitherto been wounded, was struck by a Minié ball, and plunged and fell in the midst of my men, carrying me down with him. Ordinarily the killing of a horse in battle, though ridden by the commander, would scarcely be worth noting; but in this case it was serious. By his death I had been unhorsed in the very crisis of the battle. Many of my leading officers were killed or disabled. The chances for victory or defeat were at the moment so evenly balanced that a temporary halt or slight blunder might turn the scales. My staff were bearing orders to different portions of the field. But some thoughtful officer sent me a horse and I was again mounted.

THE DESTRUCTION OF EARLY'S ARMY

▲ Major-General Philip Sheridan, on the black horse centre waving the sword, leads a cavalry assault on the crumbling Confederate defences in this post-war lithograph of the Battle of Cedar Creek. In fact, Sheridan wore a small black slouch hat instead of the kepi shown here.

found this out. After a visit from Grant, Sheridan moved on 19 September to attack Early's divided army. He struck Early's division at Winchester, forcing it to fall back and Early called three divisions down from the north to reinforce this position. A Confederate counter-attack hit a gap in the Federal line, but the line still held and drove the Confederates back. The Confederates retreated to form a new line east and north of Winchester. As the Federals advanced, Early ordered this line abandoned, with a general retreat after a loss of almost 4,000 men. The Federals lost around the same.

Early felt lucky that he had managed to get as many men away as he did, and by the next day his troops were in defensive lines south of Strasburg on Fisher's Hill. Sheridan, holding high ground at Strasburg, sent one of his divisions around the Confederate left during the night of 21 September. Late the next afternoon they advanced, capturing Confederate works in the rear and flank as two other divisions stormed Fisher's Hill. The routed Confederates ran four miles south before their officers could rally them. Early had lost another 1,235 men, while Federal losses were only 528.

The Confederates fled to New Market while Sheridan halted, pleased with his successes. Three days later the Federals hit the road again, but moved slowly, burning railways and other property on their way to Staunton and Waynesboro. Early fell back to Brown's Pass in the Blue Ridge. It seemed that the entire Valley was Union. The Confederates had not given it up, however, and their cavalry struck Federal cavalry near Fisher's Hill on 6 October. Sheridan sent all his cavalry against this force, hitting them at Tom's Brook 9 October and thoroughly beating them.

Then, on 10 October, Sheridan gathered his infantry north across Cedar Creek, putting them in strong lines on either side of the Valley Pike. Early advanced after him, ending up only a couple of miles south of the Federal position on 14 October. The Massanutten Mountain overlooked the Federal line and a

Sheridan arrived at Monocacy Junction on 6 August and received orders to clear the Valley. His main force was the VI and XIX Corps and three divisions of cavalry. In total, he would have almost 35,000 infantry and artillery and 8,000 cavalry.

Early's men, close to 14,000, had fallen back to Bunker Hill, Virginia, to await Sheridan's move. As Sheridan's men gathered, the Confederates retired to Winchester. The Federals were on the road after them, and on 11 August, aware of overwhelming numbers against him, Early pulled back towards Cedar Creek. There his men dug in. Sheridan's men reconnoitred the Confederate line, which they found stiff, and, fearing for the safety of their supply line, retreated towards Berryville. Early did not realize the Federals were pulling back immediately, but on 17 August the Southern infantry got under way after Sheridan, who had withdrawn his main force towards Charles Town, West Virginia.

The Confederates followed, launching an attack on 21 August which failed largely because of a lack of coordination between the two forces which were making the attack. Early then sent troops towards Harper's Ferry. By 25 August, his troops were giving every appearance of making another drive towards Washington. Sheridan didn't send men across the Potomac, however, as Early had hoped, instead going to Berryville where his troops dug in fortifications that the Confederates could not possibly take. Moreover his position threatened Winchester.

Early's time was up. He was forced to send a full division to Lee's hard-pressed troops at Petersburg, and Sheridan quickly

◀ General Philip Sheridan, seen here as commanding general of the army, a post he was given on the retirement of William T. Sherman in 1884. He came into the army as a U.S. Military Academy cadet in 1852. He died a full general in 1888.

Confederate topographical engineer who had been on top of this mountain claimed that he could see how an attack could destroy the Federal position. Some of Early's generals made the climb to the top and agreed, and Early made plans to attack.

On the morning of 19 October, in a heavy early morning fog, the Confederates attacked. Unable to see the enemy until they were overrun, Federal artillery and even infantry were unable to put down enough fire to stop the attack. By the time the sun burned off the fog, most of the Union camp was in Confederate hands. Only the VI Corps, forced to a position north and west of Middletown, stood. However, much of the vigour had disappeared from the attack. Hungry Confederates stopped to rummage through Federal tents for food and clothes. Formations fell apart. In the meantime, it was noted that the Federals had not been routed, but simply walked away. It would not take much to turn the battle around.

Sheridan himself was in Washington when the attack hit. Receiving telegraphed news of the battle, he immediately boarded a train and headed back to the Valley. From the nearest station he mounted his horse and rode at a gallop towards his beaten army. Riding along his lines, waving his hat, he soon turned his men around and launched a counter-attack. The Confederates, who were expecting victory were shocked, and ran from the field, losing as many as 8,000 men in the process. Federal casualties were 5,665, but from this point on Early had no army left and the Valley was largely Union.

▼ Union cavalry attacks, their only mounted opponent being a Confederate artillery major, in this post-war lithograph of the 3rd Battle of Winchester. Behind the cavalry, centre, come a line of attacking Union infantry.

COLONEL J.H. KIDD, 6TH MICHIGAN CAVALRY REGIMENT

The full scope of the calamity which had befallen our arms burst suddenly into view. The whole battle field was in sight. The valley and intervening slopes, the fields and woods, were alive with infantry, moving singly and in squads. Some entire regiments were hurrying to the rear, while the confederate artillery was raining shot and shell and spherical case among them to accelerate their speed. Some of the enemy's batteries were the very ones just captured from us. It did not look like a frightened or panic stricken army, but like a disorganized mass that had simply lost the power of cohesion.

DEATH OF THE CONFEDERACY

27 OCT **1864** CSS *Albemarle* sunk at Plymouth, North Carolina

8 NOV Lincoln re-elected

16 NOV Sherman begins his march to the sea

21 NOV Hood begins his attempt to take Nashville, Tennessee

29 NOV Spring Hill, Tennessee – Hood fails to trap a Federal column

30 NOV Battle of Franklin, Tennessee – Hood massacres his army

2 DEC Siege of Nashville – Hood digs in to capture Nashville

10 DEC Sherman's army reaches Savannah, Georgia

13 DEC Fall of Fort McAllister – Union ships can now attack Savannah

15 DEC Battle of Nashville – Federals destroy Hood's army

20 DEC Evacuation of Savannah – Hardee's troops escape Sherman's men

24 DEC Attack on Fort Fisher, North Carolina – Federals fail to close the last Southern port

15 JAN **1865** Second attack on Fort Fisher – Federals close the last Southern port

19 JAN Sherman orders a march into South Carolina

5 FEB Battle of Hatcher's Run – Federals again probe Lee's right

17 FEB Fall of Columbia, South Carolina

22 FEB Fall of Wilmington, North Carolina

11 MAR Fall of Fayetteville, North Carolina

16 MAR Battle of Averasborough, North Carolina – Confederates unsuccessfully attempt to stem Sherman's march through the Carolinas

19 MAR Battle of Bentonville, North Carolina – Confederates make a last major try to destroy Sherman's army

25 MAR Battle of Fort Stedman – Lee's last offensive is an attempt to capture a point in Union lines at Petersburg

31 MAR Battles of White Oak Road and Dinwiddie Court House, Virginia – Confederates forced back on their right

1 APRIL Battle of Five Forks, Virginia – Lee's right folds and he must abandon Petersburg

2 APRIL Evacuation of Richmond – Confederate government flees as Federals enter southern Petersburg lines

3 APRIL Union occupation of Petersburg and Richmond

6 APRIL Battle of Sailor's Creek – Federals press Lee's army

9 APRIL Surrender of the Army of Northern Virginia at Appomattox Court House

12 APRIL Surrender of Mobile, Alabama

14 APRIL Assassination of Abraham Lincoln

16 APRIL Surrender of the Army of Tennessee near Durham Station, North Carolina

4 MAY Surrender of the Department of Alabama, Mississippi, and East Louisiana

12 MAY Battle of Palmito Ranch, Texas – Last land battle of the war, a Confederate victory

26 MAY Surrender of the Army of Trans-Mississippi

3 JUNE Surrender of Confederate Navy forces on the Red River

6 NOV Surrender of the CSS *Shenandoah* – The last Confederate flag to be struck

Many Southerners realized after Vicksburg and then Atlanta fell, as they watched Lee's mighty army dwindle in Petersburg's trenches, and as port after port was permanently closed, that the end was near and it would not end favourably for the South. Still, there was always that hope that shortage of cotton would lead foreign powers to intervene, or casualties would finally force the North to end the war and grant the South independence. Lincoln and his generals were determined otherwise, however, and they pressed forward as their men told themselves that the next battle would have to be the last.

SHERMAN BEGINS HIS MARCH

On 7 November 1864, Grant gave his final approval to Sherman for his planned march from Atlanta to a point on the Atlantic coast. Sherman's last concern was for Nashville, but Thomas, who commanded there, telegraphed him on 12 November that he had no fears of coming to any harm, adding that he believed that Sherman should have a clear road. On receiving that, Sherman telegraphed back 'all right', then ordered the telegraph lines cut and a bridge burned to the rear. Sherman's forces were on their own.

Sherman broke his army into wings, the right containing the XV and XVII Corps; the left with the XIV and XX Corps. The cavalry was organized as a separate division under a general who had been a West Point cadet as recently as 1861, Judson Kilpatrick. In all, he had 59,329 infantry, 5,063 cavalry, and 1,812 artillery. Sherman wrote later, 'The most extraordinary efforts had been made to purge this army of non-combatants and of sick men, for we knew well that there was to be no place of safety save with the army itself; our wagons were loaded with ammunition, provisions, and forage, and we could ill afford to haul even sick men in the ambulances . . .'

The army brought only 65 cannon with it, in batteries made up of only four guns instead of the standard six. In all, the army would be accompanied by 2,500 wagons and 600 ambulances. Each wagon was to carry all the forage its team would need. Each soldier would bring 40 rounds of ammunition with him, while enough for 200 rounds per man was carried in the wagons.

The men themselves were full of fight and ready to go. James Connolly, a field grade officer in the 123rd Illinois Infantry, wrote home on 9 November: 'I suppose this is my last chance for writing until we reach some coast either at Mobile or Savannah, so I will take advantage of it. The weather is fine, the army in excellent spirits, and I am really anxious for the campaign. After the triumph which I am sure the Union cause met with at the ballot box yesterday, it will be glorious to ride clear through the Confederacy. There is to me something really romantic in the conception of this campaign, and I am really charmed with it.'

On 14 November Kilpatrick led his cavalry out of Atlanta, while infantrymen in the city began to destroy its public buildings, ranging from the clothing manufacturing depots to the train station. The XX Corps went north to Decatur and Stone Mountain to destroy bridges and tear up railroads there. It became clear that the Confederates could not move back into the city and begin production of war-time goods there immediately after Sherman had left. Indeed, it would be years before the city reached its pre-war standard of living, and Atlanta's residents today still feel ill-will against Sherman and his troops.

The Federals had two concerns. The first was the Confederate military but the second was bad weather, which would turn dirt roads into bogs. Nonetheless, full of confidence, on the morning of 15 November most of the infantry headed off south-east towards Jonesboro. Their route took them to threaten both Macon and Augusta, both places where much Confederate war material was produced. The actual goal, however, was Georgia's capital, Milledgeville, some 100 miles away. The rest of Sherman's army left Atlanta mostly in ashes on the 16th. Behind them a tower of black smoke indicated where Atlanta was.

Georgia had its own state army and its governor, Joe Brown, now called all men between the ages of 16 and 55 to arms to stop Sherman. But the state army consisted of only a handful of men, and not many were left from one military organization or another to join an emergency militia. With Hood concentrating on operations in Tennessee, there were relatively few Confederate troops to get in Sherman's way.

Sherman's men learned how to destroy railroad tracks quickly. Special tools had been devised for ripping up the rails and twisting

▼ Sherman divided his forces going from Atlanta to Savannah into two main columns which swept through Georgia with essentially no defending force facing them. Beauregard, in Charleston, South Carolina, had only 17,000 men to defend all the Carolinas and Georgia, which also faced Union troops on their coastlines.

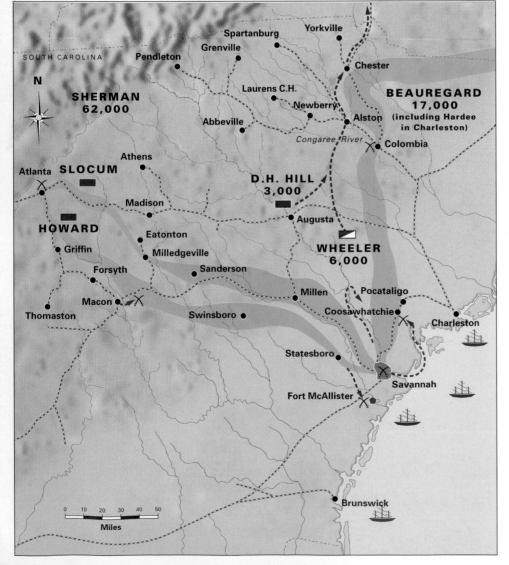

▲ A post-war painting by Stanley M. Arthurs of Sherman's men marching through Georgia. The wearing by one officer of a sash in the field, especially this late in the war, is suspect, but otherwise the painting is a good representation of Union troops in 1864.

CHAPLAIN LEVI GLEASON, 2ND MINNESOTA VOLUNTEER INFANTRY REGIMENT

I was surprised to find the people of the South so ignorant. I think but a small part of the common people can read or write. I was often asked, 'What state are you from?' and when I would answer 'Minnesota,' they would reply, 'Minnesota! Why I never hearn of that yer State.' Almost everybody from eight years old and upward in the South smoke and chew tobacco. It looked rather odd to see little girls chew tobacco. The common people have but little force of character. They are poor, ignorant, dirty imbecile creatures. The rich count labor dishonorable.

them around a telegraph pole or tree when red hot. A group from the head of the column would stop and do this task while the rest of the army passed, then move out towards the end of the army.

General orders issued at the beginning of the march called for the men to 'forage liberally on the country'. Bands of some 50 hand-picked soldiers under an officer or two, often riding mules, roamed the country around the army's flanks and followed these orders to the letter. Called 'Sherman's bummers', they brought back great amounts of vegetables and meat to supplement the small supply of hard tack and salt pork the army quartermasters brought with them. Sherman himself noticed a soldier 'with a ham on his musket, a jug of sorghum-molasses under his arm, and a big piece of honey in his hand'. The soldier proceeded to quote Sherman's orders to the amused general. While Sherman didn't discipline the soldier, he did tell him that those orders pertained only to the regular authorized bands of bummers.

THE MARCH TO THE SEA

Sherman's men spread out while Sherman himself stayed with the left wing. Luck was with them in that the weather was cold but clear. Sherman personally directed the destruction of the railway line at Lithonia on 17 November so that passing infantry saw the buildings burning as they marched through there. On 18 November, they marched between the Ocmulgee and Oconee rivers in Georgia, with troops destroying some four miles of track on the Yellow River. The army had enough pontoons to make a 900-yard bridge for each corps whenever they had to cross a river and the advanced parties soon became adept at quickly improvising bridges from available lumber.

Civilians hid their valuables ahead of the advancing army. Their slaves, however, often revealed the hiding places so that soldiers became bedecked with valuable jewellery, their knapsacks filled with silverware. At least one soldier was seen wearing a uniform coat from the Revolutionary War, obviously a family heirloom.

Many of the slaves who pointed out hiding places of valuables joined the column carrying everything they owned. Freedom with an unknown future was better than slavery with a predictable one. Many of them were hired by Federal soldiers to carry their knapsacks and muskets. Rain began to fall on the afternoon of the 19th and continued to the 21st, worrying some of the officers who feared being trapped in Georgia as Napoleon had been in Russia. Indeed,

that is exactly what Davis and other high ranking Confederates had said would happen. But the rain stopped and within a day the roads were reported excellent for marching. So they would continue for the rest of the raid.

On 21 November, some of Kilpatrick's cavalry entered the town of Griswoldville, site of one of the Confederacy's few revolver-manufacturing facilities. They burned down the plant, along with the railway station and some other buildings. The next day a small body of Confederate cavalry hanging around Sherman's flanks attacked some of the troops there, causing minor casualties before being driven back by infantry who took up defensive positions around the Duncan Farm. The largest battle of the campaign was fought when an apparently drunken Georgia militia general, P.J. Phillips, sent inexperienced boys against hardened Federal infantry again and again. Driven back every time, and finally retreating in the safety of darkness, the Confederates suffered over 500 casualties compared to Federal casualties of 62.

The following day Federal troops entered Georgia's capital of Milledgeville on the heels of a fleeing Governor and members of the state legislature, whose last action was to pass a levy en masse for troops. Delighted soldiers held their own legislative session, rescinding Georgia's measure of secession. Piles of state currency were discovered and used for lighting cigars. Other soldiers

▼ *Left*: Sherman's men became expert in destroying rail lines during their march through Georgia. Rails were heated red-hot, then twisted around trees to become 'Sherman's bowties'. The Confederacy, with few industrial resources, was largely unable to repair these lines.

▼ Outraged by the Confederate use of land-mines, called 'torpedoes' then, Sherman ordered Confederate prisoners at the head of his column to find and unearth mines with picks and shovels. Confederates pioneered the use of land mines during the Peninsular Campaign in 1862.

162

plundered the state library, carrying off useless law books by the armful. On the 25th the army left Milledgeville, blowing up the state arsenal and burning the bridge across the Oconee once they had crossed it.

Confederate cavalry, fearing that Augusta was Sherman's next goal, placed their men between Milledgeville and Augusta. Hardee was ordered to command such troops as he could find in Georgia to make a stand before Sherman wherever he should go. Sherman, however, was not planning to going to Augusta. Instead, on 26 November, his troops entered Sandersville while cavalry from both sides clashed on the 27th at Waynesborough. In the day-long fight of attack and counter-attack, dismounted Federal cavalry drove the Southerners off. Again, more miles of railroad were destroyed by Sherman's experienced vandals.

The Confederates now had troops on the way to Augusta, while Hardee's men were between Sherman and Savannah. By 1 December, however, Sherman's army was at the halfway point between Atlanta and Savannah. Two days later he personally entered the town of Millen where he waited for word from his various columns.

Among measures Davis instigated to stop Sherman was the use of land-mines, then called torpedoes. On 8 December, the horse ridden by a staff officer in the XVII Corps stepped on one of these mines, killing the horse and blowing all the flesh off one of the officer's legs. Outraged, Sherman ordered Confederate prisoners at the head of the column to find and unearth these mines with picks and shovels. Fortunately for all concerned no more mines were discovered until the army was outside Savannah.

By 8 December, the army was near the sea. The land had changed, with fields of corn giving away to rice fields. By the next day their advance elements reached the areas south of Savannah, skirmishing at Cuyler's Plantation, Monteith Swamp, and on the Ogeechee Canal between Eden and Pooler Stations. Finally on 9 and 10 December Sherman's leading corps were outside the defences of the city, the XIV Corps on the left, touching the Savannah river, the XX Corps next, then the XVII, and on the right, the XV. Savannah was completely invested. But its defences were formidable and its commander, Hardee, was one of the army's top soldiers. Sherman's men were not safe yet. Outside Savannah's harbours the Federals knew ships filled with much needed food, clothing, and rations were waiting. Now would come the hardest part of the march to the sea.

▼ Southern refugees on the move from their destroyed homes. They headed into Confederate-held territory where they were highly unpopular as they did no work but used precious resources such as housing, fuel, and food.

CAPTAIN JULIAN W. HINKLEY, 3RD WISCONSIN VOLUNTEER INFANTRY

Our first work was to destroy the Milledgeville arsenal, in which was stored a great quantity of Confederate arms and ammunition. We carried out and threw into the river, all of the ammunition in the magazine, and burned up all the arms and equipment. Besides several thousand stands of good arms, there were a lot of old-fashioned rifles and shot-guns, and thousands of pikes and bowie knives that had been manufactured by the State for the militia, with which to repel Yankees.

THE SIEGE OF SAVANNAH

Inside the city's defences, which had been prepared over a period of years, were some 10,000 Confederate regulars and militia under the command of William Hardee. The garrison was of mixed quality. Next to the 1st Georgia Regulars, a battle-tested regiment that had seen continuous service since 1861, was an inexperienced regiment of junior reserves, with no one over 18 years old.

Before he could tackle these defences, though, Sherman had to make contact with the fleet he knew was waiting offshore and get the vitally needed supplies they had. Fort McAllister prevented such a move; it sat high on a bluff on the south bank of the Ogeechee River, 15 miles below Savannah. The fort walls were made of logs and earth, holding some 22 heavy-calibre guns and 150 men who had defied all previous attempts to overrun it. U.S. Navy warships had made several attempts to blast the fort into submission, but all had failed.

Sherman detached a 1,500 man division of the XV Corps under Brigadier-General William Hazen to work their way around the city and attack the fort. During the afternoon of 13 December, troops

were in position to assault the fort. The fort's commander, Major George W. Anderson, was determined to hold the fort to the end. He and his men had spent the days before the 13th adding to its landward-side defences. They'd built *chevaux-de-frise*, logs through which were driven sharpened wood stakes that faced an enemy like a row of bayonets, and *abatis*, brush cut down and piled facing the enemy, both of which were excellent for breaking up charging unit formations. They had also buried 13-inch shells with fulmite of mercury fuses as land mines outside the fort's walls.

Nervously Sherman watched as to where Hazen's attack would fall. Finally, an hour before dark, he 'saw Hazen's troops come out of the dark fringe of woods that encompassed the fort, the lines dressed as on parade, with colors flying, and moving forward with a quick, steady pace. Fort McAllister was then all alive, its big guns belching forth dense clouds of smoke, which soon enveloped our assaulting lines. One color went down, but was up in a moment. On the lines advanced, faintly seen in the white sulfurous smoke; there was a pause, a cessation of fire; the smoke cleared away,

▲ Civilians flee Savannah after Sherman's troops captured Tybee Island in December 1864. Stories of Sherman's men looting and burning wherever they went preceeded the Union columns, but Savannah escaped with little harm.

▶ William J. Hardee was the author of the stand drill system used by both sides at the beginning of the war. Although offered army command, he declined it and rose no higher than a corps commander in the Confederate Army.

CAPTAIN JULIAN W. HINKLEY, 3RD WISCONSIN VOLUNTEER INFANTRY

The country was broken up into a mass of ditches, dykes, and canals. We found that our only road was along a narrow dyke, and that we should either have to return or charge them in single file. We did not retreat. In less time than it takes to tell this story, we had the mill. They gave us one volley and hit nobody. We did not fire a shot. They escaped with their guns and ammunition, but we captured all their provisions, including their breakfast cooking on the fire. For the first time in three days we had all that we wanted to eat.

and the parapets were blue with our men, who fired their muskets in the air, and shouted so that we actually heard them, or felt that we did.'

In all, there were 71 Confederates casualties, while Union troops had 134 casualties, most of which were caused by the land mines.

That night Sherman and his staff went out by boat to the Federal ships and three days later the first of the many Federal transports arrived up the Ogeechee with their much needed rations and clothing, as well as heavy artillery for the siege of Savannah. Perhaps even more important for the men were the bags of mail waiting for them. Finally they could start writing home again.

With the fall of Fort McAllister, it was obvious to all that Hardee could not hold the city in a long siege against Sherman's numbers. On 17 December Sherman sent a message to Hardee calling on him to surrender and avoid such a siege. Hardee requested a day

◀ Hardee pulled his garrison safely out of Savannah over a narrow bridge so that they could fall back north, join up with survivors of the Army of Tennessee and attempt to defend the Carolinas from Sherman's men.

to consider the demand and then, a day later, sent his refusal. The Federals were ordered to be ready to make an attack on Hardee's entire line. At the same time, Sherman met the commander of Union forces already in South Carolina, Major-General John G. Foster, and arranged for Foster to seal Savannah from the east so that Hardee's forces would be completely trapped.

Hardee, however, did not wait to be trapped. His engineers, lacking regulation pontoons, gathered all the rice barges they could and tied them end to end to construct a makeshift bridge over the Savannah River. On 20 December, under cover of darkness, the Confederates marched out of their works, leaving their cannon behind, across the rickety bridge to safety in South Carolina. Panic hit the streets of the city they were leaving, with soldiers remembering scenes of women and children running and screaming in the streets, while looters knocked down doors looking for anything of value, and guns being fired everywhere.

The Confederates were thoroughly demoralized. Many of them fired their weapons in the air on their retreat. One staff officer, after vainly ordering them to desist, dismounted, grabbed a weapon, and shot a private just who had just fired his weapon into the air, and killed him on the spot. Despite this, Hardee had managed to drum up the largest force to face Sherman. It would need time and work to rebuild. The question was, would there be enough time?

In the meantime, the first Federals entered the city of Savannah the next day and immediately set about removing the many mines from the river and turning the city into a major Federal supply point. Now the men had completed their march to the sea and could take a brief rest, while Sherman presented the city of Savannah as a Christmas present to Abraham Lincoln and a delighted northern population.

THE BATTLE OF FRANKLIN

As Sherman had apparently lost interest in Hood and his Army of Tennessee, Hood also looked elsewhere for his grand stroke. He now planned to cross the Tennessee River, seize Nashville, and then invade Kentucky. From there he would head east to threaten Grant's flank and rear. By 21 November 1864, he was on his way from Florence, Alabama with a combined force of some 8,000 cavalry and 30,000 infantry.

The next day Major-General John Schofield began pulling back towards Columbia. Both Federal and Confederate forces headed towards Columbia. In fact, it was Federal troops who first got to Columbia in any strength. There they found cavalry skirmishing, but their heavier columns cleared the town. The rest of Schofield's men arrived there on the 24th, taking an important crossing of the Duck River that Hood much needed. Schofield dug in both south and north.

By the evening of 27 November, the Army of Tennessee was in position on Schofield's southern front. Expecting Hood to turn his position, Schofield moved his entire force from the southern side of the river to the northern side under cover of darkness, afterwards partially destroying the railway and pontoon bridges on which his men had crossed. A concern to Schofield was the information, actually false, that Forrest had already crossed the Duck to the east above Columbia. In fact, Forrest did not cross until the evening of the 28th, and Hood's men followed him rather than attempting a river crossing under fire.

By the afternoon of the 29th, most of Hood's army was near Spring Hill, Tennessee, on the main road to Nashville, some 10 miles behind Schofield and apparently in a position to trap him and his troops who were so vitally needed for the defence of Nashville. Forrest led the way, but came upon two Federal regiments in Spring Hill, who drove him off and then just past noon fell back east of the town and began entrenching. Hood apparently did not intend to trap Schofield, however, but planned instead the next morning to head for Nashville to capture that city before Schofield's men could arrive. He therefore did not give positive orders to seize the Columbia-Franklin Pike. However the Confederates attacked the Federal position there, but were unable to carry it. Hood sent one brigade to cut the pike towards the north, but otherwise was apparently little concerned. The brigade's attack failed, and the Confederates were allowed to stand down, cook their meals, and turn in for the night.

Meanwhile Schofield, determined that Hood was moving on the pike, started his troops moving quickly from Columbia towards Franklin through Spring Hill. That night Schofield got his men past the sleeping Confederates into Franklin's pre-prepared fortifications. The two forces were so close that the Federals were reported coming over to Confederates gathered around fires to light their pipes. Hood was awoken with news of the passing Federals, but only called for a skirmish line to fire into their ranks, and promptly rolled over and

▶ This post-war lithograph of the Battle of Franklin shows terrain far more rugged than the flatter area around Franklin. The Confederates, too, are much more uniform than they actually appeared. But fighting was as close and even more deadly than shown.

▶ U.S. Military Railroad Construction Corps men were amazing in their ability to build huge bridges very quickly over deep gorges. The result was that little permanent damage was done by Confederate cavalry raids. Lincoln said one looked as if it had been built of bean poles.

▲ John Schofield, a West Point graduate, was teaching physics at Washington University, St. Louis, Missouri, when the war began. Originally commissioned as a major of volunteers, by 1864 he rose to command of the Army of the Ohio, left behind to defend Tennessee when Sherman began his march.

went back to sleep. The advance troops of Schofield's men reached the fortifications around Franklin about dawn.

Hood, however, was furious to discover Schofield's escape. He put his men on the road after Schofield immediately and by noon his first troops reached a small valley some 3.5 miles from Franklin. Hood himself, strapped into the saddle with his wooden leg rubbing his stump raw, went to the front an hour later. Against the advice of all his subordinates, he immediately called for a frontal assault on the strong Federal works. The Federal rear rested on the Harpeth River, and troops crossing on either flank could cut off Schofield, but this alternative was rejected out of hand. Moreover, he would not wait for his artillery and third infantry corps, but advanced with the two corps in the field. Hood hoped that if he smashed Schofield at Franklin, Thomas would have to give up Nashville.

At about 4.00 p.m. on 30 November, Hood's columns emerged from the woods, advancing across a broad plain towards the Federal entrenchments. They ran into two detached brigades in a forward work, which they overran. Then the Confederates hit the main works occupied by five Federal brigades who held. The Confederates finally poked through a point on the main line, near the Carter house, but a reserve brigade rushed forward and retook the ground. Men pinned down on either side of the works lay close to the earth, loading and then holding their muskets over the works and firing blindly into the mass just yards away on the other side.

FIRST SERGEANT ROBERT A. JARMAN, 27TH MISSISSIPPI VOLUNTEER INFANTRY REGIMENT

We did not find Bate's division, but instead, when about forty steps from the works we received a volley of musketry that made a considerable thinning in our lines, but we raised a shout and went at them with loaded guns and carried the works by storm, except where Manigault's brigade was; they ran, and left us exposed on our right to a terrible cross fire down our lines that told sadly next morning from the dead and wounded on the field. During the fight we ran short of ammunition; but caught a Federal ordnance bearer from the opposite side of the works and pulled him over to us with a box full of cartridges, about one thousand, when we were again in good shooting fix . . .

Hood ordered wave after wave to attack. After dark the guides on either side of the regiments, who normally held small flags to mark the regimental front alignment, held torches, making perfect targets. But the Confederates could not break the Federal lines and by 9.00 p.m. gave it up. Six Confederate generals were killed in the assault, including one of their best, Patrick Cleburne, known as the 'Stonewall Jackson of the West' as well as 6,200 men, a larger number than died in Pickett's Charge. Schofield lost 2,326 men and that night withdrew to Nashville.

THE SIEGE OF NASHVILLE

By 1 December 1864, Schofield's troops had reached Nashville and begun taking their places in the semi-circle that formed the defence south of the Tennessee state capital. Both flanks rested on the Cumberland River. Hood pressed his battered troops on after Schofield's men without taking time to reform smashed units or even adequately to take care of the many wounded left in the little town of Franklin.

Hood himself was no longer operating in a world of reality. The march to and the battle of Franklin, he felt, created an 'improved morale of the army'. Captain James Dinkins, a staff officer with the Army of Tennessee, was more accurate when he later said that after Franklin the men's 'hearts were filled with gloom and sorrow'. Moreover, by now the average Confederate soldier was poorly clad in below freezing temperatures, marching over snow-covered icy roads. Overcoats, never well supplied in the Confederate Army, were largely missing.

Even Hood could see that he could not force his way through the well designed works around Nashville with the troops he had on hand. He might have tried to bypass Nashville, cutting Thomas's supply line to the rear, but instead he opted to dig in along a line parallel to the Federal defences. He did not want to starve Thomas out; indeed, as both lines left the rear of the city open, with its supply line to the North, it would have been impossible. Instead he hoped for a rash attack by the Virginia-born Thomas which would allow him to counter-attack against a badly bloodied Federal force.

Nor did Hood ever consider retreating after the battle of Franklin. He felt that the men should have a chance of one final effort to revive the Confederacy's declining hopes. His numbers were so thin that his infantry alone could not match the Federal front, and he was forced to use dismounted cavalry on either flank to fill the gaps between the end of his infantry lines and the river.

▲ The view from the state capital on a tall hill in the center of Nashville, Tennessee, shows a relatively rural town beyond. The capital was well fortified by Union troops throughout the war, part of whose garrison used the officer's wall tent in the foreground.

Back with Meade's army, Grant tried to get Thomas to hit Hood's troops immediately. 'If Hood is permitted to remain quietly about Nashville,' he telegraphed Thomas on 2 December, 'you will lose all the road back to Chattanooga and possibly have to abandon the line of the Tennessee. Should he attack you it is all well, but if he does not you should attack him before he fortifies.' Later that day he telegraphed again, 'After the repulse of Hood at Franklin, it looks to me that instead of falling back to Nashville we should have taken the offensive against the enemy where he was.'

Thomas was not going to attack until he was fully prepared, although he planned to attack as soon as he thought his chances for success were good enough. He waited for cavalry that had been in the countryside to return, as well as for more infantry reinforcements. Moreover, Thomas considered the weather was too bad to allow an attack and that the longer he waited, the more it would demoralize the Confederate forces. As one 59th Illinois infantryman wrote home on 2 December, 'It rained all night and cold as blixen this a.m.' Indeed the weather varied from snow to rain that froze as temperatures fell below zero. The mud and frozen ground proved difficult for the gloveless Confederates in which to dig entrenchments, something that did not bother the Federals who were protected by fortifications that had been prepared a long time before. Of course, the resulting Confederate works were of poor quality as a result, making an eventual Federal attack more likely to succeed.

Grant was furious. 'Attack Hood at once and wait no longer for a remnant of your cavalry,' he telegraphed on 6 December. Thomas replied that he would, although he considered moving without his cavalry risky. And, in fact, he did not attack on that day or the next.

'Why not attack at once?' Grant telegraphed Thomas on 8 December. Thomas did not attack. 'If Thomas has not struck yet, he ought to be ordered to hand over his command to Schofield,' Grant telegraphed Washington. 'I am in hopes of receiving a dispatch

CAPTAIN WILLIAM G. LE DUC, QUARTERMASTER CORPS, U.S. ARMY

On the arrival of reinforcements (A.J. Smith and his veterans) the weather turned cold and severe for the latitude of Nashville. Rain, snow, sleet and freezing nights were bad for the rebel army, unfed, unclothed, and with no suitable tent covering. Every day's delay was for their ruin. This was not understood at Washington or at Grant's headquarters. They feared that the deliberate Thomas would allow Hood to cross the Cumberland River into Kentucky; but of that there was never the least danger at any time. Hood had reached the limit of his rash move.

from you to-day announcing that you have moved,' he telegraphed on 11 December. 'Delay no longer for weather or reinforcements.' Thomas said again that he would as soon as weather would allow.

Never terribly patient, Grant now authorized a trusted subordinate to go to Nashville and relieve Thomas as soon as he got there. At the same time, he told his subordinate not to deliver the order or have it published until he got to the city and handed it personally to Thomas. Had Thomas finally attacked by that point, he was simply to destroy the order and forget it had ever been issued.

Even this wasn't enough. Grant decided to go to Nashville himself. When he reached Washington, however, he found a dispatch from Thomas announcing that the weather was right, his reinforcements were on hand, and he was definitely going to move right away. Grant waited near the telegraph office in the War Department, next to the Executive Mansion, to await word of Thomas's eventual attack.

▼ This view of part of Fort Negley, on the left of the Union trenches, is typical of the well developed line of Union fortifications that Hood's battered army had no chance of defeating.

► John Bell Hood, an adopted son of Texas, was an excellent regimental and brigade commander but higher command was beyond him. In poor health, with a missing leg and useless arm, during the campaign, he squandered resources in useless attacks.

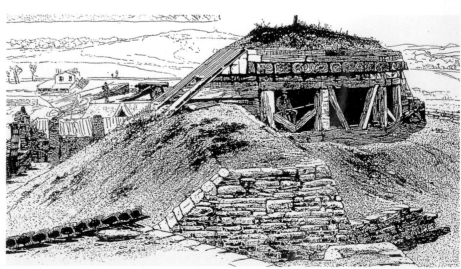

THE DESTRUCTION OF HOOD'S ARMY

The goal of every senior Civil War general in battle was essentially the destruction of his opponent's army. Lee tried this at Chancellorsville and again at Gettysburg. But, with the exception of the army surrendered at Vicksburg, no army was destroyed in battle until Thomas pounced on Hood. That battle, agonizing as the wait was for Grant, proved the most successful single battle of the war.

Thomas's men were in two lines, the combat troops, including a number of U.S. Colored Troops, were in the first line, while garrison and quartermaster troops filled the second line. On his right were 12,000 cavalrymen armed with new repeating carbines and rifles, while the IV and XXIII Corps filled the rest of the line. along with the U.S.C.Ts and troops recently arrived from Missouri.

At 3.00 a.m. on 14 December 1864, Thomas called in his top commanders to a meeting. He issued his orders for the battle that would begin the next day, briefing each of them on the role that his troops would play. According to his plan, the troops would be roused at 4.00 a.m. and be ready to attack across the 20-mile-wide front two hours later. The subordinates went back to their commands, and briefed their division and brigade commanders. By the evening the whole army knew that the 15th would be the day.

Anxious for the event, the Federals rose early and were ready well before 6.00 a.m. Indeed, word of the attack had spread among the civilians and hundreds of them gathered on a high hill behind Federals lines to watch the attack. A dense fog, however, delayed their attack. The sun burned off the fog only slowly, and as the hours ticked by, many high ranking Federals despaired of making the attack. Thomas was sure to lose his command. Shortly after 8.00 a.m., however, the orders for the attack were given. Confederate artillery opened up, but there were not enough guns available to stop the Federal forces.

'When the great array of the troops began to move forward in unison the pageant was magnificently grand and imposing. Far as the eye could reach the lines and masses of blue, over which the nation's emblem flaunted proudly moved forward in such perfect order that the heart of the patriot might easily draw from it the happy presage of the coming glorious victory,' wrote the IV Corps commander.

Some 40,000 Federals hit the first Confederate line. Demoralized and without adequate food, shelter, or clothing, The Confederates fought surprisingly bravely. Hood, whose headquarters were at the Overton Farm six miles away from the angle in the Confederate line that was first hit, was unaware what was going on. However, as soon as he heard of the attack, at around 11 a.m., he sent a brigade to reinforce the threatened point. More reinforcements were called for, but before they could arrive the line was battered by Federals from both the north and west. Reinforcements arrived, but the Federals were already there in force. By 4.30 p.m. the last of the line broke, and the Confederates fled south towards Granny White Pike.

Hood managed to rally his men along a point two miles to the south, but he had, in his hurry, picked a poor defensive line. The Overton Hill range commanded the position, while his weakest point in the line faced the strongest Federal point. Moreover he was lacking cavalry, as earlier he'd sent Forrest with two divisions to Murfreesboro, while his remaining division had been separated from the main body during the Federal assault. Because of this lack of cavalry, Hood was unaware that Federal cavalry had now positioned itself on one of two retreat routes to Franklin.

On the morning of the 16th, well-placed Federal artillery opened fire on the exposed position. At 8.00 a.m. Federal cavalry attacked the Confederate left, while infantry attacks were made later that morning against Confederates on Peach Orchard Hill. Hood thought further attacks would occur there and reinforced the position.

He was wrong. In the late afternoon, through a drizzling rain, the XXIII Corps attacked from the west, while the XVI Corps attacked from the north and the cavalry came from the south. Within minutes Hood's Army of Tennessee dissolved into a rabble, throwing away their weapons and accoutrements and abandoning their artillery and wagons. One corps retreated in decent order, but even this group lost 16 cannon before the rest could be hitched up and driven off.

Hood's army was no longer capable of any further stands. As a driving snow beat on the weary men marching over icy roads, the Federals followed. By Christmas Day the Confederates began crossing the Tennessee River near Florence, Alabama. In January, Hood resigned, while some of the units that could be reorganized were sent to the Alabama-Mississippi Department and others to Georgia to help stop Sherman. The Army of Tennessee no longer existed.

▶ Soldiers, with a woman on the right, look from the heights of Nashville towards the Union lines. The leafless trees suggests that this photo was taken during the winter around the time of Thomas' assault on Hood's lines.

▶ Howard Pyle's post-war painting of Thomas' troops attacking during the Battle of Nashville. Pyle suggests the torrent that Thomas unleashed against Confederates who were tired, hungry, cold, and ill-supplied, unable to stop the Union drive.

PRIVATE SAM R. WATKINS, 1ST TENNESSEE INFANTRY REGIMENT

Hood's whole army was routed and in full retreat. Nearly every man in the entire army had thrown away his gun and accouterments. More than ten thousand had stopped and allowed themselves to be captured, while many, dreading the horrors of a Northern prison, kept on, and I saw many, yea, even thousands, broken down from sheer exhaustion, with despair and pity written on their features. Wagon trains, cannon, artillery, cavalry, and infantry were all blended in inextricable confusion. Broken downand jaded horses and mules refused to pull, and the badly-scared drivers looked like their eyes would pop out of their heads from fright.

THE FALL OF FORT FISHER

By December 1864 the only seaport left through which blockade runners could bring in the ammunition, equipment, clothing, armaments, and civilian goods needed to keep the Confederacy running was Wilmington, North Carolina. The bar that guarded the inlets leading to that town's wharves was mainly defended by Fort Fisher. Colonel William Lamb, 26 years old when placed in command, wrote, 'I determined at once to build a work of such magnitude that it could withstand the heaviest fire of any guns in the American navy.' Across the Cape Fear River at the rear of Fort Fisher was Fort Lamb, while the Old Inlet into the river was guarded by Forts Campbell, Caswell, Holmes, and Johnston. Two artillery posts were further up the river from Forts Fisher and Lamb, while several batteries were placed north of Fort Fisher on the Atlantic coast. Fort Fisher, however, was the main point of defence for this vital port.

Fort Fisher was made of earthen walls, with openings for heavy artillery pieces, mostly smoothbore Columbiads, surrounded by sandbags, and bomb-proofs between each gun to protect the garrison during enemy bombardment. In all, 24 guns were mounted facing the sea, while another 20 faced land approaches to the fort. The most important gun in the fort was a British-made 150-pounder Armstrong rifled cannon whose long range would keep U.S. Navy ships a safe distance from the fort. Unfortunately only 13 rounds were available for this weapon. Lamb's men also laid a minefield some distance from the log palisade that faced the Northern approach to the fort by land, while the southern approach was protected by a line of rifle pits. The mines were electronically detonated on an enemy's approach by a man inside the fort who fired them by use of an electric battery.

While the fort was physically imposing, its garrison was considerably less so. Lamb's main force was the 36th North Carolina, a heavy artillery regiment that had spent the war in garrison duty and had no combat experience. Moreover, the regiment, officially close to 1,000 strong, mustered fewer than 600 men. Most of them spent their days in boring building and repair work under a hot sun in summer and in bitter winds in winter. Desertion was not uncommon. Back towards Wilmington, the fort could also call on reinforcements that included both veteran infantry and junior reserves.

Benjamin Butler, whose record in the Bermuda Hundred was so poor that he was no longer holding a command, suggested that an old Navy ship should be filled with gunpowder, towed to the fort's sea-face, and exploded. The blast would surely so level the fort's walls that it could be easily taken. The idea was accepted and the USS *Louisiana* was filled with some 200 pounds of gunpowder, and brought with a flotilla followed by more transports

▲ Colonel William Lamb, a Virginia newspaperman married to a New Englander, became colonel of the 36th North Carolina Artillery and in July 1862 was given command of Fort Fisher. He was the single commander of this fort which he largely designed himself.

▶ A contemporary Currier & Ives print of the successful attack of Union combined forces on Fort Fisher in January 1865. With the fall of this fort, the Confederacy was no longer able to import much needed military and civilian supplies, or export cotton to pay for its war.

with 6,500 soldiers, to a point off the fort's walls. At approximately 1.45 a.m. on 24 December, the ship was exploded. A huge ball of fire spread out for some distance, but even the marsh grass on the fort's walls was unharmed. The expedition was a fiasco.

The next day the fleet bombarded the fort as planned, and that evening told the army representatives that the fort was ready for the taking. In fact, only two cannon had been disabled, while several others that had been damaged were still workable. Only four Confederates had been killed. Reinforcements poured into the area.

Still, Butler landed his troops north of the fort in the early morning hours of Christmas Day. Hardly had the first wave set foot on shore, when the fort's garrison opened fire, pinning down the hapless troops. Butler himself returned to sea late that afternoon to examine the fort from the sea in case troops could be landed there. This was, he learned, impossible, and he then withdrew his troops, stranding some 700 who had been unable to get to the ships' boats in time. When he returned to Fort Monroe, on the 27th, he told Grant he had called off the attack, and Grant immediately and with pleasure relieved Butler. He then gave command of a new expedition to Major-General Alfred H. Terry, wiring the naval commander to wait for an increased force to try again.

On 8 January 1865, the army and naval commanders met at Beaufort and planned a new attack. On the 13th the ships and transports were again off Fort Fisher. The navy blasted the fort again, but from close range, disabling several cannon, destroying part of the land-face, and cutting the wires that activated the

mines. At the same time, Terry landed three white and one U.S.C.T. division north of the fort. The U.S.C.T. troops dug works facing north, to prevent Confederate reinforcements.

At 4.00 p.m. on 14 January, the navy sent 2,000 sailors and marines against the fort's north-eastern salient, while the army attacked the land-face parapet. The maritime forces suffered heavy casualties, but diverted the garrison's attention from the main attack. The Confederates fought bravely, but by 9.00 p.m., Lamb severely wounded, the fort was in Federal hands. The Confederacy's last gateway to the world was no more.

▲ The Confederate defenders of Fort Fisher fought bravely, but when they saw the American flag planted on the fort's walls, they realized that the battle was over and escaped as quickly as they could up river to Wilmington, North Carolina.

SEAMAN ROBERT WATSON, C.S.N.

At 3.30 p.m. the Yankee infantry advanced on Fort Fisher and were repulsed three times but on the 4th charge they gained a footing on the left of the works. Unfortunately all the guns of the left were disabled, if this had not been the case they never would have gained a footing, but our men fought them bravely until after dark with musketry and contested every inch of ground. The slaughter was great. As soon as we saw that the enemy had gained a footing and planted their hateful flag on the left of the works we knew that the fort was lost and Captain Chapman had all hands mustered, the roll called, and he then informed us that the fort was lost ...

SHERMAN'S MARCH THROUGH SOUTH CAROLINA

▼ Sherman's troops marching north from Georgia through the Carolinas could depend on supplies sent from the coastal regions where Union troops had long held southern territory. This Union supply base at Port Royal, South Carolina, also supplied U.S. Navy blockaders.

By mid-January, Sherman's army was ready to renew operations. This time it would be a drive northward to join the Army of the Potomac and finish off Lee's army. His right wing, consisting of the XV and XVII Corps was grouped near Pocotaligo, South Carolina. The left wing included the cavalry, the XIV and XX Corps. It was near Sister's Ferry, 40 miles north of Savannah. He left a garrison in Savannah which became part of the Department of the South. In total, Sherman had 60,069 men and 68 cannon.

Sherman's goal was to march 425 miles north to Goldsborough, North Carolina, to arrive before many of the old Army of Tennessee could be transferred to his front. The garrisons at Charleston and Augusta, he felt, would not by themselves be able to stop his veteran troops, but he had no intention of going to Charleston.

The route of the march would pass first through South Carolina. Since secession was voted on initially in South Carolina, indeed that convention was the only one with a unanimous vote for dissolving the Union, the average Federal soldier felt this was the time for retribution. As Major James Connelly of Sherman's army wrote home, 'The army burned everything it came near in the state of South Carolina, not under orders, but in spite of orders. The men "had it in" for the State and they took it out in their own way. Our track through the State is a desert waste.'

Even senior officers felt this way. Sherman's chief of artillery, Major Thomas Osborn, wrote home, 'I visited today the residence of William Gilmore Simms, the South Carolina novelist and author of 'Marion' etc. He has evacuated but has left a very ardent secesh family to protect the residence and library for him. He has a fine Library. I think it will be saved. I should have no objection to seeing it burned. His influence has been very great in carrying on the war.'

After a fortnight of preparations, on 1 February, Sherman's troops headed north in their two columns. Ahead of them Confederates felled trees across the roads and burned bridges across the many creeks. By this time, however, Sherman's expert battalion of pioneers who marched in the vanguard of the column were expert at clearing away such obstacles. Desperate Confederate authorities sent every soldier or would-be soldier they could to Hardee whose force was the only substantial one in Sherman's path. They tried to defend a line on the Salkehatchie River, but by 3 February Sherman's right wing had passed over three miles of swamp, and had forced the defenders away from River's Bridge. From there they headed directly towards the state capital, Columbia. The next day, the left wing crossed the Savannah River, swollen by recent rains, and were well under way.

Confederates tried unsuccessfully to slow the advance at Cowpen Ford and near Lane's Bridge on the Little Salkehatchie on 6 February. However, terrain was more of an obstacle than the handful of poorly trained, led, and equipped Confederate military forces, most of whom were cavalry under native son Wade Hampton, who had been sent from Virginia to take command in the state. Federals crossed the North Edisto on 12 February and the Congaree River on 14 February. On 17 February, Sherman's men entered Columbia, which was surrendered without a fight. Fleeing Confederate cavalry left behind them burning bales of cotton.

Trouble happened in Columbia. While a number of soldiers gathered in the new State House, which had yet to be finished, to hold a mock legislative session to repeal the ordnance of secession, others wandered in the streets. Happy blacks and citizens who wished to remain safe brought out whisky and gave it to the tired soldiers. Soon most of them were drunk and breaking into stores to plunder freely. At the same time, a strong wind fanned the flames of the cotton bales and spread sparks to some nearby wooden buildings. By evening most discipline had broken down, while the city burned. Powder hidden in cellars exploded. Sherman

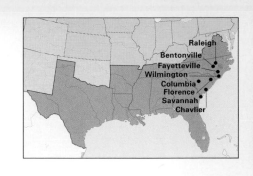

brought in fresh troops to clear the streets, arrest drunken soldiers, and form bucket brigades to extinguish the flames.

Shortly after midnight everything was largely under control. Federal provosts reported killing as many as 40 of their own men who resisted arrest, while many more drunken soldiers were killed in burning buildings. In all, some three quarters of the town, made up largely of wooden buildings, was destroyed in the fire. The college, now the University of South Carolina, survived, as did many buildings on the south and eastern edges of town, but almost nothing remained of the centre. Wade Hampton would accuse Sherman of deliberately burning the city.

The next day, however, Sherman finished the destruction by having all public buildings such as railway depots and supply houses, most of which were on the outskirts of town, burned down. On 19 February, they destroyed the state arsenal, which housed part of the state's military academy, as well as military stores, machine shops, foundries, and railway lines. Federals also found a number of train engines with their carriages which they destroyed.

▼ While Sherman's men were keen on retaliation in South Carolina, the state which they believed caused the bloody war, the burning of Columbia was essentially accidental. Even so, the state's capital was largely destroyed in the fire.

REV. A. TOOMER PORTER, D.D., CHAPLAIN, C.S.A.

On my way to the Market House I saw the first bale of cotton take fire. The soldiers who were sitting and lying on the cotton had begun to light their pipes, and a spark or a lighted match must have fallen on the loose cotton, which of course took fire. I was within twenty feet of the first cotton fired that day. The flames soon spread, and the men, cursing those who had deprived them of their resting-place, quickly got away from the burning piles.

SHERMAN'S MARCH THROUGH NORTH CAROLINA

By 20 February, Sherman's men had outflanked the Confederate line on the west bank of the Cape Fear River and were headed straight towards Wilmington, North Carolina. Confederates there had only enough men for a token resistance and began torching the city's shops. Braxton Bragg, who had been serving as Davis' military adviser, arrived in Wilmington on 21 February and ordered an evacuation to attempt to buy time while building up as large a force as possible. The last of the Confederates left Wilmington on 22 February, with the Federals entering the undefended city only hours later. The soldiers behaved differently in North Carolina to South Carolina: they paid for what they took and they did not burn private homes or take revenge on the locals as they had earlier.

On 23 February, Joseph Johnston, in semi-retirement at his home in Lincolnton, North Carolina, received a telegram from Richmond directing him to take command of whatever troops were available in the Department of South Carolina, Georgia, and Florida, and drive Sherman back. What he found were some 11,000 troops, including 5,000 survivors of the Army of Tennessee. Around 2,000 were near

Charlotte, site of an important naval station and army hospitals, another 1,000 were nearby at Newberry, while another 2,000 were between Newberry and Augusta and heading for Charlotte. Survivors of the Charleston, South Carolina, garrison were marching towards Cheraw. That same day the Federal XX Corps crossed the Catawba River in South Carolina headed for the North Carolina border.

By 5 March Sherman's men were concentrated around Cheraw, ready to march to Fayetteville, North Carolina. Fayetteville was home of one of the Confederacy's major arsenals, in which excellent rifles were made on machinery taken from the ruins of the Harper's Ferry Arsenal in 1861. Hardee's men from Charleston changed their line of march to go to Fayetteville rather than Cheraw. Meanwhile, Federals under Major-General Jacob Cox established a supply base in New Berne, which they found easier to use than Wilmington. On 8 March, Confederates under Bragg attacked the Federals there, breaking through a newly organized brigade before being stopped at the Battle of Kinston. Fighting there would continue during 10 March.

▲ The Confederates paused for a day after their first day's successes at Bentonville, allowing fresh Union troops to reinforce their lines. Then Sherman struck, and Johnston was forced to give up his last attempt to beat Sherman's forces in detail.

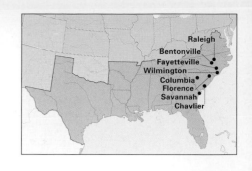

Rain now slowed Sherman's march, but his first troops entered Fayetteville unopposed on 11 March. Ahead of him, Hardee's infantry and Hampton's cavalry fled, burning the bridge across the Cape Fear River that Sherman had hoped to capture intact. Sherman then set up his headquarters in the arsenal, which had been a U.S. Army arsenal before the war, and made contact with the navy and, through it, the War Department in Washington and Grant at City Point. From what Sherman could deduce, Johnston had gathered an army of 30,000 and Hardee brought another 20,000 from Charleston. All this force, one almost as large as his, was ahead of him.

Sherman's army spent some time in Fayetteville. The constant duty, often in swampy and wooded areas, tore their clothes and wore out their shoes, so that many were barefooted and almost naked. Some men were even wearing Confederate uniforms taken from the many Southern quartermaster depots they captured on the march. New clothes were needed and supplies were brought in by boat.

Finally, on 15 March, Sherman's men were back on the march, with one wing aimed towards Goldsborough and another at Averasborough, where Hardee had entrenched his 6,000 troops with the Black River on one flank and a swamp on the other. The Federals struck the front on 16 February, while sending a brigade to turn the Confederate right. The Confederates fell back slowly but in good formation, however, and fighting ended in darkness with both sides still in good order. That night Hardee evacuated his position, having lost 865 men and three cannon. The next day the Federals found Hardee gone, and headed towards Bentonville. A gap had developed between the two wings, and Johnston decided this would be his best chance of preventing the Federals from concentrating at Goldsborough.

Johnston, with 21,000 men, struck this column on 19 March at Bentonville. The Federals dug in along an arrow-shaped front, the point aimed at the Confederate line. A semi-impenetrable swamp anchored the Federal right. The Confederates attacked time and again but could not break the line. The next day the field was quiet as Johnston dug in and hoped for a Federal attack his men could

destroy. Neither side moved, although Sherman brought up reinforcements during the day.

The next morning Sherman struck the Confederate front, at the same time sending a division around the Confederate left. The Confederates fended off this threat and held their lines, but Johnson realized his gamble had failed. He ordered his army back to Smithfield. It was a slow retreat since his army lacked ambulances and had but few wagons required to remove the wounded to hospitals in the rear. But by 2.00 a.m. on the 22nd Johnston's army, minus the 2,606 lost at Bentonville, were retreating again. Sherman's losses were some 1,645.

▼ **Confederates under Braxton Bragg attempt to stop Sherman's march through North Carolina at the Battle of Kinston, March 8–10, 1865. The Federals prevailed there, capturing Goldsborough a week later.**

THE POLITICAL FRONT

As the war started and progressed, neither side attempted to negotiate a peace, nor did they have time to think about what would happen after the war ended. Now, however, both things were needed. Confederate officials would try a last desperate attempt to work out terms with the Federal government that would give them an independent country. At the same time, Federal officials would deal with the thorny problem of what the reunited country would look like.

It would not be a slave-holding state. In the U.S. Congress a 13th amendment to the U.S. Constitution was proposed. It would outlaw slavery throughout the country. Passed easily enough in the Senate, it stalled in the House of Representatives. Speaking for the amendment, which he initially introduced on 14 December 1863, J.M. Ashley, Republican of Ohio, said, 'Mr. Speaker, if slavery is wrong and criminal, as the great body of enlightened Christian men admit, it is certainly our duty to abolish it, if we have the power.' For the other side, Robert Mallory, Democrat of Kentucky, pointed out that 'the Constitution does not authorize an amendment to be made by which any State or citizen shall be divested of acquired rights or property or of established political franchises.'

In the meantime, states that had been slave states but in which a large percentage of the population had mostly been against slavery began to change their own state constitutions to forbid the practice. Tennessee's people ratified an amendment to their constitution forbidding slavery on 22 February 1865 in a popular election. Missouri abolished slavery on 11 January. Finally, on 31 January the House passed the 13th Amendment, with a vote of 119 in favour, 56 opposed, and eight abstentions. Now it had to go to the states for ratification. Illinois acted quickly, ratifying it on 1 February, but two-thirds of the states required to ratify it delayed until 18 December 1865.

It was mostly members of the Democratic Party, which had been the majority party in the south prior to the war, who resisted abolishing slavery. As a result, they were in favour of ending the war as quickly as possible before slavery was abolished and perhaps even political equality for African-Americans became national law. Francis P. Blair, Sr., an older Democratic leader from Maryland, whose house in Silver Spring had been burned by Early's troops, went to Lincoln to arrange permission to travel to Richmond to force Davis to enter into peace negotiations. In mid-January he made this trip, bringing back to Washington a letter from Davis in which he agreed to meet 'with a view to secure peace to the two countries.'

Unfortunately, such a meeting was doomed from the start, since it was a firm principle of the Lincoln administration that there was one country, not two. Lincoln declined the offer. But the idea for such a meeting did not totally die. On 22 January 1865 Davis appointed

▼ The USS *River Queen* steams towards the James River after the fall of Richmond. The boat was the scene of the last attempt to negotiate a peace between the two warring sides. Lincoln also held a conference of war there with both Grant and Sherman.

► Major-General Francis P. Blair, seated centre, and his staff. A lawyer from a prominent family, he enlisted seven regiments personally and was awarded a major-general's commission in November 1861. He resigned in November 1865, having spent almost all his money in the support of the Union.

three men, Vice-President Alexander Stevens, Virginia Senator R.M.T. Hunter, and Assistant Secretary of War John A. Campbell to represent the Confederacy in talks with Federal officials.

Although initially Lincoln declined to meet unless the group explicitly agreed that there was only one country involved, wanted to end the war before the more radical members of his Republican party could impose a harsh peace. Therefore, when Grant got the delegates to agree to omit references to two countries, Lincoln and Secretary of State William Seward met the three on 3 February on the Presidential steamer *River Queen* off Hampton Roads.

The Confederates opened the conference by asking how an end to the war could be achieved. Lincoln replied that the only way was for those who were resisting the laws of the Union to cease. Campbell asked terms, then, if the Confederacy returned to the Union. Lincoln replied that the states would return to their pre-war status, but this could not be done while Southerners were still in arms. Moreover, slavery was to be abolished. Seward told a shocked delegation that the 13th Amendment had passed through Congress and was certain to be ratified by the states.

With this news, the Confederate delegates accepted the fact that there would be no negotiated peace. The war would continue until no Confederate soldiers were left in the field.

However, this did not concern Federal government officials. On 4 March 1865, the Congress set up a Bureau for the Relief of Freedman and Refugees. It was to spend a year helping newly

J.B. JONES, CLERK, CONFEDERATE WAR DEPARTMENT

February 5th [1865]. – Clear and cold. Our commissioners are back again! It is said Lincoln and Steward met them at Fortress Monroe, and they proceeded no further. No basis of negotiation but reconstruction could be listened to by the Federal authorities.... All hope of peace with independence is extinct – and valor alone is relied upon now for our salvation. Everyone now thinks the Confederacy will at once gather up its military strength and strike such blows as will astonish the world. There will be desperate conflicts!

freed African-Americans get a basic education with a network of schools, to find work, and to settle on public lands under the 1862 Homestead Act. It also set wages and terms of employment contracts so former slave-owners would not be able to take advantage of their recent property.

The Confederates, too, were thinking of the African-Americans, but as a desperate last measure. On 13 March, after much debate, the Confederate Congress approved the recruiting of African-Americans into their army. This was too late and too little, although by the war's end two companies of African-American Confederate soldiers paraded through the streets of the Southern capital.

DEFENDING THE JAMES

There was one more way to reach Richmond and that was by the James River which allowed ships of fairly deep draught to reach Richmond's gates, its docks at Rocketts. Initially the Confederate Army blocked the way up the river with a series of batteries which featured heavy naval ordnance. But the Federal Navy had already proved from New Orleans to Mobile Bay that land defences alone could not wholly defend a position against a determined squadron. Initially, too, the Confederate Navy was not strong enough to defend against the overwhelming force the U.S. Navy could throw against it.

Distinguished Southern scientist Matthew Fontaine Maury, known before the war for his charting of the ocean currents, after resigning from the U.S. Navy and joining the Confederate Navy, was named to recommend ways to defend Virginia's waterways. He immediately considered mines, then called torpedoes, as a cheap, quick, and efficient way to equalize the odds. Experimenting at first in his cousin's Richmond home, he soon designed and ordered a number of torpedoes, that worked both by firing electrically from shore and mechanically by coming in contact with an enemy ship.

By 1862, the Confederate Submarine Battery Service had set up a line of torpedo defences in the James. It had its first success in early August 1863 when a Federal expedition, moving up river, passed the first mine station. One of its ships, the *Commodore*

Barney, a ferry boat in New York City before the war that had been converted to river warfare use, passed near one of the torpedoes which was immediately exploded. The explosion threw the boat out of the water, tossing 20 sailors into the water, but she settled back with only minimal damage.

Although only two sailors were killed, the effect was to slow down U.S. Navy voyages up the river. It was not be until May 1864 that another squadron moved up the river to take the fortifications at Drewry's Bluff. Although shore parties moved along the river banks to find mine stations and electric cords, the Confederates were well hidden in the swamps, and when one of the lead ships, the *Commodore Jones*, passed a torpedo that had been in the water 22 months, the operator exploded it. The explosion was a success for the Confederates, with the ship being sunk and 40 of her officers and men lost with her. The expedition turned back.

Knowing that torpedoes alone were not enough to stop the U.S. Navy, the Confederate Navy took advantage of the time they had bought to initiate a squadron on the river, centred around three iron-clads built on the design of the CSS *Virginia*. They were the *Richmond*, launched in July 1862; *Virginia II*, launched in June 1863; and the *Fredericksburg*, launched in November 1863. A fourth iron-clad, the *Texas*, was begun but was not be finished in

▼ The shot-riddled smokestack of the CSS *Virginia II* guarded by a Union soldier after the fall of Richmond. Such damage on the stack caused the already inefficient engines to work even more poorly than usual.

▲ Most Confederate mines, called 'torpedoes,' were made around wooden kegs filled with gunpowder and fired either electronically by a wire running to the shore or by a fuze on the torpedo that was released when a ship brushed by it.

time to help the war effort. The squadron also included a number of auxiliary gunboats, civilian craft converted for war use with guns placed on their decks. The squadron largely served as a 'fleet in being', which threatened but did not attack, the Federal ships further down the river. Nonetheless, the Federals built a line of fixed defences that included piles, rafts, sunken hulks, and their own torpedoes lower in the river to stop the Confederate squadron suddenly appearing among them.

Anxious to help as much as possible in the Confederacy's fight, in late 1864 the Navy Department ordered the James River Squadron to pass down river, strike the enemy ships there, and, block the river around City Point to force Grant's withdrawal. After some delay, the squadron set sail in the night of 23 January 1865. The *Fredericksburg*, the lightest iron-clad, mounted with a boom on her bow to sweep enemy torpedoes, led the squadron through a narrow channel. Confederate torpedo positions were marked by coded stakes placed beforehand. By 8.00 p.m. on the 24th the squadron approached a Federal position, Fort Brady, whose guns overlooked the river. Moving with their port shutters closed and as silently as possible, the ships were initially undetected. As they reached the fort, however, a sentry spotted them, and the cannon opened fire. No significant damage was done.

Once past, one of the smaller craft ran aground, and much time was spent by another ship's crew in attempting vainly to free her, and then to transferring her crew and destroying her munitions before rejoining the squadron. By 9.00 p.m. the *Fredericksburg*

had cleared Federal obstacles from the channel and that night anchored in the larger channel, awaiting the rest of the squadron's ships. The flagship *Virginia II*, however, ran aground by midnight and spent three hours, helped by other boats, in attempting to get free. The *Richmond* also ran aground. The *Fredericksburg* was recalled to defend her sisters as they attempted to get free, while, as day broke, Federal guns opened on the stalled squadron. The U.S. Navy brought up its ships, including *Monitor*-class boats with two turrets which outgunned the Confederate ships badly. The Confederates managed to withdraw and the last major naval battle of the war was over.

▲ **The naval defenders of Charleston, South Carolina, also tried a submarine, the *Hundley*, painted here by a Confederate soldier/artist, Conrad Wise Chapman. The man-powered craft actually sunk a Union blockader but was swamped and lost returning to port.**

R.O. CROWLEY, ELECTRICIAN, C.S. NAVY

The *Commodore Jones* steamed up to the wharf at Deep Bottom, and found our quarters deserted. This looked suspicious, and the order was then given for her to fall back. Our man now concluded that the entire fleet would retire, and he determined to destroy the *Commodore Jones*. As she retreated she passed immediately over one of the two torpedoes planted there. All at once a terrific explosion shattered her into fragments, some of the pieces going a hundred feet in the air. Men were thrown overboard and drowned, about forty being instantly killed.

THE ATTACK ON FORT STEDMAN

The longer the Army of Northern Virginia stayed in the trenches of Petersburg, the less capable it was of winning the war. Families wrote to their men in the trenches, pleading for them to desert a losing cause and return home to save them from starvation. Many men responded, and a steady trickle of deserters turned into a torrent. 'I have the honor to call your attention to the alarming frequency of desertion from this army,' Lee wrote to the Secretary of War in January 1865. 'You will perceive, from the accompanying appears, that fifty-six deserted from Hill's corps in three days. I have endeavored to ascertain the cause, and think that the insufficiency of food and non-payment of the troops have more to do with the dissatisfaction among the troops than anything else.'

Lack of food led to weaker troops, more prone to disease than ever. The many hospitals around Richmond were packed with soldiers suffering from diseases such as dysentery, as well as from wounds received in the constant shelling of the Petersburg lines. At the same time, the south had largely reached the bottom of its manpower reserves. Even the newly approved African-American combat units, of which only two companies were actually organized, would be unable to make up for the losses.

Lee therefore knew that his only chance was to do something with the men he had already on hand before the army haemorrhaged any more irreplaceable losses. He began scouting along the lines looking for any spot in the Federal line that would appear vulnerable. With so much of Grant's attention taken by affairs in the Valley and further south and west, there might have been an excuse for inattention to detail on the Petersburg front. True, such a move might be another Pickett's Charge, but then again it might be another flank march at Chancellorsville.

◀ Major-General John B. Gordon, a Georgia politician, turned out to be one of Lee's better corps commanders by the end of the war. He was well respected by both sides and after the war was over he became the governor of his native state.

One of Lee's better generals, John Gordon, found what he felt to be just such a weak point in his front, Fort Stedman. The fort was located especially close to the Confederate works, which would mean a short sprint across the no-man's-land to the position. Gordon proposed making the attack well before dawn. The leading men would be equipped with axes to chop through the chevaux de frise and stakes connected with tangled wires that lay in his path to the front. These obstacles cleared, the main body of troops would cross into the fort, held by Federal heavy artillery. From there they would spread out and take three small forts the Confederates believed to the rear of Fort Stedman. These would be taken by small bands who would approach the forts calling out, 'The rebels have taken Fort Stedman and our front lines.' Unsuspecting Federals would let themselves be overwhelmed by these attackers. From there, reinforcements would enfilade the Union lines and attack the route to the City Point supply base. In all, Gordon asked for, and received, three divisions to make the attack.

On 25 March 1865, at 4.00 a.m., Gordon's men jumped out of their trenches and dashed across to the Federal defences. In such a short time that Federal gunners were unable to loose off one shot, Confederate pioneers cleared the way and the infantry dashed into the fort. Some Federals fled, firing back into the fort as they left. On the Federal lines to the left of the fort, the noises of chopping wood followed by scattered musket fire alerted the defenders, who stood their ground successfully. By dawn the Confederates held Fort Stedman firmly. Then they moved out to find and take the three smaller forts.

At this point fortune changed to favour the Federals. There were no three smaller forts. The attackers actually hit several other points, Fort Haskell and Battery 9, but the defenders at both posts were fully ready for them, and repelled every attempt at capture. In other places, units roamed the area behind Fort Stedman as the sky grew brighter looking for some non-existent forts to capture. The Federals also reacted quickly. Brigadier-General John F. Hartranft was first on the scene and put together a force to counter-attack. He swiftly gathered a ring of troops around the attackers, based on the positions in the area that had not fallen. Within a short time the Confederates were being fired on from three directions. Federal fire swept the ground between the Confederate main line and Fort Stedman, while Pickett's Division, assigned a reinforcement role, failed to come up in time to help Gordon's men. Lee, on the spot, saw that the attack was a failure, and by 8.00 a.m. ordered a retreat.

Some of the Southern troops dared to dash back under fire to their own lines. Many others, however, weary from the fighting, hungry, and no longer in favour of dying for a cause that seemed lost, simply took cover in the fort and surrendered when the Federals retook it. By the day's end, the Confederates had lost 4,400 troops either killed, wounded, or taken prisoner, as opposed to only 1,500 Federal losses.

▲ Brigadier-General John F. Hartranft, a Pennsylvania lawyer, organized the 51st Pennsylvania and was its first colonel. Made a brigadier-general in May 1864 for his service at Spotsylvania, he was brevetted major-general by the war's end.

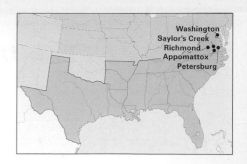

▼ Fort Stedman was the site of the Army of Northern Virginia's last offensive effort to break Grant's army. Despite initial successes, the Confederates there were soon cut off by Union reinforcements and the attack eventually failed.

MAJOR-GENERAL JOHN B. GORDON, C.S.A.

Although it required but a few minutes to reach the Union works, those minutes were to me like hours of suspense and breathless anxiety; but soon was heard the thud of the heavy axes as my brave fellows slashed down the Federal obstructions. The next moment the infantry sprang upon the Union breastworks and into the fort, overpowering the gunners before their destructive charges could be emptied into the mass of Confederates. They turned this captured artillery upon the flanking lines of each side of the fort, clearing the union breastworks of their defenders for some distance in both directions. Up to this point, the success had exceeded my most sanguine expectations.

BATTLES NEAR HATCHER'S RUN

In early February 1865, Grant ordered his men to move to the left yet again, sending over 35,000 men against Confederates holding the Boydton Plank Road, over which they believed supplies were brought into Petersburg. The Federal 2nd Cavalry Division set off on 5 February in dreary, rainy weather, taking the Dinwiddie Court House on the way. Then, under orders, they fell back. Behind them came infantry, with the II Corps reaching Hatcher's Run near the Vaughan Road Crossing, three miles below Burgess' Mill, and digging in there. Right across from them the Confederates had also dug in.

In the late afternoon of 6 February, the Confederates attacked the new Federal positions, and were beaten off, holding on the road. During that fighting Confederate Brigadier-General John Pegram, in command of the division making the assault, was shot through the heart and killed. According to Lee, he died 'while bravely encouraging his men'. Pegram's funeral was held at St. Paul's Church in Richmond, where only three weeks earlier he had celebrated his wedding.

Federals also attacked towards Hatcher's Run. On the 7th, they fell back from their Boydton Plank Road positions to fortify new lines to Hatcher's Run at the Vaughan Road Crossing. Confederate lines were stretched to breaking point. Lee had some 46,000 men holding almost 37 miles of trenches from Richmond to the west of Petersburg. Brigade commanders reported having to hold on to their lines with men placed six to ten paces apart. But after the last Federal push, the lines grew quiet for a time. Lee took advantage of the lull to write directly to Grant offering to meet to find 'a satisfactory adjustment of the present unhappy difficulties by means of a military convention'. Grant, always aware of political overtones, replied that he had no authorization to hold such a meeting.

After the failure at Fort Stedman, Lee began seriously to consider abandoning Petersburg, and with it, Richmond, and attempting to link up with Johnston's army, either in North Carolina or Southern Virginia. 'Our line is so long,' he wrote to Longstreet, 'extending nearly from the Chickahominy to the Nottoway, and the enemy is so close upon us that if we are obliged to withdraw, we cannot concentrate all our troops nearer than some point on the line of railroad between Richmond and Danville. Should a necessity therefore arise, I propose to concentrate at or near Burkeville. The route for the troops north of the James River would have to be through Richmond, on the road to Amelia Court House, the cavalry passing up the north branch of the river and crossing at some point above Richmond. Pickett's Division would take the route through Chesterfield Court House, crossing the Appomattox at Goode's Bridge. With the army concentrated at or near Burkeville, our communications north and south would be by that railroad and west by the South Side Railroad. We might also seize the opportunity of striking at Grant, should he pursue us rapidly, or at Sherman, before they could unite.'

He ordered his quartermaster and supply officers to begin putting together trainloads of provisions that would be needed for

▲ Lieutenant General U.S. Grant watches the Army of the Potomac drive against Lee's Army of Northern Virginia. One observer said that Grant always had the face of a man determined to drive his head through a brick wall.

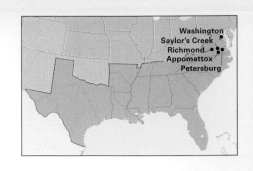

such a march. In the meantime, he waited for better weather to dry and harden the roads. As he would have to retreat to his right, he sent troops under George Pickett and Fitzhugh Lee to hold the line there open, ordering them to the Five Forks area.

The Federals again began pushing along in that same area at the end of March. Cavalry under Philip Sheridan, newly arrived with reinforcements from the Valley, followed by heavy infantry columns, pushed out on 29 March towards Dinwiddie Court House. Infantry of the V Corps found Confederates dug in at the junction of the Boydton and Quaker Roads, whom they forced back and so held that important position. The fighting continued the next day in driving rain, with the V Corps then moving to take a line towards Gravelly Run. Cavalry was beaten back by Confederate cavalry near Five Forks, however.

While fighting towards the west was going on, Federal officers sent scouts out to probe all the rest of the Petersburg lines to find if they were as strongly held as ever. Their reports indicated that, indeed, they had been weakened and a final assault would have a good chance of taking the lines.

On 31 March the rains finally sputtered to a stop. Now the Federals could move in earnest. The odds were heavily on their side, with more than 50,000 of them against a defending force that numbered no more than 10,000. Sheridan's cavalry advanced from Dinwiddie Court House, only to be met by dug-in infantry, who forced Sheridan's men back to their main lines at the Court House itself. Federal infantry had mixed results. The V Corps ran into strong works on the White Oak Road, the Boydton Road, Crow's House, and Hatcher's Run. Still, even as generally poor a soldier as Pickett realized that his men would eventually be destroyed by the advancing Federals, and on 31 March he withdrew them towards Five Forks.

►► *Far right:* Major General Fitzhugh Lee, a nephew of Robert E. Lee, was a professional soldier before the war and became a Confederate cavalry officer in 1861. By 1863 he was a major general in the Army of Northern Virginia's Cavalry Corps.

► Major-General George Pickett commanded an all-Virginia division in Lee's army. Finishing at the bottom of his U.S. Military Academy class, he was vain and not all that intelligent. He lost Lee's confidence at Gettysburg and even more so at Hatcher's Run, but followed the army, without a command, until Appomattox. At the end, Lee dismissed him from the Army of Northern Virginia shortly before its surrender.

COLONEL THOMAS W. HYDE, 1ST MAINE VOLUNTEER INFANTRY REGIMENT

I asked a mortally wounded artillery officer who was propped up against a limber what battery it was. 'Captain Williams of Pogue's North Carolina battalion," said he. 'And who was the officer on the gray horse,' I continued. 'General Robert E. Lee, sir, and he was the last man to leave these guns,' replied he, almost exhausted by the effort. What a prize we had missed! this gallant old man, struggling like a Titan against defeat. He had ordered his battery commander to die there, and had done all one brave man could do to save his fortunes from the wreck.

THE BATTLE OF FIVE FORKS

Five Forks, the post that Lee told Pickett to hold 'at all hazards' the morning of 1 April 1865, was a crossroads in a flat, thickly wooded area, cut up with numerous ravines. In the dark of early morning, Pickett put cavalry on the right and left, with five brigades of almost 9,200 men and a six-gun battery in between. The artillery, commanded by an expert cannoneer, William Pegram, was posted with three cannon at the crossroads, and another three further west, where they covered open farmland. Four horse artillery cannon were posted on Pickett's left. The men immediately started digging a trenchline and cutting down pine trees, which they threw in front of the trench, covering the trees with earth. The line that they held ran about 1.75 miles, with the left slightly bent back for added protection. Then, after digging in, the men rested, glad that there would appear to be no fighting that day.

They were wrong. Sheridan was at the front and unhappy with the progress of Warren's V Corps the previous day. He ordered the infantryman to bring his corps into line near Gravelly Run Church. The corps, with 12,500 men in three divisions, moved on up as skirmishing broke out between cavalry and Pickett's men.

Major-General Thomas Rosser, who commanded the reserve, had had the good fortune to get hold of some shad and he invited both Pickett and cavalry commander Fitzhugh Lee to dinner that day. Both accepted, with Pickett leaving the front to ride two miles to Rosser's headquarters at about 3.00 p.m. Both generals would be out of touch if anything were to happen to their command.

By 4.30 p.m. all of Warren's men were in line and began their advance, crossing the White Oak Road and a half hour later striking the eastern flank of Pickett's line. The outnumbered Confederates

▲ A fanciful post-war lithograph of the Battle of Five Forks. The Confederates, marked with red for artillery service, were not at all dressed as shown, while Union cavalry wore as many plain blouses as dress jackets shown here, and would not wear their brass shoulder scales in action.

could hardly resist, with an entire brigade dissolving almost immediately. Many were captured, while some managed to escape to the west. Other Federals struck other Confederate positions. The far right of the Confederate right was held by the 2nd Maryland Infantry Battalion, made up of Southern sympathizers long cut off from home. Only 250 men strong, the battalion, as were the others in its brigade, was pushed back through its winter encampment, losing a number of men and seven officers before survivors managed to run from the field. Officers at the site did their best to rally their men, but in the absence of the senior commanders they were unable to stop the rout.

Those commanders were having a fine time completely unaware of what was going on. A combination of soaked woods and high humidity hid the sounds of gunfire from them. It was not until the generals actually saw a line of Federal infantry advancing towards their position that they understood what was going on. Pickett and Fitzhugh Lee instantly mounted, riding towards Five Forks. Their way was blocked by Federal infantry, but Pickett ducked down besides his horse's head and neck and dashed through their lines to reach his own. Lee was unable to do the same, and returned to organize forces on the north side of Hatcher's Run.

Pegram, who had been asleep when the attack hit, woke, mounted and rode towards his three guns at Five Forks. As he rode into his battery, he suddenly started and fell heavily from his horse. He had been badly wounded on his left side, and as he declared, 'I'm mortally wounded, take me off the field', he was carried away. The Confederacy had lost yet another promising officer.

When he reached his position, Pickett called for a brigade to drive out the Federals in their rear. This attempt failed, but at the same time two other brigades held open a door west despite attempts by Federal cavalry to trap them. Everything lost, the men, including their general, fled that way, leaving some 2,400 of their comrades behind them.

BUGLER H.P. MOYER, 17TH PENNSYLVANIA VOLUNTEER CAVALRY REGIMENT

It was about this time that General Sheridan appeared on the field and, seeing our men coming back, he rushed in the midst of the retiring troops and cried out 'Where is my flag?' The sergeant who carried the flag rode up to him, when Sheridan seized the flag, waved it above his head, cheered on the men and made great efforts to rally them and close up the ranks. Bullets were flying thick and fast, one pierced the general's flag, one killed the sergeant who had carried the flag, and another wounded Captain McGormigle, and others struck several of General Sheridan's staff officers.

That evening, Federal artillery all along the line opened fire on the Confederates. Behind them infantry gathered for the front-wide assault Grant ordered for the next morning. At dawn they hit. In some places the Confederates appeared to hold; the rabbit warren of trenches proved complicated to clear out quickly, and combat went on slowly. One point in the line, Fort Mahone, was taken and retaken time and again. One man recalled firing over 200 rounds that day. But when the sun set, the Federals had lost many of their initial gains. The Confederates had not retaken every captured trench, but they had taken enough of them to hold their line.

Now Lee had to face reality. 'This is a bad business, Colonel,' Lee told one of his staff officers. 'Well, it has happened as I told them at Richmond it would. The line has been stretched and it has broken.' Overwhelmed on his right, his one way out, and heavily pressed by overwhelming numbers in the front, Lee sent word to Richmond that night advising 'that all preparations be made for leaving Richmond to-night.' In fact, his telegraph did not arrive in the War Department telegraph office until the next morning.

▼ **Regulars of the 1st U.S. Cavalry Regiment. The officer standing left front wears an enlisted man's overcoat, without its cape, which was allowed as the dark blue officers' model made officers stand out as ready targets. The men wear their dress uniform jackets.**

► **William J. Pegram was one of the bravest Confederate artillerymen of the war. Terribly nearsighted, even with the glasses rarely worn then but shown here, he fought his guns near the Union lines, he said, so he could see the enemy.**

THE BATTLE OF SAILOR'S CREEK

On Sunday 2 April 1865 Jefferson Davis was at the morning service at St. Paul's Church in Richmond. In the midst of the service a messenger opened the doors, walked down the nave to Davis's pew, and handed him a note that said Lee's men were abandoning their lines. He quickly scanned it, rose, and strode to the door. He was followed by Stephen Mallory and a number of other government officials, although many remained to receive the Eucharist that last day of Confederate Richmond.

At government offices, clerks and officials were busy packing necessary documents and equipment for a government on the run and sending them to the railway that ran towards Danville. Government hard currency, mostly foreign coins, and local bank specie were also packed, guarded by midshipmen from the C.S. Naval Academy, which had been located on the CSS *Patrick Henry* until its destruction.

Also that day, A.P. Hill riding with an orderly towards Lee's headquarters, ran across several Federal infantrymen. The two Confederates pointed their pistols at the Federals, who had their muskets aimed at the mounted men. As Hill called for their surrender, they fired, killing one of the South's famed lieutenant generals.

Luckily for Lee, the Federals did not press their attack on 2 April, but concentrated on straightening their lines and cleaning out pockets of resistance. Depending on two small forts, Gregg and Whitworth, which had been built to protect the Confederate rear if the right were turned, Lee slowly began to withdraw his troops around midnight. Forts Gregg and Whitworth held, pushing back one early afternoon attack, until overwhelmed in the late afternoon as the last action of the day. The last of the Confederates were out of Petersburg, crossing the Appomattox River well before dawn and setting fire to the bridges they used.

Behind them, some Federals entered the city whose church spires they'd looked at for so long. Most, however, would not have the honour, being put on the road after Lee's men as soon as the abandonment of the city was discovered. At the same time, Federal scouts entered Richmond through the flames that had been started as retreating Confederates set fire to valuable stores there. Within hours the U.S. flag flew over the building that had housed the Confederate Congress.

Lee had ordered rations to be sent from Richmond to Amelia Court House before he had abandoned his positions. His army reached there on 4 April in a drizzling rain. The railway carriages they found there, however, contained ammunition, not rations, through a mix-up at both his army headquarters and the commissary department in Richmond. Rather than continue the retreat, however, Lee decided to halt there and sent supply wagons into the countryside to find food. As he waited Federal cavalry, with infantry not far behind, were in hot pursuit of his men.

On 5 April, having rested and fed his men, Lee started west again. As the army marched, however, it also dissolved. Men, finding themselves the sole survivor of their company, simply stopped by the side of the road or headed off in the general direction of home. Some were passing their homes during this retreat and stopped there, having had enough.

On the afternoon of 6 April, the army crossed Sailor's Creek, a slightly hilly area cut with boggy spots. Here a gap developed between the head of the army and the two corps commanded by Richard Anderson and Richard Ewell. As the Federals were pressing behind them, the Confederate corps halted and deployed for battle. They turned back an attack on their centre, then, delighted to be finally out of the trenches and in open field battle, charged the Federals. Many of them, such as the sailors from the James River Squadron who had been formed into a Naval Brigade, had only served in the trenches and were inexperienced in such battles. Federal infantry and artillery smashed their impromptu attack. Then, at about 6.00 p.m. the Federal artillery let up and the infantry

▲ General Richard Anderson, the last of Lee's corps commanders, was not the type of aggressive leader that other Army of Northern Virginia commanders like Stonewall Jackson and A.P. Hill were.

► Soldiers and civilians stream across the last bridge across the James on the night of 2 April, 1865, leaving a burning city of Richmond behind. This Currier & Ives print dates from only shortly after the actual event.

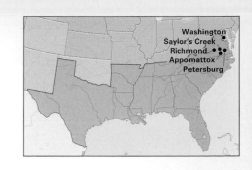

▲ Confederate troops burning military supplies started the fires that spread throughout much of the City of Richmond and left it the ruins seen here shortly after its Union capture. Ironically, the first Union troops in the city were African-American and they helped put the fire out.

PRIVATE EDWARD A. MOORE, ROCKBRIDGE ARTILLERY, ARMY OF NORTHERN VIRGINIA

As we started in haste to retire, he and Poindexter being mounted, expressed great concern lest I, being on foot, should be captured. Just as they left me, however, and while the air seemed filled with flying lead and iron, I came upon one of the ambulance corps who was trying to lead an unruly horse. It was a Federal cavalry horse, whose rider had been killed in pursuit of General Pickett. In the horse's efforts to break loose, the two saddles he was carrying had slipped from his back and were dangling underneath, which increased his fright. I suggested to the man that, to escape capture, he had better give me the horse, as he seemed to be afraid to ride him. To this he readily assented . . .

advanced. Soon they enveloped most of the formations that survived to oppose them, the Naval Brigade being the last to accept defeat. Anderson reported that his small corps was virtually wiped out. Wagons, stuck in the mud of the creek beds, were also captured. In all, 8,000 Confederates, including Ewell and five other general officers, had been taken prisoner at Sailor's Creek, the most Americans ever captured in combat alone.

'My God!' Lee exclaimed, 'Has the army dissolved?' Later, in describing the army's situation to a courier from Davis, he admitted,

'A few more Sailor's Creeks and it will be over - ended - just as I have expected it would end from the first.'

In all the Union loss was 1,180 killed or wounded. Still, Lee's Army of Northern Virginia constituted a fair force after this final battle, and the survivors headed off to Farmville on 7 April. Sheridan's men were right behind, with Sheridan telegraphing Grant, 'If the thing is pressed, I think Lee will surrender.' Lincoln, at Grant's headquarters, read Sheridan's message and ordered, 'Let the thing be pressed.'

APPOMATTOX

On 7 April 1865, Longstreet's men arrived in Farmville where they finally managed to get issued some rations. They had little time to enjoy them, however, as the Federals continued to snap at their heels. Lee decided to move the remainder of his army to the north side of the Appomattox, ordering the bridges at High Bridge and Farmville to be burned to protect his force for a time. Federals managed to take spans at High Bridge before they could be destroyed, so Lee sent troops to block the Federals moving from High Bridge to intercept his line of march.

That afternoon Federals arrived in Farmville and Grant sent his first message to Lee suggesting that the Army of Northern Virginia surrender. 'Not yet,' said Longstreet when Lee showed him the note. Lee replied that he would not surrender, however he wondered what Grant's terms would be. Grant wrote back that he had only one positive term and that would be that the officers and men would not be allowed to take up arms against the U.S. government again until properly exchanged.

Lee continued his retreat, stopping at New Store to order that Richard Anderson, Bushrod Johnson, and George Pickett be relieved of command due to the smallness of the army. In fact, their poor performance in these final days contributed to Lee's decision. Pickett and Johnson were apparently not notified, and continued with the army. While there, the army's chief of artillery, William Pendleton, a long-time friend of Lee and rector of the church to which Lee would eventually belong, told the commander that his officers agreed that the time had come to negotiate surrender with the enemy. Lee turned down the idea, saying instead that as soldiers they should die at their posts.

Federal infantry reached New Store late in the afternoon of 8 April. The Confederates marched on, although with every stop and start fewer remained with the column. Ahead of them lay, they believed, Federal cavalry, their only block to escaping to unite with Johnston's force. Lee ordered a breakout, with Fitzhugh Lee's cavalry leading, supported by John Gordon's infantry. At 3.00 a.m. on 9 April, the Confederates were in the streets of Appomattox Court House, moving out to attempt the breakout. Lee, wearing a dress frock coat rather than the sack coat he usually wore, watched as the dawn rose from a hilltop. Asked why the dress uniform, he replied that he expected that day to be Grant's prisoner and wanted to make his best appearance.

The attacking force engaged the enemy, skirmishers out front, by 8.30 that morning. Very quickly, however, they discovered the enemy in their front was not cavalry, but infantry. The road west was blocked. Lee therefore wrote to Grant asking to meet to discuss his army's surrender. The last shots fired appear to have been by some Confederate engineer troops who killed a Federal horseman who appeared at their front at about 10.00 a.m.

Federal staff officers looked for a place for the two commanders to meet and picked the home of Wilmer McLean, a farmer who had moved from Manassas for safety after the 1861 battle there. Grant and his staff reached the house at approximately 1.30 p.m., shortly after Lee and his one military secretary. After some small talk, mostly about their mutual service in the Mexican War, they discussed terms. Grant allowed the officers and men to be paroled and the officers to keep their side arms. Lee pointed out that most Confederate soldiers owned their own horses, which would be needed for spring planting. Grant agreed that

▲ Union troops pose in front of the Wilmer McLean house at Appomattox Court House, scene of the surrender of the Army of Northern Virginia. McLean had moved to Appomattox to get away from the war after selling his first house on the site of First Bull Run battle.

MAJOR WILLIAM F. OWEN, WASHINGTON ARTILLERY, C.S.A.

When my march brought me to the hill I espied Generals Longstreet and Alexander, chief of artillery, sitting on a log. Alexander got up and came towards me. I said to him, 'Gen. Lee instructed me to stop here for orders. What do you want me to do?' He replied, 'Turn into that field on the right and park your guns.' Then added, in a low tone, 'We are going to surrender today!' We had been thinking it might come to that, sooner or later; but when the shock came it was terrible. And was this to be the end of all our marching and fighting for the past four years? I could not keep back the tears that came to my eyes.

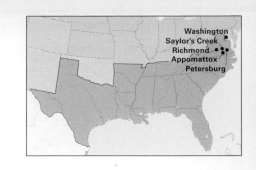

they could take them home. In addition Grant promised 25,000 rations for the hungry prisoners. The terms were drafted, and by 3.00 p.m. the Agreement had been signed and the war was finished for the armies of Northern Virginia and the Potomac.

Lee rode back through mobs of weeping soldiers. Some Federal soldiers fired off their guns in celebration, but Grant, sensitively, quickly quashed any celebrations. Finally individual Federal soldiers drifted between the lines, to see close-up those men who had kept them from Richmond for so many years. They shared food from their haversacks with hungry Confederates who were astonished to see issued items like butter and real coffee. Federal authorities eventually forbade these crossings of the lines.

The formal surrender ceremony took place on 12 April 1865. The honour of receiving the weapons, accoutrements, drums, and flags of the vanquished enemy fell to Brigadier-General Joshua Chamberlain, the Maine college professor whose valiant defence of Little Round Top helped win Gettysburg for the Union. John Gordon was given the task of leading the Confederates who had fought so many battles to surrender their implements of war. As they marched down towards the Federals at about 9.00 a.m., Chamberlain ordered his men to salute their brave foes. Gordon, seeing this honour given, returned the honour by giving Chamberlain a salute with his sword himself, then ordering the men following to give the marching salute as they passed. It was, as Chamberlain later wrote, 'honor answering honor.'

Then each regiment, some no more than a dozen men, filed into line, stacked arms, slung their accoutrements from the musket stacks, laid their colours - those who had not previously cut up their colours into pieces and distributed them among the survivors – and marched off into history.

▼ **Grant, wearing a fatigue blouse, and Lee, wearing a dress uniform saved from his baggage after the Confederate wagon trains were destroyed, shake hands after the surrender. McLean lost much of this parlour furniture as Union staff officers took it for souvenirs.**

AFTER APPOMATTOX

The surrender of Lee's army meant the end for many Southerners and Northerners alike. It was not, however, the end of the war. The Confederacy still had a large number of troops in the field holding important territory, and each one of these forces would have to be induced to surrender.

On 12 April 1865, the day Lee's men stacked their arms near Appomattox Court House, the Confederacy's last major city, Mobile, Alabama, fell. Federal troops under Major-General E.R.S. Canby entered the city, as the defenders loaded up what supplies they could and burned the rest before leaving. The Confederates, under Major-General D.H. Maury marched to Meridian, Mississippi, where they halted to refit. They, as with Lee's men, planned to move from that point to join Johnston's troops in North Carolina. Also on the 12th, cavalry under young leader Brigadier-General James Wilson occupied Montgomery, Alabama, where Jefferson Davis had been sworn into office as the Confederacy's first and last President four years before.

Davis himself was in Greensborough, North Carolina on the 12th. There he met with Johnston, Beauregard, and several other cabinet members who had left Richmond with him. Davis was keen to continue the fight and was shocked when his two top generals recommended negotiating instead of fighting. All but Secretary of

State Judah Benjamin agreed with the generals against Davis, so reluctantly he granted Johnston permission to meet Sherman to discuss surrender. In the meantime, he and Benjamin planned to travel to Florida with the idea of sailing out of there to safe territory. Travelling with them would be a small fortune in gold, the Naval Academy midshipmen and some trusty cavalry troops.

On 14 April a pleased Abraham Lincoln accepted an invitation to Ford's Theatre with his wife to see *Our American Cousin*. Earlier a group with ties to the Confederate Secret Service, the Southern intelligence agency associated with the Signal Corps, plotted to kidnap the President and bring him South in exchange for, at best, independence, at worst, the wholesale release of thousands of prisoners of war. Now that independence seemed impossible, the group, headed by Maryland actor John Wilkes Booth, changed their plot to include the murder of Lincoln, his Vice-President, and his Secretary of State. Booth decided to strike at Ford's Theater, a place he knew well. He also knew that at one spot in the play only one actor was on the stage, so he could shoot the President, use his noted athletic abilities to leap from the President's box to the stage, and escape to where a horse would be waiting for him in the alley behind the theatre. Luck was with him, as Lincoln's normal bodyguard was in Richmond, and the man he wanted as a substitute had been requested to work at

▶ **John Wilkes Booth shoots Abraham Lincoln in a box at Ford's Theater, Washington, D.C., during a performance of *Our American Cousin*. The officer also in the booth was badly cut in the arm attempting to catch the murderer.**

▶ **Brigadier-General James Wilson, seated in the short jacket and sky blue trousers, looking to his left, and his staff. Obviously a field photo, these staff officers all wear the type of clothes they would wear while on active service.**

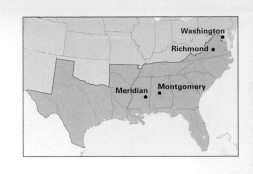

CAPTAIN GEORGE A. BOWEN, 12TH NEW JERSEY VOLUNTEER INFANTRY

Personally I sat down on a pile of rails, saying nothing, trying to comprehend the fact and all it included. 'The war over.' I had lived to see the Union Arms triumph.

The Union was saved. The many weary marches, the many hard fought battles, the colds of winter, the heats of summer had not been braved in vain. 'The War Over.' I could not begin to realize what it meant to me. I was afraid it was a dream, that if I stirred I would awaken.

the War Department that evening. The Lincolns would be accompanied by only a staff officer and a woman friend.

Things worked out almost perfectly for Booth, who, at the right moment entered the small room behind the President's box and then stepped out to fire a single shot into the president's brain. The major with Lincoln attempted to stop Booth, but Booth slashed him with the bowie knife he also carried, and leapt to the stage. Unfortunately for him, his spur got caught in the Treasury Department flag hanging from the front of the booth, and Booth fell awkwardly, breaking a leg. Still, he managed to get to his horse, and away, towards the eastern shore of Maryland, where his secret service connections could whisk him away to the South.

Another of Booth's gang attacked the Secretary of State in his bed where he was recovering from a serious accident. Only the brace the Secretary had been forced to wear because of the accident saved him. The last player left his card at the hotel of the Vice-President, but lacked the courage to try to find and kill him, heading instead towards Rockville, Maryland.

Lincoln was borne from the theatre, mortally wounded, to a boarding house across the street. Dozens of senior officials visited the deathbed that night, and finally on the morning of 15 April at 7.22 a.m., the President drew a large breath and exhaled his last. 'Now,' Secretary of War Edwin Stanton said, 'he belongs to the ages.'

On the whole Southerners were aghast at the murder, feeling they had a better chance of a peaceful reconciliation under Lincoln. Booth's fellow gang members were soon rounded up, but Booth himself managed to get his leg set by a Confederate Secret Service agent who was a doctor, and who later claimed not to have recognized the actor. Then Booth and one of his fellow conspirators headed South again, aided by other agents. Finally on 25 April pursuing U.S. cavalrymen had a tip-off that Booth was in a barn on the farm of Richard H. Garrett. They surrounded the barn and, when Booth refused to come out, set fire to it. A shot was heard, and they found a mortally wounded Booth. While one cavalryman claimed responsibility, it is just as likely that Booth simply committed suicide.

▲ **President Andrew Johnson, by trade a tailor from Tennessee, took office on Lincoln's death. He, too, was scheduled for killing, but the man assigned that task lost his nerve. Johnson, a moderate on southern reconstruction, was largely ineffectual in getting his programs through a radical-dominated Congress.**

THE WAR IS OVER

On 17 April 1865 Sherman and Johnston met in a small farmhouse near Durham Station, North Carolina, to discuss the surrender of those Confederate forces that still survived in the area. On being told that Lincoln had been killed, Johnston called the news a great calamity for the South. They met again the next day and signed what they called a 'Memorandum or basis of agreement,' which went far beyond what Grant and Lee had managed. The paper called for all armies in the field to recognize an armistice, while Confederate forces were to disband, returning their arms to state armouries. Each soldier would then agree to recognize state and Federal authority, while the U.S. President would recognize existing state governments, their officials having taken an oath of allegiance to the U.S., Federal courts would be re-established. What would prove especially intolerable to U.S. officials later was that rights of person and property, which could be interpreted to include slaves, were to be guaranteed, while Southerners would not be disturbed as long as they lived in peace and all Confederate officials would be given a general amnesty.

Sherman sent copies of this document to Grant and War Department officials, offering to take charge of carrying out the terms. These officials took time out on 19 April from the official funeral service of the President to discuss Sherman's terms. They were adamant that these terms were absolutely unacceptable, as, crossing into political policy making, they were way beyond the General's authority. They sent Grant personally to North Carolina to emphasize their rejection. Grant arrived at Sherman's Raleigh headquarters on 24 April and passed the word on, telling Sherman that he had to give Johnston 48 hours notice, and then was to begin action against his army unless he was to surrender on

essentially Lee's previous terms. Sherman was furious, claiming he did nothing beyond what Lincoln had wanted. Still, he obeyed orders and notified Johnston, who had previously received Davis's approval for the terms.

Johnston knew that he could not fight even Sherman's army, let alone a combined army with the Army of the Potomac, and he returned to meet Sherman on 26 April. That afternoon, he agreed to Grant's terms as forwarded by Sherman. Grant approved the surrender, and the Confederacy's second major army, some 30,000 men strong, had surrendered.

On 30 April, Federal Major-General E.R.S. Canby and Confederate General Richard Taylor agreed a truce prior to the surrender of Confederate forces in East Louisiana, Alabama, and Mississippi. Canby telegraphed Grant that Taylor had accepted essentially the same terms as Lee had accepted on 2 May, and received word that the surrender was accepted. The two generals met at Citronelle, Alabama, some 40 miles north of Mobile, to sign the agreement. In addition, Canby allowed Taylor's officers to continue controlling local railways and steamers so they could transport the paroled soldiers home, something that had not been done in other surrender ceremonies after when each soldier had had to make his way home as best he could. On 11 May Brigadier-General M. Jeff Thompson surrendered his Missouri command at Chalk Bluff, Arkansas, under Lee's terms.

The only surviving major Confederate force was the Trans-Mississippi Department under General E. Kirby Smith. Grant ordered Canby to move into the area to receive its surrender too. Before that, however, the last land battle of the war took place on 12 May when Federal troops attacked Palmito Ranch on the banks of the Rio

▼ *Left*: General Joseph E. Johnston surrenders the survivors of the Army of Tennessee to Major General William T. Sherman April 26, 1865, in this period engraving. Sherman's initial generous terms were rejected by the U.S. Government, and Johnston eventually surrendered with the same terms as had Lee's army.

▼ The CSS *Shenandoah*, a commerce raider, was in northern Pacific waters when her commander eventually learned of the war's end long after it had actually happened. Rather than surrender her to U.S. officials, he took her halfway around the world to surrender in England.

▲ For days first Grant's army then Sherman's army paraded through the streets of Washington, D.C., in triumph. This lithograph shows the reviewing stand on Pennsylvania Avenue in front of the president's residence, the White House, from where political and military leaders took their soldiers' salutes.

LIEUTENANT-GENERAL RICHARD TAYLOR, C.S.A.

We then joined the throng of officers, and although every one present felt a deep conviction that the last hour of the sad struggle approached, no allusion was made to it. Subjects, awakening memories of the past, when all were sons of a loved, united country, were, as by the natural selection of good breeding chosen. A bountiful luncheon was soon spread, and I was invited to partake of patis, champagne-frappe, and other 'delights' which to me had long been as lost arts. As we took our seats at table, a military band in attendance commenced playing 'Hail Columbia'. Excusing himself, General Canby walked to the door. The music ceased for a moment, and then the strain of 'Dixie' was heard. Old Froissart records no gentler act of 'courtesie'.

Grande River in Texas. Although the Federals were initially successful, a Confederate counter-attack gave them victory, ironic as it was. Despite this, Southern state representatives met Smith and urged him to surrender. Smith sent Lieutenant-General Simon Buckner, who had so long ago surrendered Fort Donelson to Grant, to meet the Federal representative, Major-General Peter J. Osterhaus, on 26 May. The two agreed to the Appomattox terms, Smith approving them on 2 June, at which point the Confederacy ceased to exist.

At least it ceased to exist for the army. The Confederate Navy existed a little longer, with naval forces on the Red River surrendering on 3 June. However, the CSS *Shenandoah*, the last of the Confederacy's commerce destroyers, was at that time in the Bering Sea, far from being in touch with its command, and still capturing and

destroying U.S. shipping. It was not until 2 August that her officers received a copy of a newspaper from a British barque that told them the war was over. Lieutenant James Waddell, the ship's commander, could have taken her to the nearest U.S. port, which in this case would have been San Francisco, California, to surrender. However, he did not want to surrender to Federal authorities, but rather return her to the country of his ship's birth. He plotted a course that would take him to the tip of South America, around the Horn, and then back to Great Britain. There, on 6 November 1865, he dipped the last Confederate flag ever flown in earnest on entering Liverpool harbour, and surrendered his vessel to British authorities.

On 2 April 1866, President Andrew Johnson declared 'that the insurrection which heretofore existed . . . is at an end . . .'.

THE EYEWITNESSES

AUGUSTUS PITT ADAMSON, was born in Georgia in 1844. A farmer with what he admitted was 'limited education', he joined Co. E, 30th Georgia Infantry, on its formation in October 1861. He was elected third corporal on the regiment's reorganization in May 1862, and promoted to first corporal in 1863. He was badly wounded at Chickamauga and then captured in May 1864. He was finally discharged from prison in Rock Island, Illinois, in 1865. He returned to farming, but also taught at school and was active in local politics. He served as secretary to the 'Reunion Association of the Thirtieth Georgia Regiment', writing the regimental history, from which his account is taken.

WILLIAM HILL ANDREWS was born in Georgia in 1838. At the outbreak of war, he was an overseer and a member of the Fort Ganines Guards, a local volunteer militia company. When war broke out, in February 1861 he joined the 1st Regiment of Georgia Regulars as a private. He surrendered as first sergeant of Company D of that regiment with Johnston's forces in North Carolina in 1865. In 1891 he published a short account called *1st Georgia Regulars Through the War Between the States*, and he wrote further accounts in later editions of the *Atlanta Journal*, the first of which was published in 1901.

LUCIUS BARBER was born in New York in 1839 and his family moved to Illinois to farm when he was 11. He joined Co. D, 15th Illinois Infantry in April 1861. Captured in October 1864, he spent time in Andersonville and Millen, but was exchanged seven weeks later. Promoted to sergeant, he was discharged in September 1865. After the war he wrote his *Army Memoirs*, which were published in 1894. He did not live to see the published version, dying of consumption, supposedly brought on by his treatment as a prisoner, in March 1872.

T.E. BESSELLEIN was a soldier in the 2nd South Carolina during the Battle of Brandy Station. After the war he started his own medical practice in Savannah, Georgia. He published his account in the *Philadelphia Times* on 24 March 1883.

AMBROSE GWINNETT BIERCE, one of America's major writers of the late 19th century, was born in 1843, his family moving to Indiana in 1848. He was working there in a shop when he joined Co. C, 19th Indiana Infantry in April 1861 as a private. His regiment's service lasted only three months and he re-enlisted when he returned home, being quickly named a sergeant and then sergeant-major of the 9th Indiana Infantry. He was commissioned second lieutenant in December 1862, first lieutenant the following February and was sent to a brigade headquarters as a topographical engineer. He was badly wounded at Kennesaw Mountain in June 1864 and needed a long hospital stay. He returned to serve at Franklin and Nashville as a staff officer, being discharged in January 1865. After the war he went to California where he worked as a writer and correspondent. In 1913 he went to Mexico where he disappeared, never to be seen again.

JOHN D. BILLINGS, a Massachusetts native, wrote several of the best known of Civil War veterans' works, including his classic account of private soldier life, *Hardtack and Coffee*, and the history of his own unit, the 10th Massachusetts Light Artillery.

THEOPHILUS F. BOTSFORD was born in Alabama in 1830 or 1831. A poor farmer, who had only 93 days of schooling his entire life, he joined Co. D, 47th Alabama, in May 1862. He survived the war and published a short history of his regiment in 1909, with a revised edition coming out in 1911, and a third edition in 1914.

GEORGE A. BOWEN joined Co. I, 12th New Jersey Infantry in August 1862 as a private when he was 19 years old. He was quickly named the company's 3rd sergeant, rapidly moving to the commissioned ranks of lieutenant and captain, the rank he held when the war ended and he was mustered out in June 1865. He was offered the rank of major, but declined. Serving in every battle of the war, he later said he never missed a day because of illness or wounds. A copy of his diary is in the collection of the Salem County Historical Society, New Jersey.

GEORGE N. CARPENTER joined the 8th Vermont Infantry as a private when the regiment was formed in 1861 and was soon named the regiment's sergeant major. In June 1862 he was commissioned as 1st lieutenant, and became captain of Co. C in August 1863. He later served as acting adjutant of the regiment and an aide-de-camp on the brigade staff. He resigned in July 1864 to accept an appointment as captain and commissary of subsistence of U.S. volunteers. During the last year of the war he served on the staff of General R.A. Cameron. After the war he wrote the History of the 8th Regiment, Vermont Volunteers, from which his accounts are taken.

HENRY W. CARRUTHERS was born in Illinois in 1835. When he was a child his father died and his mother returned to her home in Pennsylvania, where Henry became apprenticed to a printer in West Chester. He later became a lawyer. When the Civil War started he joined the 9th Pennsylvania Infantry, a three-months' regiment, as a private. After it was mustered out, he joined the 97th Pennsylvania Infantry as a first lieutenant. He quickly became the regiment's adjutant, serving as such until he was mortally wounded at Strawberry Plains, Virginia, in August 1864. His account of Bermuda Plain is from a letter to William Wayne now in a private collection.

JOHN OVERTON CASLER was born in Virginia in 1838 and was a farmer in various places before the war began. In June 1861 he joined as a private a company which eventually became Co. A, 33d Virginia Infantry. Often missing without leave from the army, he nevertheless seems to have avoided serious punishment. He finally deserted the regiment in January 1865, unofficially joining the 11th Virginia Cavalry, in which he served for a month before being captured. His was released in May 1865 and returned to take up contracting in Virginia. He moved to Texas and then Oklahoma where he continued

contracting. He published his *Four Years in the Stonewall Brigade* in 1893 and died in 1926.

FRANK CHURCH took advantage of a rapidly growing U.S. Marine Corps to become commissioned as a second lieutenant in the organization in July 1862. He was promoted to first lieutenant in August 1864. After the war, Frank, who by then was married with a son, found promotion slow and pay low. He therefore resigned from the Corps in 1869, after the birth of his second son, and took a job with the Title Guarantee and Trust Co. in Chicago, Illinois. His wife died at an early age, and he moved about the mid-west of the country, dying in Kentucky in 1910 and his body was returned to Chicago to be laid next to his wife. His diary is in the collection of the U.S. Marine Corps, Histories and Museums Division.

ACHILLES V. CLARK joined the 20th Tennessee Cavalry, C.S., in January 1864. He was promoted to sergeant shortly before the Fort Pillow massacre, which he so vividly described. Serving to the end of the war, he was paroled as a captain under Forrest's command in 1865. This letter to his two sisters was written two days after the battle and is now in the Confederate Collection, Manuscripts Section, Tennessee State Library and Archives.

WILLIAM L. DANIEL was born in South Carolina in 1832. A medical doctor, he chose to serve in the ranks in the 2nd South Carolina as a private. He wrote this account of the Battle of Mechanicsville, Virginia, to his mother on 13 July 1862. He was killed in the Battle of Gettysburg and his letter was finally published in *Progressive Farmer Magazine* in July 1938.

CHARLES DEVENS, JNR., was born in Massachusetts in 1820. A Harvard University and Harvard Law School graduate, he served before the war as a lawyer, state senator, United States martial, and state militia officer. When the war broke out he was commissioned major of the 3rd Massachusetts Rifles, which served only 90 days. Thereafter he was given command of the 15th Massachusetts Infantry. In 1862 he was appointed a brigadier general of volunteers and given command of an IV Corps brigade. He served at Balls Bluff, Fair Oaks, and Chancellorsville. On returning to service after Chancellorsville, he was given command of a division of the Army of the James. After the war he commanded the District of Charleston, South Carolina, until 1867 when he was appointed a judge. He was named a justice of the Massachusetts Supreme Court in 1873 and served as Attorney General of the United States under President Rutherford B. Hayes. He died in 1891. This account is taken from his testimony before the Congressional Joint Committee on the Conduct of the War.

JAMES DINKINS was born in Mississippi in 1845. He served in the 18th Mississippi Infantry in the Army of Northern Virginia for the first two years of the war. Named a first lieutenant of cavalry in April 1863, he then served as an aide-de-camp to

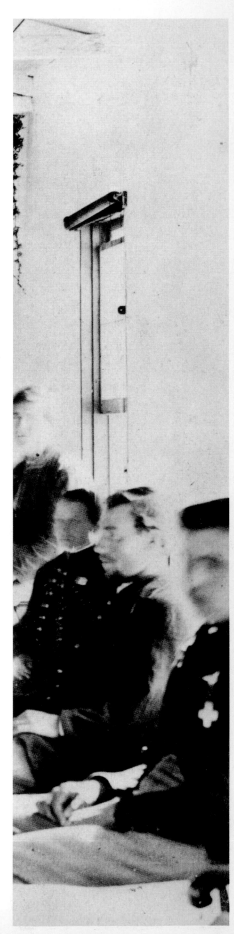

General James R. Chalmers, part of Nathan Bedford Forrest's cavalry after January 1864. After the war he married, managing his father-in-law's plantation until 1873 when he got a job with the Illinois Central Railroad Co. He founded a bank in 1903 in Louisiana and remained a banker until his retirement in the 1930s. He died in North Carolina in 1939. His memoirs were titled: *1861 To 1865. Personal Recollections and Experiences in the Confederate Army. By an 'Old Johnnie.'*

ABNER DOUBLEDAY, often incorrectly said to have invented the American game of baseball, was born in New York in 1819. A graduate of the U.S. Military Academy class of 1842, he served in the Mexican-American War and was stationed in Charleston, South Carolina, when the war broke out. He was quickly appointed a brigadier-general of volunteers and served in the Army of the Potomac during Gettysburg, after which he served in Washington D.C. He was promoted major-general in 1865 and was named colonel of the 35th U.S. Infantry Regiment in 1967. He retired in 1873 and wrote *Reminiscences of Forts Sumter and Moultrie* in 1860-61 in 1876. He died in 1893.

LUIS FENOLLOSA EMILIO was born to a Spanish father in Massachusetts in 1844. In April 1861, he joined the Union Drill Club in Salem as a private, the company becoming Co. F, 23rd Massachusetts in September. He was promoted corporal, and then sergeant in August 1862. In February 1863 he was named a lieutenant in the new African-American 54th Massachusetts. He became a captain in the regiment in March. After the war he moved to San Francisco, California, where he married. He published his regiment's history, *A Brave Black Regiment*, in 1891. He returned to New York in 1881, dying there in 1918.

LEVI GLEASON, a Methodist minister when the war broke out, joined Co. I, 2nd Minnesota Infantry as a private. He later became the regimental chaplain, serving until discharged with his regiment in July 1865. He wrote the letter describing the people he met during Sherman's march to the sea to his hometown newspaper, the *St. Paul Pioneer*, which published it on 27 April 1865.

JOHN BROWN GORDON was born in Georgia in 1832. Trained in the law, when the war broke out, he was developing coal mines and was immediately elected a company commander. He quickly rose to the rank of brigadier general, being appointed in 1862. His appointment as major-general came in May 1864. He was so badly wounded at Antietam that he only avoided drowning in his own blood because of a hole in his cap which drained it. Well regarded and highly popular during the war, he entered politics after the war and was Governor of Georgia, as well as one of the state's U.S. senators three times. He published his memoirs, *Reminiscences of the Civil War*, in 1903 and died the following year.

HIRUM ULYSSES GRANT was born in Ohio in 1822. He graduated from the U.S. Military Academy in 1843 and was cited for gallantry during the Mexican War as an infantry regiment's quartermaster. He resigned from the Army in 1854 to avoid a

court martial for drunkenness and worked at several occupations in Illinois until the war broke out. He was then commissioned colonel of the 21st Illinois Infantry and quickly named a brigadier general. He soon caught the public eye and was promoted to major-general and then, in March 1864, to lieutenant-general and named overall Union commander. After the war he remained in command of the U.S. Army. In 1868 he was elected President, the first of two terms. After a presidency marred by scandal, he lost his fortune in a bad financial venture and wrote his memoir, *Personal Memoirs of U.S. Grant*, which became a bestseller. He died in New York in 1885.

CONSTANCE CARY HARRISON was a loyal Virginian and supporter of the Confederate cause. She, and her two cousins, made the first three Army of Northern Virginia battle flags, the familiar dark blue St. Andrew's cross on a red field. Her account of life in 1861 Virginia was published in *Battles & Leaders of the Civil War*.

RUSH HAWKINS was born in 1831 and saw service in the Mexican War. At the outbreak of the Civil War he organized the 9th New York Infantry, a Zouave regiment best known as 'Hawkins' Zouaves'. He was promoted to brigadier general of U.S. Volunteers and discharged in May 1863. Husband of one of the founders of Brown University in Rhode Island, he specialized in collecting incunabula, affordable because he made a fortune in real estate and investments. He died in 1920.

JULIAN WISNER HINKLEY was born in Connecticut in 1838 and moved with his family to Wisconsin when he was 11. He became first sergeant of Co. E, 3rd Wisconsin Infantry on its inception in April 1861. Commissioned second lieutenant in February 1862 and first lieutenant that November, he became a company commander and captain in May 1863. In the last few months of the war he served as acting major of the regiment and was discharged in August 1865. After the war he was involved in construction. His accounts are taken from the regimental history, *Service with the Third Wisconsin Infantry*, which he wrote.

FREDERICK L. HITCHCOCK was commissioned as adjutant of the 132nd Pennsylvania Infantry in August 1862. He was twice wounded at Fredericksburg, but recovered and was promoted to the rank of major in the regiment in January 1863. He mustered out with the regiment in May 1863. In 1904 he published his regiment's history, *War from the Inside.*

OVANDO J. HOLLISTER was born in Massachusetts in 1834 and raised in a Shaker community in New York. His early life was spent farming in Kansas and then Colorado. He joined the 1st Colorado Infantry on its organization in 1861 as a private, eventually becoming a sergeant. He served with the regiment in New Mexico and on its return to Denver, Colorado, where he was invalided out in January 1863. Afterwards he served as the editor for the Denver Daily *Commonwealth and Republican*, the *Black Hawk Mining Journal*, the *Denver Rocky Mountain News*, and other newspapers. He wrote the

Colorado Volunteers in New Mexico, 1862, from where this account was taken, among a number of other books. He died in Salt Lake City in 1892.

THOMAS WORCESTER HYDE, who was born in Italy, entered the Union army as the major of the 7th Maine in August 1861. He was promoted to lieutenant-colonel in December 1863 and was transferred to the 1st Maine Veteran Infantry in September 1864. He became the regimental colonel in October 1864 and was promoted to brigadier general of U.S. Volunteers in April 1865 for service at Petersburg. In 1891 he was awarded the Medal of Honor for his service at Antietam. He died in 1899.

JOHN DANIEL IMBODEN was born in Virginia in 1823. Educated at Washington College, he was a schoolteacher and practised law. Entering the Confederate army as the commander of the Staunton Artillery, he organized the 62nd Virginia mounted Infantry. He became a brigadier general in January 1863. He became ill with typhoid in late 1864 and served thereafter on prison duty. After the war he returned to law and worked in the mining industry in Virginia, where he died in 1895. His account is from the *Battles and Leaders of the Civil War*.

ROBERT AMOS JARMAN was born in 1840 in Mississippi. A student at the University of Mississippi at the outbreak of war, he immediately joined his hometown company, Co. K, 27th Mississippi Infantry and became the company's first sergeant. His account is from a memoir in the collection of the Mississippi Department of Archives and History.

JAMES D. JOHNSTON, southern born, was a career U.S. Navy officer, having entered the service as a midshipman in 1832. He was named a passed midshipman in 1838, and a lieutenant in 1843. When the war broke out he was one of the many naval officers who resigned their commissions to go south. He received a commander's commission in the Confederate Navy and was on the Tennessee at the battle of Mobile Bay. His article on the battle first appeared in *The Century Magazine* and was later reprinted in *Battles and Leaders of the Civil War*.

JOHN BEAUCHAMP JONES, who spent his boyhood on the frontiers of Kentucky and Missouri, was born in Maryland in 1810. At the beginning of the war he was a successful author in New Jersey, but he quickly returned south with the idea of taking a job in the Confederate government and publishing his diary after the war's successful conclusion. He found a job, pursuing his ultimate goal in the Confederate War Department. He did, in fact, publish *A Rebel War Clerk's Diary* in 1866.

JAMES H. KIDD was a first-year at the University of Michigan in 1860, where he served in the pre-war militia company the Tappen Guard. In 1862, at the end of his second undergraduate year, he obtained a commission to raise a company for the 6th Michigan Cavalry, which he accomplished by September. The unit became Company E. He was named major in May 1863 and became the regiment's colonel in May

1864. He was twice wounded and promoted to brigadier general of U.S. Volunteers for war service at the war's end. In 1908 he published his history of the Michigan Cavalry Brigade, *Personal Recollections of a Cavalryman*.

JOHN HENRY LEWIS was born in Portsmouth, Virginia, in 1835. A carpenter when the war broke out, he was also married with two children. In April 1861 he joined the Portsmouth Rifle Company, part of the 3rd Virginia. In May 1862, on the regiment's reorganization, he became his company's first sergeant. He became a junior second lieutenant in March 1863 and was captured at Gettysburg. Released in July 1865, he moved to Washington, D.C., after the war where he worked as a builder and carpenter, becoming rather prosperous. He published his *Recollections from 1860 to 1865* in 1895. He died in 1917.

WILLIAM GATES LE DUC was born in Ohio in 1823. Educated at Kenyon College, he became a lawyer and moved to St. Paul, Minnesota in 1850. He practised law there, as well as operating a book shop and stationers. He also participated in a number of building projects in this frontier city. In 1862 he was commissioned as a captain in the U.S. Army Quartermaster Corps and was discharged as an acting brigadier general of volunteers in 1865. After the war he served as United States Commissioner of Agriculture from 1877 until 1881. He died in Minnesota in 1917. His memoirs are in the collection of the Minnesota Historical Society.

ALFRED THAYER MAHAN was born in New York in 1840 and graduated from the U.S. Naval Academy in 1859. One of the great strategic thinkers of his time, he was appointed President of the Newport War College in 1886-89 and 1892-93. He is best known for his books *The Influence of Sea Power upon History, 1660-1783* and *Sea Power in its Relation to the War of 1812*, as well as his memoirs. He retired from the Navy in 1896 but was sent to the Hague Conference in 1899 as an official delegate. He died in 1914.

EDWARD A. MOORE was born of an old and distinguished Virginian family in 1842. When the war broke out he was a student at the University of Virginia and he soon joined the Rockbridge Artillery Company, then commanded by the Rev. William Pendleton, a West Point graduate and Episcopal priest, who would later become chief of artillery of the Army of Northern Virginia. Moore served throughout the war, being wounded at Antietam and the Second Cold Harbor. He was paroled at Appomattox and published his wartime memoirs, *The Story of a Cannoneer under Stonewall Jackson*, in 1907.

GEORGE WASHINGTON MORGAN was born in Pennsylvania in 1820. He served as an officer in the Texas Army during the state's fight for independence against Mexico and then attended the U.S. Military Academy, although he did not graduate. A lawyer, he became colonel of the 2nd Ohio Volunteers in the Mexican-American War and was then appointed colonel of the 15th U.S. Infantry Regiment. He was minister to Portugal at the beginning of the Civil War, quickly resigned and returned to be commissioned as a brigadier

general of volunteers in the U.S. Army. After the war he served three terms in Congress, as well as writing about the war in the *Battles and Leaders of the Civil War*. He died in Virginia in 1893.

HENRY P. MOYER of Lebanon, Pennsylvania, was mustered in as one of the two buglers in Co. E, 17th Pennsylvania Cavalry in September 1862 and was mustered out in the same position with his company in June 1865. After the war he was active in the Seventeenth Pennsylvania Volunteer Cavalry Association and ended up writing the regiment's history, *History of the 17th Reg't Penna. Volunteer Cavalry*, which was published in 1911.

ST. CLAIR AUGUSTIN MULHOLLAND was born in Lisburn, Ireland, in 1839. His family moved to America, settling in Philadelphia, Pennsylvania, in 1850. Working as an artist when the war broke out, he was quickly commissioned as a lieutenant-colonel in the 116th Pennsylvania Infantry, a largely Irish unit, in September 1862. The regiment was assigned to the Army of the Potomac's Irish Brigade. He was named colonel and the regimental commander in early 1864 and was later promoted to brigadier and major-general, serving as a brigade commander. Badly wounded several times, he managed to stay with the regiment until it was disbanded after Appomattox in 1865. He later served as Chief of Police in Philadelphia, retiring to paint, mostly landscapes. He also wrote his *Story of the 116th Regiment*, which was published in 1899. He died in 1910.

MATTHEW O'BRIEN was born in Ireland in 1837 and his parents came to Tuscaloosa, Alabama, when he was six. In 1852 he went to work as an apprentice in a foundry and he was there when the war broke out. He was commissioned third assistant engineer in the Confederate Navy in May 1861 and served on the C.S.S. *Sumter*. On that cruise's end, he was assigned to the C.S.S. *Alabama*. Appointed a chief engineer he was finally assigned to the C.S.S. *Shenandoah*, the last vessel to strike its colours. After the war he went to work for the Morgan Steamship Line, later becoming the U.S. supervising inspector of steam vessels in New Orleans.

THOMAS WARD OSBORN was born in New Jersey in 1836. A graduate of Madison University (now Colgate University) in 1860, he became a lawyer. He became a first lieutenant in Battery D, 1st New York Light Artillery, when the war broke out and was soon promoted to be the battery commander. He was promoted major and named Chief of Artillery of the XXI Corps in June 1863 and in July 1864 became chief of artillery of the Army of the Tennessee, in which position he served until the end of the war. He was promoted to lieutenant-colonel and colonel after the war and became an assistant commissioner of the Freemen's Bureau in Alabama, then later Florida. Active in the state's post-war politics he became a member of the Florida Senate and then, from 1868 to 1873, the U.S. Senate from Florida. Afterwards he practised law in New York City. Copies of his journals are in the Bowdin College Library and the Colgate University Library.

WILLIAM W. OWEN, a citizen of New Orleans when the war broke out, joined the Washington Artillery, a well-known pre-war militia unit. He was soon afterwards appointed first lieutenant and adjutant. In 1863 he was named a major in the battalion that consisted of the four Washington Artillery batteries on duty with the Army of Northern Virginia. He was later named Chief of Artillery in Preston's Division of the Army of Tennessee, returning to the Washington Artillery in April 1854 as the second field officer. He became the battalion commander, a lieutenant colonel in 1865. Surviving the war, he wrote *In Camp and Battle with the Washington Artillery of New Orleans*, which was published in 1885.

WILLIAM HARWAR PARKER was born in New York in 1826 to an old Virginian family. He entered the U.S. Navy in 1841 as a midshipman, making a number of cruises before being assigned to the new U.S. Naval Academy from which he was graduated in 1848. He wrote a number of texts on gunnery and naval tactics. He resigned his commission in 1861 and joined the new Confederate Navy. He served on the C.S.S. *Virginia* in its fight with the U.S.S. *Monitor*; in Charleston he commanded the Palmetto State; and as commander of the C.S. Naval Academy outside Richmond. After the war he became a professor of engineering and then President of the Maryland Agricultural College, now the University of Maryland. He left the college and was named U.S. Minister to Korea, but served only a short time and retired to Washington. He died there in 1896. He left his memoirs, Recollections of a Naval Officer.

ORLANDO METCALFE POE was born in 1832 and graduated from the U.S. Military Academy in 1856 as an officer in the Topographical Engineers. Commissioned colonel of the 2nd Michigan Infantry in 1861, he served until 1862 when he was commissioned a brigadier general of U.S. Volunteers. His commission expired in 1863 and he was named a captain of the Corps of Engineers, serving as a chief engineer on several staffs. After the war he served in the Corps on the Great Lakes and, as a colonel, as an aide-de-camp to General William T. Sherman when he was commander of the U.S. Army. He published his war memoirs as *Battles and Leaders of the Civil War*. He died in 1895.

THE REV. A. TOOMER PORTER, the witness to the burning of Columbia, South Carolina, was born in the state in 1828. He became an Episcopal priest before the war, serving as the rector of St. Michael's Church in Charleston. He organized a factory there with sewing machines to teach poor women a skill. It was taken over to make uniforms by the state at the start of the war. He then went to Washington to become chaplain to the Light Infantry, resigning and returning to Charleston and his church before the war was over, which was where he spent the rest of his life. He died in 1898. His account comes from his autobiography, *Led On!*

HENRY ROGERS PYNE was born in Connecticut in 1834. An Episcopal priest, he was mustered in as chaplain of the 1st New Jersey Cavalry in September 1861. He remained with the regiment until mustered out in September 1864. In

August 1865 he married in Washington where he was rector of St. John's Church. He published his history of the regiment, *Ride to War*, in 1870. He died in 1892.

J.W. REID, a native of South Carolina, joined the 4th South Carolina Infantry as a private on its inception in spring of 1861. He was discharged in July 1862 and was sent home. A year later he was caught in the net of the Conscript Act and sent to the state's camp of instruction. There he was recruited into the 1st Regiment of Engineer Troops, then being raised for service with the Army of Northern Virginia, as a sergeant. He served with Co. K, a pontoon bridge specialist company, until the surrender of the army. After the war he worked at various jobs in South Carolina and Georgia. In 1891 he published his wartime memoirs, *History of the Fourth Regiment S.C. Volunteers from the Commencement of the War until Lee's Surrender.*

WILLIAM STARKE ROSECRANS was born in Ohio in 1891. A graduate of the U.S. Military Academy in 1842, he retired from the Army in 1854 to work as an architect, a civil engineer, and a coal and oil refiner. Named a colonel of engineers of Ohio Volunteers in 1861, he became the commander of the 23rd Ohio Infantry that June. At almost the same time he became a brigadier general of volunteers and was promoted to the rank of major-general in March 1862. He resigned from the Army again in 1867 and served as Minister to Mexico the next year until 1889. After a short time in the Army again, he later served as a congressman and a rancher in California. He died in 1898.

EDMUND HASTINGS RUSSELL, from Pittsburgh, Pennsylvania, was serving as a first lieutenant in Co. G, 9th Pennsylvania Reserves, when he was detailed in August 1861 to the Signal Corps. He served at first with the Army of the Potomac, being sent to the Department of the Gulf in June 1862. He was promoted to the new corps as a first lieutenant in January 1863. After a short term with the Department of the Cumberland, he returned to the east as commander of the corps camp of instruction outside Washington, D.C. He was appointed a captain in March 1863 and assigned to various headquarters commands until mustered out, with the rank of brevet major, in August 1865.

WILLIAM H. SHERFY, a native of Indiana, joined the 97th Indiana Infantry as a 1st lieutenant on the regiment's organization. In January 1863 he was detailed to the U.S. Signal Corps. He was commissioned as a 1st lieutenant in that organization in July 1863. For his service he was promoted twice, ending the war as an acting major. He was mustered out of service in September 1865 and returned to Indiana where he died in 1877.

WILLIAM TECUMSEH SHERMAN was born in Ohio in 1820. When his father died in 1829, he was raised by Thomas Ewing, a U.S. Senator, who sent him to West Point, as a member of the Class of 1840. After service in Florida and the Mexican War, he resigned from the army, to become a businessman in California and Superintendent of the Louisiana State Seminary of Learning and Military Academy. On the war's outbreak he was commissioned the Colonel of the 13th U.S. Infantry Regiment, becoming a brigadier general of volunteers in May 1861. He became a major-general a year later. A close friend of Grant's from when they served in the West together, he was named to command all Western troops when Grant went east. He accepted the surrender of the Army of Tennessee on 17 April 1865. After the war he was promoted to lieutenant-general, then General-in-Chief of the army when Grant became President. He published his *Memoirs of General William T. Sherman* in 1875 and died in New York in 1891.

THOMAS L. SNEAD was born in Virginia in 1828. A law graduate of the University of Richmond, he moved to St. Louis and was a pro-Southern citizen of Missouri when the war began. He served as aide-de-camp to the state's Governor as well as Acting Adjutant-General of the Missouri State Guard, a member of the Confederate Congress, and Chief of Staff to the Confederate Army of the West with the rank of major. After the war he settled in New York where he became managing editor of the New York Daily News. He wrote a number of articles on the Western War in the *Battles and Leaders of the Civil War*. He died in New York in 1890.

GEORGE T. STEVENS was a medical doctor in New York City when the war broke out. He was the second surgeon to the 77th New York Infantry, replacing Dr. John L. Perry in January 1862. He served until December 1864 when he resigned and settled in Albany, New York. He began writing his book, *Three Years in the Sixth Corps*, almost immediately after his discharge, and it was published in 1866.

RICHARD TAYLOR, the son of famed Mexican War general and U.S. President Zachary Taylor, was born in Kentucky in 1826. A Yale graduate, he served as his father's military secretary during the Mexican war but that was his only military service before the Civil War. A planter in Louisiana when the war broke out, he became the colonel of the 9th Louisiana Infantry, being quickly promoted to brigadier general in October 1861, to major-general in July 1862, and lieutenant-general in April 1864. As such he commanded the Department of Alabama and Mississippi. He died in New York City in 1879.

ADIN BALLOU UNDERWOOD was born to an old Massachusetts family in 1828. A graduate of Brown University in 1849, he studied law at Harvard and was admitted to the bar in Boston. In May 1861 he became a captain in the 2nd Massachusetts Infantry, transferring as lieutenant-colonel to the 33rd Massachusetts Infantry in August 1862. He became that Regimental Colonel in April 1863. He was badly wounded, and thereafter crippled, in October 1863. Appointed a brigadier general in November 1863, he was promoted major-general in August 1865. Discharged from the army in August 1865, he returned to Boston to become the surveyor of the port. He also wrote his regiment's history, *The Three Years' Service of the Thirty-Third Mass. Infantry Regiment.* He died in 1888.

HENRY WALKE was born in Virginia in 1808. He was appointed a midshipman in the U.S. Navy in 1827 and a lieutenant in 1839. He was a commander by the war's outbreak, commanding the gunboat Carondelet in the Mississippi under Flag Officer Andrew Foote. He was promoted to captain in 1862 and to rear admiral in 1870. He retired the next year, dying in New York in 1896. His account of the gunboats at Fort Henry was published in *Battles & Leaders of the Civil War.*

ANDREW WALKER was born in Missouri in 1836 where he was raised on a farm. He stayed there, save for several trips working on the railways, until the February 1862, when he went to Arkansas to participate in the Confederate Army. Deserting, he surrendered to Union authorities that winter, shortly after joining Quantrill's band. After Quantrill's 1863 campaign, he fled first to Texas and then to Mexico for safety, staying there for 19 months. He then moved to California, followed by Oregon until March 1867, when he returned to Missouri to resume farming. Later he moved to near Weatherford, Texas, where he lived the remainder of his life. He produced his story of the raid for the *Kansas City Journal* of 12 May 1888.

SAM R. WATKINS was born in Tennessee in 1839. A student in Jackson College, he enlisted in the 1st Tennessee when it was raised in 1861 and served until the war's conclusion. After the war he married and, 20 years later in 1881, began writing his memoirs for his local newspaper. Eventually he bound his accounts together as a book titled *Co. Aytch*. He died in 1901.

ROBERT WATSON, a native of Key West Florida, joined a Florida coast defence unit that became Co. K, 7th Florida Infantry, in April 1862. In March 1864, in response to a plea for seamen from the Confederate Navy, Watson with some of his comrades, was transferred to the Navy and assigned to the C.S.S. *Savannah*. In December 1864 the ship was scuttled and Watson's crew headed north to join the defenders of Fort Fisher. He escaped to find himself at the defences of Richmond when it fell and was captured on 8 April 1865, leaving the city. After the war he made his way to Havana, Cuba, and back to Key West from there where he was married in 1868. A copy of his Civil War diary is in the Cornell University Library.

WILLIAM WATSON, a native of Great Britain, found himself at the outbreak of the Civil War in New Orleans on business. While not in favour of secession, he joined the Confederate army as a private in 1861 both in sympathy to his Southern friends and to maintain his business position. Originally a first sergeant, after the fall of Corinth he was named acting Assistant Adjutant General of an infantry brigade. He decided to leave the army, which as a British subject he was legally entitled to do, and returned to New Orleans and, from there, back to Britain in 1863. He continued his military interests there, serving in the 1st Renfrew and Dumbarton Artillery Volunteer Corps when he published his memoir, *Life in the Confederate Army*, in 1887.

SELECT BIBLIOGRAPHY

Alexander, E. Porter, *Fighting for the Confederacy*, Chapel Hill, North Carolina, 1989

Andrews, WH, *Footprints of a Regiment, A Recollection of the 1st Georgia Regualrs, 1861-1865,* Atlanta, Georgia, 1992

Blackford, WW, *War Years With JEB Stuart*, New York, 1945

Boatner, Mark M. III, *The Civil War Dictionary,* New York, 1988

Burton, E. Milby, *The Siege of Charleston, 1861-1865*, Columbia, South Carolina, 1970

Carter, Samuel III, *The Final Fortress,* New York, 1980

Cavanaugh, Michael A., and William Marvel, *The Battle Of The Crater,* Lynchburg, Virginia, 1989

Cleaves, Freeman, *Meade of Gettysburg*, Norman, Oklahoma, 1960

Connolly, James A., *Three Years in the Army of the Cumberland*, Bloomington, Indiana, 1959

Connelly, Thomas L., *Autumn of Glory, The Army of Tennessee*, 1862-1865, Baton Rouge, Louisiana, 1971

Coski, John M., Capital Navy, *The Men, Ships and Operatons of the James River Squadron*, Campbell, California, 1996

Cozzens, Peter, *No Better Place to Die*, Urbana, Illinois, 1990

Cozzens, Peter, *This Terrible Sound*, Urbana, Illinois, 1992

Cozzens, Peter, *The Shipwreck of Their Hopes*, Urbana, Illinois, 1994

Cozzens, Peter, *The Darkest Days of the War*, Chapel Hill, North Carolina, 1997

Davis, Burke, *The Long Surrender*, New York, 1985

Davis, William C., *The Battle of New Market*, New York, 1975

Davis, William C., *Battle at Bull Run*, Baton Rouge, Louisiana, 1977

Dinkins, James, *1861 to 1865. Personal Recollections and Experiences in the Confederate Army*, Dayton, Ohio, 1975

Dowdey, Clifford, *Lee's Last Campaign*, New York, 1960

Dowdey, Clifford and Louis H. Manarin, *The Wartime Papers of R.E. Lee*, New York, 1961

Early, Jubal A. *Narrative of the War Between the States*, Philadelphia, Pennsylvania, 1912

Farwell, Byron, *Ball's Bluff*, McLean, Virginia, 1990

Ferguson, Ernest B., *Chancellorsville 1863*, New York, 1992

Gragg, Rod, *Confederate Goliath: The Battle of Fort Fisher*, New York, 1991

Harwell, Richard and Philip N. Racine, *The Fiery Trail: A Union Officer's Account of Sherman's Last Campaigns*, Knoxville, Tennessee, 1986

Hennessy, John J., *Return to Bull Run*, New York, 1993

Hoehling, A.A., *Last Train from Atlanta*, Harrisburg, Pennsylvania, 1958

Hughes, Nathaniel C., Jr., Bentonville: *The Final Battle of Sherman & Johnston*, Chapel Hill, North Carolina, 1996

Hughs, Nathaniel C., Jr., *The Battle of Belmont*, Chapel Hill, North Carolina, 1991

Johnson, Robert U. and Clarence C. Buel, *Battles and Leaders of the Civil War*, New York, 1956

Judge, Joseph, *Season of Fire, The Confederate Strike on Washington*, Berryville, Virginia, 1994

Katcher, Philip, *Building The Victory, The Order Book of the Volunteer Engineer Brigade*, Shippensburg, Pennsylvania, 1998

Kennedy, Jos. C.G., *Preliminary Report on The Eighth Census*, 1860, Washington, 1862

Kennett, Leo, *Marching Through Georgia*, New York 1995

Krick, Robert K., *Stonewall Jackson at Cedar Mountain*, Chapel Hill, North Crolina, 1990

Krick, Robert K., *Conquering the Valley*, New York, 1996

Livermore, Thomas L, *Numbers and Losses in the Civil war in America 1861-65*, Dayton, Ohio, 1986

Long, E.B., *The Civil War Day by Day, An Almanac 1861-1865*, New York, 1971

Longacre, Edward G., *Army of Amateurs*, Mechanicsville, Pennsylvania, 1997

Luraghi, Raimondo, *A History of the Confederate Navy*, Annapolis, Maryland, 1996

Grant, Ulysses, *Personal Memoirs of U.S. Grant*, New York, 1885

McClellan, H.B., *The Campaigns of Stuart's Cavalry*, Secaucus, New Jersey, 1993

McDonough, James Lee and Thomas L. Connelly, *Five Tragic Hours, The Battle of Franklin*, Knoxville, Tennessee, 1983

Manley, R. Wayne, *Marching to Cold Harbor*, Shippensburg, Pennsylvania, 1995

Matter, William D., *If It Takes All Summer*, Chapel Hill, North Carolina, 1988

Perry, Milton F., Infernal Machines, *The Story of Confederate Submarine and Mine Warfare*, Baton Rouge, Louisiana, 1965

Sears, Stephen W., *Landscape Turned Red*, New York, 1983

Sears, Stephen W., *To the Gates of Richmond*, New York, 1992

Shea, William L. and Earl J. Hess, *Pea Ridge*, Chapel Hill, North Carolina, 1992

Sheridan, Philip, *Civil War Memoirs*, New York, 1888

Silverstone, Paul H., *Warships of the Civil War Navies*, Annapolis, Maryland, 1989

Soley, J. Russell, *The Blockade and the Cruisers*, New York, 1883

Sommers, Richard J., *Richmond Redeemed*, New York, 1981

Starr, Stephen Z., *The Union Cavalry in the Civil War*, Baton Rouge, Louisiana, 1961

Sunderland, Glenn W., *Five Days to Glory*, New York, 1970

Swanberg, WA, First Blood, *The Story of Fort Sumter*, New York, 1957

Sword, Wily, *Shiloh: Bloody April*, New York, 1974

Taylor, Richard, *Destruction and Reconstruction: Personal Experiences of the Late War*, New York, 1955

Trudeau, Noah Andre, *Bloody Roads South*, New York, 1989

Trudeau, Noah Andre, *Out of the Storm*, New York, 1994

Various, *The War of the Rebellion: A Compilation of the Official Records of the Union and Confederate Armies, Washington, 1880-1901*

Warner, Ezra J., *Generals in Gray*, Baton Rouge, Louisiana, 1959

Wert, Jeffry D., *From Winchester to Cedar Creek, The Shenandoah Campaign of 1864*, New York, 1987

INDEX

ACKNOWLEDGEMENTS

AKG, LONDON 8–9, 46 Top, 74 right, 92 right, 129, 166 left, 175,/Timothy O'Sullivan 83.

BRIDGEMAN ART LIBRARY, London/New York /Private Collection, Howard Pyle (1853–1911) *The Nation is at War and Must Have Men* Illustration from 'Young' by William Gilmore Beymer, pub in Harper's Magazine 1909 19 left, /Private Collection Julian Oliver Davidson (1853 – 94) *The Monitor and the Merrimac, the First Fight between the Ironclads in 1862* (litho) pub. By Louis Prang &co., 1886 36, /Private Collection Charles macaroon (20th century) *Battle of Vicksburg, May 19th, 1863* 75, /Private Collection Charles Prosper Sainton (1861–1914) *Pickett's Charge, Battle of Gettysburg in 1863* 82, /Detroit Institute of Arts, USA Founders Society purchase and Dexter M.Ferry Jr. Fund Winslow Homer (1836–1910) *Defiance: Inviting a shot before Petersburg, 1864* oil on panel 130, /Library of Congress, Washington D.C., USA pub by Kurz & Allison, Chicago 1888 (engraving)(b/w photo) by American School (19th century) *The Death of General James B Macpherson at The Battle of Atlanta, July 22nd, 1864* 137 Top, Philadelphia Museum of Art, Pennsylvania, PA, USA Edouard Manet (1832 – 83) *Battle of Kearsage and Alabama, 1864* 142 Bottom Left, Yale University Art Gallery New Haven CT Currier and Ives *The Capture of Atalanta by the Union Army, 2nd September, 1864* 148, /Library of Congress, Washington D.C., USA pub by Kurz & Allison, Chicago 1890 (engraving)(b/w photo) by American School (19th century) *The Battle of Cedar Creek, Oct. 19th, 1864* 156 Top, Private Collection (litho)N.Currier (1813–88) and J.M.Ives (1824–95) *The Fall of Richmond, Virginia, 2nd April 1865* 188 Bottom, Private Collection Jean Leon Jerome Ferris (1863–1930) *Let Us Have Peace* 191.

CORBIS UK LTD 18 right, 20 left, 21 Bottom, 34 Bottom, 49 Top, 57 right, 59, 60, 67 Bottom, 71 right, 85, 89 Top, 91 right, 114, 115 right, 117 Top, 125 left, 126, 131 Top, 131 Bottom, 134, 139, 142 Bottom Right, 149 right, 151, 154, 162 right, 164, 165 Bottom, 173, 176, 177, 180 left, 182 Bottom, 187 left /Bettmann 15 Bottom, 27 Top, 86 left, 102 Top, 106 Bottom, 107, 118, 133 left, 140, 153 Right, 190, 193 left, /Hulton-Deutsch Collection 14 Top, /Medford Historic Society Collection 4 Top,4 Centre, 4 Bottom, 10–11, 23 Top, 26 right, 28 Bottom, 31 Centre, 37 Centre, 41 left, 41 Centre,42–43, 44 left, 44 centre right above, 44 centre right below, 47,51 left, 52–53 Centre, 53, 54 left, 57 left, 76–77, 78 79, 84 Top, 84 Bottom, 88, 91 left, 92 left, 95, 96 right, 97,98 left,99 left,99 right, 105 left,109 left, 109 right, 111 Bottom, 116, 117 Bottom, 119 Centre, 120 Bottom Left, 120 Bottom Right, 121, 124, 125 right, 132, 133 right, 134–135, 135,144,145 right,155,165 Top, 168, 171 Top, 174, 178, 179, 180 right, 183,192,193 right, 201,/Minnesota Historical Society/Howard Pyle 171 Bottom.

GRANGER COLLECTION 54 right,/Kurz + Allison 157.

CHRIS HEISEY confederate and union flags throughout the book and on cover.

HULTON GETTY PICTURE COLLECTION Front Cover, Back Cover, 3, 5 Top, 6–7, 12 Bottom Left, 13 Bottom, 14 Bottom Left, 16, 17, 19 right, 24 right, 25 right, 28 Centre, 29 Top, 38 left, 38 right, 39 left, 39 right, 41 right, 46 Bottom, 49 Bottom, 51 right, 52, 56 Bottom Left, 58, 58–59, 61 Bottom Right, 63 Bottom, 66, 67 Top, 68 left, 70, 71 left, 72 left, 73, 74 left, 81, 86–87, 87, 90 Top, 98 right, 100, 104, 106 Top, 110, 122–123, 127, 128, 136, 142 Top, 143, 145 left, 146 right, 147, 149 left, 162 left, 163, 167, 172 Bottom, 186, 189, 194 right 195, 196–197.

PETER NEWARK'S AMERICAN PICTURES 5 Bottom, 18 left, 20 right, 22 Top, 45, 48, 61 Bottom Left, 63 Top, 68 right, 80 right, 94 Bottom Right, 101, 102 Bottom, 103, 105 right, 112 left, 112 right, 113, 119 left, 158–159, 194 left, /painted by Conrad Wise Chapman 181,/Stanley M Arthurs 161.

PRIVATE COLLECTION 12 Bottom Right, 14 centre right above, 14 centre right below, 21 centre left above, 21 centre left below, 22 Centre, 22 Bottom, 24 right, 25 left, 26 left, 27 Bottom, 30 Top, 31 left, 31 right, 32 right, 33 right, 34–35 Top, 35 right, 35 Centre, 37 Bottom, 55 Top, 55 Bottom Left, 55 Bottom Right, 61 Top, 62, 64 Top, 64 Bottom, 65 Top, 65 Bottom, 69 Bottom Left, 69 Bottom Right, 80 left, 89 Bottom, 94 Centre Left, 94 Bottom Left, 96 left, 111 Top, 119 right, 120 Top, 137 Bottom, 138, 141 left, 141 right, 146 left, 152, 153 left, 156 Bottom, 166 right, 169 left, 169 right, 172 Top, 182 Top, 184, 185 left, 185 right, 188 Top.